OPEN ECONOMY MACROECONOMICS IN EAST ASIA

For my parents

Open Economy Macroeconomics in East Asia

Edited by

AHMAD ZUBAIDI BAHARUMSHAH
Universiti Putra Malaysia, Malaysia

ASHGATE

Published by
Ashgate Publishing Limited
Gower House
Croft Road
Aldershot
Hants GU11 3HR
England

Ashgate Publishing Company
Suite 420
101 Cherry Street
Burlington, VT 05401-4405
USA

Ashgate website: http://www.ashgate.com

British Library Cataloguing in Publication Data
Open economy macroeconomics in East Asia
1.Monetary policy - East Asia 2. Finance - East Asia
3.Macroeconomics 4.Foreign exchange rates - East Asia
5.East Asia - Economic conditions 6.East Asia - Economic
policy 7.East Asia - Economic integration
I.Ahmad Zubaidi Baharumshah, 1953-
339.5'095

Library of Congress Cataloging-in-Publication Data
Open economy macroeconomics in East Asia / [edited] by Ahmad Zubaidi Baharumshah.
p. cm.
Includes bibliographical references and index.
ISBN 0-7546-4400-6
1. East Asia--Economic policy. 2. East Asia--Economic conditions. 3. Monetary policy--East Asia. 4. Foreign exchange rates--East Asia. 5. East Asia--Economic integration. 6. Financial crises--East Asia. I. Ahmad Zubaidi Baharumshah, 1953-

HC460.5.064 2005
339.5'095--dc22

2004027233

ISBN 0 7546 4400 6

Printed and bound in Great Britain by MPG Books Ltd, Bodmin, Cornwall

Contents

List of Contributors

Ahmad Zubaidi Baharumshah is a Professor in the Department of Economics, Universiti Putra Malaysia.

Chan Tze-Haw is the Senior Data Analyst in International Medical University and a Graduate Student in the Department of Economics, Universiti Putra Malaysia.

Chin-Hong Puah is a lecturer in the Faculty of Economics and Business, Universiti Malaysia Sarawak.

Evan Lau is a Research Associate and Graduate Student in the Department of Economics, Universiti Putra Malaysia.

Goh Wee-Keat is a Graduate Student in the Department of Economics, Universiti Putra Malaysia.

Hassanuddeen A. Aziz is an Associate Professor in the Kulliyah Economics and Management Science, International Islamic University, Malaysia.

Hway-Boon Ong is a lecturer in the Faculty of Management, Multimedia University, Malaysia.

Kian-Ping Lim is a lecturer in Labuan School of International Business and Finance, Universiti Malaysia Sabah.

M. Azali is an Associate Professor in the Department of Economics, Universiti Putra Malaysia.

Mansor H. Ibrahim is a Professor in the Kulliyah Economics and Management Science, International Islamic University, Malaysia.

Marwan Abdul-Malik Thanoon is a Post-Doctoral Student in the Department of Economics, Universiti Putra Malaysia.

Mohammed B. Yusoff is a Professor in the Kulliyah of Economics and Management of Sciences, International Islamic University, Malaysia.

Muhd Zulkhibri Abdul Majid is the Senior Economist at Monetary and Financial Policy Department, Central Bank of Malaysia.

Muzafar Shah Habibullah is a Professor in the Department of Economics, Universiti Putra Malaysia.

Sarinder Kumari is the Principle Assistant Director in the Ministry of International Trade and Industry (MITI), Malaysia.

Venus Khim-Sen Liew is a lecturer in Labuan School of International Business and Finance, Universiti Malaysia Sabah.

Yoke-Kee Eng is a Lecturer in the Faculty of Accountancy and Management, Universiti Tunku Abdul Rahman.

Foreword

The East Asia countries were among the fastest growing economies in the world and of growing importance to the world economy. These countries have taken the lead in adopting outward-oriented development policies.

This volume focuses on the major issues on open economy macroeconomics in the East Asia economies that will be instructive to both academics and policymakers. The emphasis is on the countries that were severely affected by the 1997/98 Asian financial crises. Thailand, Malaysia, Indonesia, the Philippines and South Korea became deeply involved while countries like Singapore escaped from the financial crises. Several aspects of exchange rate, current account, budget deficits, monetary and financial issues are considered in this book. In addition, several chapters are devoted to discussion on the issues of economic integration in the region. The contagion and the currency crisis are also discussed thoroughly in this book. Most of the papers are empirical in nature and the empirical evidence provided is based on the recent development in time series econometrics methods.

The major findings are as follows; first, the events in the East Asia countries suggest that policy measures to curb external imbalances cannot simply rely on the management of fiscal deficit. Besides managing the budget deficit, policymakers in these countries need to consider exchange rate and interest rate targeting, not to mention productivity enhanced policies. Second, the evidence shows the formation of yen block among the Asian countries is a possibility. The analysis tends to support the hypothesis that countries like Indonesia paid less to attention the movement of yen but placed more emphasis on price stability in the domestic economy. In contrast, countries like Singapore where inflation rates are low tend to favour competitive devaluation policies. Third, the Asia Pacific countries are closely interconnected to the global financial markets namely US and Japan. This finding reveals that the financial reform packages of the 1980s and early 1990s have led the markets of these countries to integrate with the global financial centres.

Fourth, real exchange rate of these countries follows a mean-reverting process. This is contrary to the widespread agreement that purchasing power parity (PPP) is unlikely to hold in the post-Bretton Woods system. The implication of this finding provides a rational for using standard monetary model or its variant for forecasting and policy analyses in these countries. Finally the evidence suggests that the banking sector in Malaysia is fragile and vulnerable to financial shocks.

Acknowledgements

This volume is a product of several research projects funded by Ministry of Science Technology and Environment (MOSTE), Malaysia [Grants No:05-02-04-0532 and 05-02-04-0046]. The articles selected for this volume were presented in several of the Faculty of Economics and Management conferences at Universiti Putra Malaysia and Asia Pacific Economics and Business Conferences (APEB). The students who have contributed directly to the idea of this book include Evan Lau, Venus Khim-Sen Liew, Marwan Abdul-Malik Thanoon, Tze-Haw Chan and Siti Hamizah Mohd.

PART I
MONEY AND GROWTH

Chapter 1

Structural Adjustment to Sustained Economic Growth in Malaysia

Marwan Abdul-Malik Thanoon

Introduction

Developing countries are usually characterised by low per capita income, higher import than export earning, low savings rate relative to investment and unequal income distributions. Thus, their economic policies have focused on increasing growth and development in order to raise the level of GDP and consequently improve the standard of living. In order to realise these objectives, investments in productive sectors of the economy have to be encouraged (Meier, 1995).

Limited resources are one of the major constraints encountered by most developing countries; especially in their strive to attain a higher level of national prosperity and living standard. The slowness of progress observed in many developing countries is partly due to their inability to save and to channel scarce resources into the most productive uses, or to obtain foreign funds through trade. Consequently, these shortages pose serious constraints to economic growth. Some of these constraints are due to domestic factors; these include savings, skills, and fiscal constraints, while others are external factors such as trade, debt and balance of payment constraints. The two-gap model proceeds by deriving the capital requirements implied by a target growth rate of GDP. These capital requirements are compared with the likely availability of savings comparative to investment; the difference is the savings gap; and the availability of export earning comparative to import; the difference is the trade gap (Ventara, 1996; Mills, and Nallari, 1997; Evangelos et al. 1999).

Malaysia's economic performance since her independence had been impressive by world standards. The fact remains, however, that its growth process had been punctuated by difficulties associated with limited domestic resources.

These had been manifested by the existence of the savings-investment and export-import gaps. As a result, the macroeconomic planning had to grapple with funding solutions to narrow these gaps so as to ensure that the economy will be on a sustainable path. The government's objective of transforming the economy through industrialisation by 2020 needs to be closely accompanied by the provision of resources required for structural upgrading. This requires a simultaneous increase in human resource skills, government revenue, domestic savings and export earnings, as well as their allocation into areas that can fulfil the demand resulting from rising levels of national and per capita income.

The present chapter attempts to analyse the nature and extent of various resource gaps, their economic manifestation and implications and alternative solutions for Malaysia to achieve sustainable economic progress. Particular emphasis is given to the impact of foreign transfers on the potential output growth rate. The recent Asian financial crisis demonstrates that foreign capitals enhance economic growth but when they leave, the adjustment process can be painful. Furthermore this chapter has also been inspired by the need to provide answers to a number of yet unsolved questions. For example, what are the causes of the resource gaps in Malaysia? Which of these gaps has been and will continue to be the binding constraint in the years ahead? Which variables are the major determinants of the gaps? Another aspect where this chapter is expected to contribute is in the policy options. The constructed models impose a discipline on the design of policy options by requiring consistency among individual relationships and ensuring that all pertinent identities are satisfied respectively. This is done by making projections based on the assumptions that include; (1) five sets of exports growth rates – low (6.5 and 7.5 percent), medium (8 percent) and high (10 and 11 percent), (2) two target rates of GDP growth of 6 and 8 percent and (3) increasing total tax by 5 percent and reducing total imports by the same rate. An alternative set of projections will be carried out from the base line estimated from the 1981-1995 period, which in turn will be used as a base for prospecting Malaysia's growth path over the next ten years from 1996 to 2005.

There are several underlying reasons in the selection of the two-gap analyses in this chapter. The first and more general reason is that it fits in with the issues in which Malaysia's economic planning will have to be concerned with in the coming years. The economy has hitherto achieved a relatively high level of development growth through industrialisation and manufactured exports. But as the country progresses and encounters the problems that will be brought about by shortage of foreign capital, population growth and the reduced prospects of her traditional primary exports, it will be necessary for it to bring about a further economic transformation. In this vein, it will be necessary to examine the nature, magnitude and evolution of the dominant constraints that will confront the economy through time, including that of capital resources. Secondly, the analytical and empirical models employed in the two-gap model can provide an effective checklist of foreign capital requirements and their necessity for growth. Thirdly, the model that is developed and employed in this chapter is able to provide operational results under a wide variety of servers. Indeed a recent chapter by the World Bank reveals that the two gap model remains the most widely used tool for making macroeconomic projections and to analysed macroeconomic policies (World Bank, 1997; Easterly, 1999). The gap approach is one of the most popular frameworks and has been used to determine financial requirements for the developing countries. The role of domestic and external resources in the process will be very critical, and its analysis will be able to shed some light on many issues that can be very useful to serve as lessons for the developing economy (Adelman and Kim, 1995).

Malaysia in the Context of Gaps

Malaysia recorded a fiscal deficit during 1965-1996. Public sector expenditure increased by nearly 13 percent over the 1965-1990 period compared with 7.2 percent over the 1990-1996 period. Government revenue registered a moderate growth of 6.6 and 7 percent over the two respective periods. The country's savings rate had been high by international standards, being at 39.4 percent of GNP in 1997. The investment rate had been even higher at 44.8 percent of GNP. This yielded a savings-investment (S-I) gap of 5.4 percent of GNP, which had to be financed through external borrowing. The current account position of the balance of payment was a negative 5.4 percent of GNP in 1997. Hence, these shortages posed serious constraints to the country's economic growth, including both domestic factors like savings, skills, and fiscal constraints and external ones such as trade, debt, and balance of payment constraints (Economic Report, 1999).

In the post crisis period, the S-I gap narrowed and by 1998 it had turned to a surplus equivalent to nearly 15 percent of GNP. A major factor that had contributed to the surplus the S-I gap is the sharp decline of the Ringgit *vis-à-vis* the major currencies. For example, the Ringgit depreciated by 35 percent against USD between 1997 and 1999. As a result of this sharp fall in the Ringgit, trade and current account balance improved significantly. Exports rose sharply while imports fell, and these led to a surplus of 69 and 35 billions in the balance of trade and the current account balance reporting in 2000 (Economic Report, 2002).

Review of Related Literature

Authors such as Rosenstein-Rodan (1961), Addison (1989), Lewis (1984), Chenery (1988) and Ardeshir and John (1992) claimed that in order to raise foreign exchange revenue and permit investment through imported capital goods to take place exports need to be expanded sufficiently. For instance, Chenery and Strout (1966) argued that foreign capital can induce economic growth and eventually allow developing countries to catch up with the industrial nations. Chenery (1988) suggested that the achievement of any planned growth rate would require changes in the structural parameters which takes time, or sufficient inflows of foreign resources to cover the binding gap. Weusskopf (1971), Thirlwall and Shibly (1981), Syrquin and Taylor (1984), Khan (1990), World Bank (1997) and Easterly (1999) all consider foreign capital as the primary source to finance development, since it can be used to expand the capacity of imports and investment.

Gersovitz (1982) used the two-gap approach to identify the resource constraints in five developing countries (Argentina, Colombia, Ecuador, Guatemala and Peru) during the 1950-1980 period. The results of their empirical investigation suggest that investment is less likely to be constrained by imports than by savings. The World Bank (1992) provided estimates of capital requirements for highly indebted countries (HICS) and low-income Asia. The development committee estimates additional capital requirements of the HICS to the order of US $11-12 billion annually and to low-income Asia, US $4-5 billion a year. In related work, David (1993) used the two-gap model for Kenya during the 1960-1990 period and provided sufficient evidence that the economy has had a trade gap constraint.

Baruah and Hazarika (1997) adopted the two-gap model for the Indian economy over the 1980-1990. The results show that the savings gap is the dominant constraint and the Indian economy needed $12.5 billion to achieve its target rate of growth. The European Bank for Reconstruction and Development in 1995 announced it was using the financing gap to project investment requirement. This projection warned the ex-communist countries that "investment finance of the order of 20 percent or more of GDP will be required" to reach "growth rates of 5 percent". All recent studies mentioned above concluded that additional funds are to be provided to LDCs in order to reach minimum growth targets. The World Bank (1998) has changed from basic approach that the bank uses for its macroeconomic projections and policy work by putting more emphasis on the relationships among savings, foreign capital inflows, investment, trade and growth. This approach is reflected in the Revised Minimum Standard Model (RMEM) that has been the basis of country economic projections in the bank for several years (Khan, 1990; Easterly, 1997).

Formulation of the Theory of Foreign Capital Requirements

The model to be presented here is a simple aggregative model of an economy based on standard macroeconomic relationships and embodying the two independent constraints on growth that have been emphasised in the literature on two-gap analysis. Such a model is necessary for an evaluation of the role of foreign capital because foreign capital inflows contribute both to the potential availability of savings, thereby easing the savings constraint, and to the potential availability of the imports, thereby easing the trade constraint. It turns out that the identification of the behavioural savings function depends on which of the constraints is in fact binding for a given country during the time period in question. The two gaps must be identical ex-post although through ex-ante they need not be so. Since foreign capital can add both to the availability of savings and to the availability of foreign exchange, and since the two-gap disequilibrium situation means that only one of the two constraints is likely to be binding at any particular time, the productivity of foreign assistance depends critically on which constraints is in fact binding. In order to estimate savings and or import functions from historical time series data, one must make a judgement about which constraint was in fact binding during the period used for estimation. Accepting the general framework of two-gap analysis, this section is addressed to the problem of identifying which of the two constraints was dominant in the Malaysian economy during the historical period 1981-1995.

The model consists of nine equations in nine variables, and two inequality constraints. The first four equations are the macroeconomic accounting:[1]

$Y + M \equiv C + I + E$ (1)
$Y = C + S$ (2)
$S = Y - C$ (2a)
The definitions of savings are expressed by the following equation
$S = I + (E - M) = I - F$ (3)
Sources of investment finance are expressed by the following equation
$I = S + F$ (3a)
Sources of import finance are expressed by
$M = E + F$ (4)
$F = M - E$ (4a)
At any point of time, the total amount of resources available to a country which it can consume and devote to investment or use for exports is equal to the country gross domestic product (Y) plus its imports.

The underlying assumption is that the growth of gross domestic product (Y) is assumed to increase at a given desired target rate exogenously (g^*) over the forecasting period

$$Y_t = \leq (1 + g^* \ )Y_{t-1}$$

$$g^* = \sqrt[t]{(Y_t / Y_0)} \ \text{-1}$$

Then the target output (Y_t^*) in the t year is:

$Y_t^* = Y_0 (1 + g^*)^t$ where t = 1, 2,3

The behavioural savings function is introduced as follows:

$S^*{}_t = \alpha_0 + \alpha_1 Y_t + u_t$ (5)

where: $S^*{}_t$ is ex ante gross domestic savings, as distinct from the ex post variable S . Y_t is gross domestic product, α_1 is marginal propensity to save, α_0 is the intercept and u_t is the error term. The level of savings and the ratio of savings to gross domestic product in developing countries are likely to be a function of many variables affecting the ability and willingness to save. Having said that evidence based on time-series and cross-section for a wide sample of countries all provide support to the Keynesian type model, that is, the level of savings is primarily a function of the level of income. Accordingly, the savings function has been specified in linear and un-lagged form in order to simplify the model. We estimate investment requirements by using the model of the growth identity by Harrod-Domard: g =s/κ, where g is the proportional rate of growth of domestic income ($\Delta Y / Y$), s is the average total savings to income (S / Y) over the period and k the incremental capital-output ratio: $\Delta i / Y$. The target or planned rate of growth g^* is given and S / Y is constant. Then an estimate of k is constant also: $k = s / g^*$. The investment ratio requirements as a proportion of output can be calculated as: $i = g^* k$ Investment requirements in period (n) are estimated as:

$$(I_t^r) = (g^* \times k)\, Y_t^* \quad \text{or} \quad i \times Y_0(1+g^*)^t \tag{6}$$

The minimum level of import necessary to sustain the current economic activity is calculated from the following equation:

$$M_t^r = (g / m^*)\, Y_t^* \tag{7}$$

where M_t^r is ex ante or required imports and m^* is incremental output-import ratio $\Delta Y / M$. This ratio can be calculated in analogous by using the simple growth formula $g = i + m$, where i is the average historical ratio of imports to GDP (M / Y). Thus $m^* = g / i$. The volume of export is largely determined by supply conditions, while earnings depend on supply and the price determined by world demand condition. Both supply and world prices are notoriously difficult to forecast, making the forecast of export earnings equally difficult. In view of these difficulties, a simple exponential trend rate of growth of export (ε) is assumed, based on historical experience. In fact, fitting an exponential trend to past data gives a better statistical fit than any of the more sophisticated export demand function.

$$\overline{E}_t = \chi_0 + \chi_1 T \quad and \quad \overline{E}_t = E_0(1+\varepsilon)^t \tag{8}$$

where ε here is the exogenous rate of growth of export.

The net availability of foreign capital are considered exogenous to the model and are defined accordingly:

$$F = \overline{F} \tag{9}$$

The two inequalities include first of all the savings and trade constraints relating ex-post to ex-ante savings and imports:

$$I_t^r \geq S_t^* \tag{10}$$

$$E_t \leq M_t^r \tag{11}$$

By substituting equations (1) to (8) into inequalities (10) and (11), the model can be expressed in reduced form as two inequality constraints on the target growth as follows:

$$(g^* \times k)\, Y_t^* \geq \alpha_0 + \alpha_1 Y^*_t \tag{10'}$$

$$(g / m^*)\, Y_t^* . \geq E_0(1+\varepsilon)^t \tag{11'}$$

There are two possible cases, each of which is defined by a pair of binding constraints.

Case I involves a binding savings constraint, that is:

$I_t^r - S^*_t \geq M_t^r - \overline{E}_t$ or

$$(g^* \times k)\, Y_t^* - \alpha_0 + \alpha_1 Y^*_t \geq (g / m^*)\, Y_t^* - E_0(1+\varepsilon)^t$$

Case II involves a binding trade constraint, that is:

$M_t^r - \overline{E}_t \geq I_t^r - S^*_t$ or

$$(g / m^*)\, Y_t^* - E_0(1+\varepsilon)^t \geq (g^* \times k)\, Y_t^* - \alpha_0 + \alpha_1 Y^*_t$$

A classification of the variables that are relevant in our analysis and their uses is presented in Table 1.1. The bulk of the data comes from: Key Indicators of Developing Asian and Pacific Countries, 2000, Vol XXXI, Oxford University press, New York and the World Bank (World Table and World Debt Table). The sample period is from 1980 to 1995 was chosen as a frame of reference in carrying out the empirical analysis.

Estimating Foreign Capital Needs for Malaysia 1996-2005

The solution to the system depends on whichever constraint is more restrictive or whichever provides a lower rate of growth. Based on the values of the relevant variables and parameters in Table 1.2, projection of external capital requirements in Malaysia for the period 1996-2005 is possible.

Analysis of the Scenarios of Export and Economic Growth Rates

As mentioned before, foreign capital needed is reflected either by the internal or external gap or both, whichever is larger. If the GDP and exports were to grow at 8 percent and 6.5 percent per annum (Alternative 1) both external and internal gaps would appear with the external gap appearing to be more dominant. As shown in Table 1.3, foreign gap increased from RM 8.1 billion in 1996 to RM 17.7 billion in 2005. Given this enlarged gap, the economy could achieve only 3.6 percent and 3.1 percent of its target of GDP growth. On the other hand, the savings gap is less bound to growth over this period; though this has also increased from RM9.9 million in 1996 to RM 1.8 billion in 2005. Resources limitations will lead to the slow-down of the economy. It allows the economy to grow at 7 percent, which is slightly lower than the target rate of growth, (see Table 1.3). An increase in the rate of growth of export to 7.5 percent (Alternative 2) would reduce considerably the financial task of supporting the national target rate of growth, and there is a significant albeit declining surplus of exports over imports during the period. This will reduce considerably the financial downside of the foreign gap to RM 7 billion in 1996 and RM 14.6 billion in 2005, supporting the growth rate at 4 percent.

A further increase of exports to 8 percent annually (Alternative 3) would reduce this gap further to around 6 billion, supporting the growth rate at 5.8 percent. In order to fill the foreign gap exports would need to grow by at least 11 percent (Alternative 4), with this rate of export growth the gap would be eliminated after 1998 and the economy could achieve its target rate of growth of 8 percent in 1999. These projections may be observed from Figure 1.1.

On the basis of a 6 percent GDP growth rate, and 6.5 percent export growth rate (Alternative 5), the external gap would become more glaring, rising steeply from RM 7.4 billion to RM 12 billion over 1996-2005. The size of the gap would accordingly become smaller than that stemming from the 8 percent of GDP growth rate. Nevertheless, with this gap the economy would be able to achieve only a 3 percent growth. In order to eliminate the foreign gap, exports would need to expand by 10 percent per annum (alternative 6). At this rate of export growth, the gap would be eliminated only after 2001. This point may be gleaned from Tables 1.4 and Figure 1.2.

The predominance of the foreign gap in the projection period appears to be a continuation of the trend that has been observed in the preceding years. This is due to the advent of high imports, and debt as well as insufficient export earnings to facilitate the inflow of goods and services for the investment. It is critical that steps be taken to overcome directly the trade constraint if the prescribed target rate of growth in the economy is to be sustained.

Analysis of the Performance Parameters

The solutions that have been proposed include increasing taxes by 5 percent per annum and reducing the imports by the same rate. The results of the projection incorporating these assumptions are discussed below.

An increase in the tax rate by 5 percent annually over the projection period of 1996-2005 will lead to a reduction in imports by the same ratio, thereby reducing the foreign gap. With the GDP growth rate of 8 percent exports needed to grow 10.5 percent to cover import requirements in the projection periods. By comparison, with a 6 percent growth rate of GDP, exports needed to increase by 9 percent to finance imports during the forecasting periods. The changes in the basic parameters from the projection may be observed from Table 1.5. Increasing the tax by 5 percent would increase public savings by 2 percent and reduce private savings by 3 percent. The share of government and private savings would come to 30 and 70 percent respectively. The total effect would be negative, leading to a reduction in total savings by 1 percent. However, this negative effect would not adversely affect the original estimation of the savings gap under both projection periods. The changes in the basic parameters may be gleaned from Table 1.5.

Concluding Remarks and Policy Conclusion

The objective of this chapter was to describe, estimate and analyse the basic model that lies behind the policy packages developed by the World Bank. The aim of the projection exercise was basically to consider the macroeconomic implications involved if such a growth target is maintained throughout the projection period. While the results indicate the scenario that would emerge, whether these would materialise would depend on a number of factors. In practice the nature and size of the resource gaps will be subjected to the actions and policies that are taken such as the planning authorities' response to the pressures, problems and opportunities confronting the economy from time to time. In particular, the external financing gap will be subject to trade, domestic investment, overall domestic financial and foreign exchange policies all of which affect aggregate demand. The main conclusions of this chapter are:

The results conform to the Neo-structure school of thought that the dominant constraint in most developing countries is the foreign exchange gap, which creates structural disequilibrium and macroeconomic imbalances. The results of the analysis suggest that the trade constraint has more often been binding than the savings constraint on economic growth, which indicates that Malaysia has taken-off to a higher stage of development. The savings – investment gap tends to diminish while the import-export gap tends to expand for any particular growth rate that is chosen.

The chapter suggests that while foreign exchange is scarce, the projected gaps between investment requirements and domestic savings and between import requirements and export earnings are of roughly equal magnitude, and that policies to raise the level of domestic savings must assume as much importance as policies to augment the quantity of foreign exchange if dependence on foreign assistance is to be reduced.

It appears therefore that the most efficient way to achieve the Malaysian targeted rate of growth in GDP is to attract a higher level of foreign resources and to regulate the fiscal regime. The most likely approach, however, should consist of a mixture of new resources together with a reduction in foreign debt interest payment through reforms in fiscal and monetary policies, and an improvement in the external sector by improving exports, implementing import substitution and managing foreign debt and FDI in the country.

The resource constraints faced by the country would imply that Malaysia would have to continue relying heavily on external capital and borrowing. The Malaysian economic forecasts are less optimistic about the short and medium term prospects of the economy. The balance of payment and the medium term prospects for the external debt and the debt service ratio is likely to remain unfavourable.

A stronger export performance will be an important contributing factor to the improvement in growth performance during the next few years. Export volume and its rate and the key factors affecting it (i.e. exchange rate, terms of trade, creating new markets and goods) require special attention. Export growth should be promoted through a broad range of export-oriented policies.

Against this backdrop, the government over the next few years should attempt to introduce additional measures to strongly improve the country's balance of payments position. These measures should aim at enhancing the competitiveness of Malaysia's exports, reducing intermediate and capital goods imports and strengthening the services trade account. The analyses that have been carried out point to the need for exports to grow by more than 12 percent to achieve both 6 and 8 percent growth. The challenge will be for Malaysia to sustain its export growth. In order to enhance the competitiveness of Malaysia's exports, various steps need to be taken to improve product quality and to adopt more aggressive marketing strategies. More active promotion of exports to both traditional and non-traditional markets has to be undertaken. A more effective system of incentives is required to promote potentially viable export activities especially during the formative stages of their development. Furthermore research and development (R&D) must be undertaken and new markets and products must be developed to sustain the dynamism of traditional exports. Pricing and exchange rate policies must be aligned in order to provide producers with the right incentive to export their products.

In the final analysis the government's objective of maintaining real GDP growth at about 8 percent annually over the next few years will be dependent not only on the continued progress of adjustments undertaken by the global economy but more importantly on the responsiveness and ability of the domestic economy to modify its structure of production to the changing world demand and the opportunities that arise with it. While some progress has been made in this area in recent years, there is a further need now to accelerate the restructuring and privatisation of public enterprises in order to reduce their reliance on budgetary subsidies and transfers, and in order to promote their overall economic efficiency.

Note

1. All of the variables are assumed to carry the same time subscript (t), which is omitted to simplify the exposition.

Table 1.1 Specification Variables of the Two-Gaps Model

Target Scenarios	Exogenous	Endogenous	Parameters	Policy
g^*	$\overline{E}$	$S^*{}_t$	κ^*	ε
	$\overline{F}$	I_t^r	m^*	T
		α_1, s , i		

Table 1.2 Values of Variables and Parameters of the Two-Gap Over 1981-1995

Average variables over 1981-1995	Symbol	RM Million
Gross domestic product	Y_0	213653
Gross investments	I_0	95571
Gross domestic savings	S_0	75882
Export of goods and services	E_0	25682.1
Imports of goods and services	M_0	69434.5
Parameters		percent
Incremental capital output - ratio	κ^*	4.3
Incremental output - import ratio	m^*	0.125
GDP growth rate	g	8percent and 6percent
Marginal saving rate	α_1	0.3076
Import/GDP ratios	i	0.64
Saving/GDP ratios	s	0.344
Export growth rates	ε	65, 7.5, 8, 10, 11

Table 1.3 Projection of Import, Export and Foreign Gap to 2005 Using Target GNP Growth Rate of 8 Percent

		Export Earnings			
Year	**Import**	**6.5**	**7.5**	**8**	**11**
1996	147676.9	70343.5	81689.4	87985.4	136394.9
1997	159491.1	74915.8	87816.2	95024.3	151398.4
1998	172250.4	79785.4	94402.4	102626.2	168052.2
1999	186030.4	84971.5	101482.5	110836.3	186537.9
2000	200912.9	90494.6	109093.7	119703.2	207057.1
2001	216985.9	96376.7	117275.8	129279.5	229833.4
2002	234344.8	102641.2	126071.5	139621.8	255115
2003	253092.4	109312.9	135526.8	150791.5	283177.7
2004	273339.7	116418.2	145691.5	162854.8	314327.3
2005	295206.9	123985.5	156618.2	175883.2	348903.3

Foreign Gap							
6.5		**7.5**		**8**		**11**	
Absolute	**percent**	**Absolute**	**percent**	**Absolute**	**percent**	**Absolute**	**percent**
81078.7	3.6	70336.9	4.18	59691	4.76	11282	7.38
88564	3.5	76350.6	4.17	64466	4.76	8092	7.59
96713	3.5	82874	4.15	69624	4.76	4198	7.8
105583	3.4	89951	4.13	75194	4.76	- 507	8.02
115236.5	3.4	97627.7	4.11	81209	4.76	- 6144	8.24
125740.6	3.3	105954	4.09	87706	4.76	- 12847	8.47
137168.5	3.3	114985.9	4.07	94723	4.76	- 20770	8.7
159599.7	3.2	124781.5	4.05	102300	4.76	- 30685	8.95
163119.9	3.2	135405.5	4.03	110484	4.76	- 40987	9.19
177822.9	3.1	146927.6	4.03	119323	4.76	- 53696	9.45

Notes: Positive sign indicates gaps and the negative sign indicates fill or closed the gaps.

Table 1.4 Projection of Export, Import and Foreign Gaps to 2005 Using Target GNP Growth Rate of 6 Percent

		Export Earnings			
Year	**Import**	**6.5**	**7.5**	**8**	**10**
1996	144942.2	70343.5	81689.4	87985.4	118008.6
1997	153868.7	74915.8	87816.2	95024.3	129809.4
1998	162857	79785.4	94402.4	102626.2	142790.4
1999	172628.4	84971.5	101482.5	110836.3	157069.4
2000	182986.4	90494.6	109093.7	119703.2	172776.3
2001	193965.4	96376.7	11727.58	129279.5	190053.9
2002	205603.3	102641.2	126071.5	139621.8	209059.4
2003	217939.5	109312.9	135526.8	150791.5	229965.3
2004	231015.8	116418.2	145691.5	162854.8	252961.9
2005	244876.7	123985.5	156618.2	175883.2	278258

Foreign Gap							
6.5		**7.5**		**8**		**10**	
Absolute	**percent**	**Absolute**	**percent**	**Absolute**	**percent**	**Absolute**	**percent**
74598.7	2.9	63252	3.38	56956	3.64	26933	4.88
78722.9	2.92	65822	3.43	58614	3.71	23829	5.07
83071.6	2.94	68454	3.48	60230	3.78	20066	5.27
87656.9	2.95	71145	3.52	61792	3.85	15559	5.46
92491.8	2.96	73892	3.57	63283	3.92	10210	5.66
97588.7	2.98	76689	3.62	64685	3.99	3911.5	5.87
102962.1	2.99	79531	3.68	65981	4.07	- 3456	6.1
108626.6	3.0	82412	3.73	67148	4.15	- 12025	6.3
114597.6	3.02	85396	3.78	68161	4.22	- 21946	6.65

Table 1.5 Change in Imports and Saving Stemming for 5 Percent Change in Tax Rate

Year	Change in import with GNP growth 8 percent	Change in import with GNP growth 6 percent	Change in savings with GNP growth 8 percent	Change in savings with GNP growth 6 percent
1996	140293	137695	68775.1	67472
1997	151516.5	145956.8	74406.9	71617.1
1998	163637.9	154714.2	80487.4	76011.5
1999	176728.9	163996.9	87058	80669.6
2000	190867.3	173836.9	94152.7	85607.1
2001	206136.6	184266.1	101814.8	90840.9
2002	222627.5	195323.1	110089.8	96388.7
2003	240437.7	207042.5	119026.7	102269.4
2004	259672.7	219465	128678.6	108502.8
2005	280446.5	232632.9	139102.7	1151103

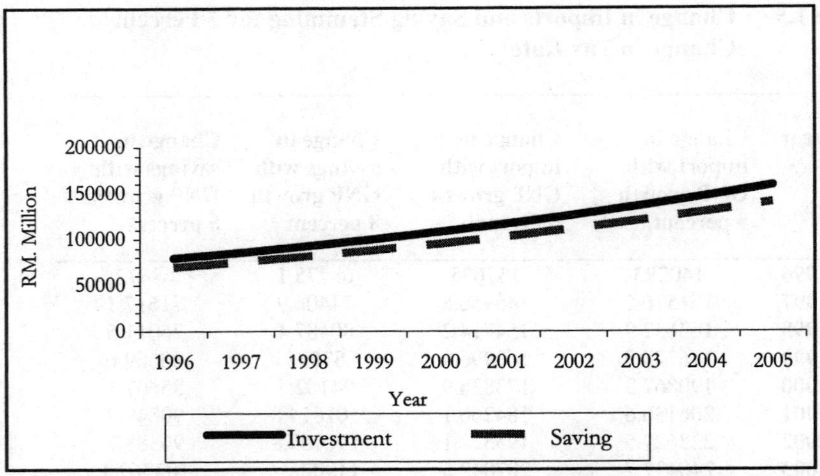

Figure 1.1 Projection of Saving, Investment and Saving Gap Using Target GDP Growth Rate of 8 Percent

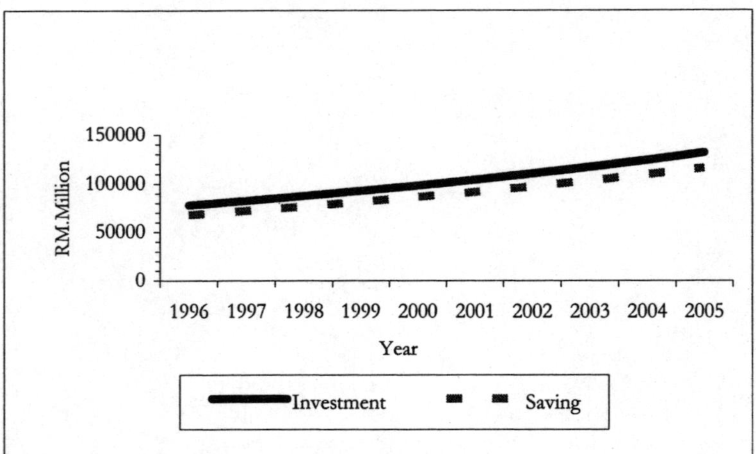

Figure 1.2 Projection of Saving, Investment and Saving Gap Using Target GNP Growth Rate of 6 Percent

Appendix

By substituting the values of the parameters into the equations given in Table 1.1, we obtained the following relationships:
Estimated Results Based on the 1981-1995 period and growth rate 0.06

$Y_t^* = 213653\ (1+0.06)^t$

$I_t^r = (0.06 \times 5.73) \times Y_t^*$

$S_t^f = -1668.8 + 0.31\ Y_t^*$

The savings gap = $I_t^r - S_t^f$ or $(0.06 \times 5.73) \times Y_t^* - (-1668.8 + 0.31 \times Y_t^*)$

$M_t^r = (0.06/0.094) \times Y_t^*$

$X_t = -878.7 + 1234.4\ T$

The external gap = $M_t^r - X_t$ or $(0.06/0.094) \times Y_t^* - (-878.7 + 1234.4\ T)$

Estimated Results Based on the1981-1995 period and growth rate 0.08

$Y_t^* = 213653\ (1+0.08)^t$

$I_t^r = (0.08 \times 2.75) \times Y_t^*$

$S_t^f = -1638.9 + 0.30817\ Y_t^*$

The savings gap = $I_t^r - S_t^f$ or $(0.08 \times 2.75) \times Y_t^* - (-1638.9 + 0.30817 \times Y_t^*)$

$M_t^r = (0.08/0.125) \times Y_t^*$

$X_t = -878.7 + 1234.4 T$

The external gap = $M_t^r - X_t$ or $(0.08/0.22) \times Y_t^* - (-878.7 + 1234.4\ T)$

The results of estimation under the two-target rate of growth of GDP are shown in Tables 1.3 and 1.4 and Figures 1.1 and 1.2.

References

Addison, D. (1989), 'The World Bank Revised Minimum Standard Model: Concepts and Issues', World Bank PPR Working Paper No. 231.

Adelman, I. and Kim, M. J. (1995), 'An Econometric Model of the Korean economy', in I. Adelman (eds), *Institutions and Development Strategies*, Britain, Edward Edgar Limited.

Ardeshir, S. and John, L. (1992), 'Uganda: Constraints on Economic Growth', *African Development Review*, vol. 4, pp. 29-46.

Chenery, H.B. (1971), *Studies in Development Planning*, Harvard University Press, London.

Chenery, H.B and Srinivasan, T. (1989), *Handbook of Development Economics*, vol 2, Elservier Science Publishers, North Holland.

Chenery, H.B and Strout, A. (1966), 'Foreign Assistance and Economic Development', *American Economic Review*, vol. 56, pp. 679-733.

Easterly, W. (1997), 'The Ghost of Financing Gap. How the Harrod-Domar Growth Model Still Haunts Development Economics', World Bank, Mimeo, pp. 1-30.

Easterly, W. (1999), 'The Ghost of Financing Gap: Testing the Growth Model used in the International Financial Institutions', *Journal of Development Economics*, vol. 60, pp. 423-438.

Evangelos, A.C, Anupam, B. and Dhaneshwar, G. (1999), 'Adjustment and Growth in Sub-Saharan Africa', IMF Working Paper No.51.

Frenkel, R., Fanelli, J. and Rozenwurcel, G. (1993), 'Growth and Structural Reform in Latin America: Where we stand, UNCTAD Discussion Papers No.62.

Gersovitz, M. (1982), 'The Estimation of the Two-Gap Model', *Journal of International Economics*, vol. 12, pp. 111-126.

Khan, M. S. Montiel, P. J. and Haque, N. U. (1991), *Macro Economic Models for Adjustment in Developing Countries*, International Monetary Fund, New York.

Khan, A. and Hoshino, E. (1990), 'Foreign Capital Inflow and Economic Growth: A Two-Gap Model for the Bangladesh', *Bangladesh Development Studies,* vol. 18, pp. 55-73.

Lewis, W., (1984), 'The State of Development Theory', *American Economic Review*, vol. 74, pp. 1-10.

Lensink. R. and Vanbergeijk, P. (1991), 'Official Finance Requirements in the 1990s', *World Development,* vol. 19, pp. 497-510.

Meier, G. (1995), *Leading Issues in Economic Development* 6th, Oxford University Press, New York.

Mills, C. and Nallari, R. (1997), 'Analytical Approaches to Stabilization and Adjustment Programs', World Bank, Seminar Paper No.44.

Moran, C. (1989), 'Imports Under a Foreign Exchange Constraints', *World Bank Economic Review*, vol. 3, pp. 279-95.

Polak, J. (1990), 'A Marriage Between Fund and Bank Models? Comment on Khan and Montiel', *IMF Staff Papers*, vol. 37, pp. 183-186.

Rosenstrin-Rodan, P.N. (1961), 'International Aid for Under Developed Countries', *Review of Economics and Statistics*, vol. 43, pp. 107-38.

Shibly, M. (1984), 'Foreign capital inflow, domestic savings and economic growth: The experience of the Sudan', Economic Development, 9, 125-45.

Shibly, M. and Thrilwall, A. (1981), 'Dual Gap Analysis for Sudan', *World Development*, vol. 9, pp. 193-200.

Streeten, P. (1987), 'Structural Adjustment: A Survey of the Issues and Options', *World Development*, vol. 15, pp. 1469-1482.

Syrquin, M. and Taylor, L. (1984), *Economic Structure and Performance*, Florida Academic Press, New York.

Taylor, L. (1994), 'Gap Models', *Journal of Development Economics*, vol. 45, pp. 17-34.

Taylor, L. (1998), 'IMF and World Bank in a Globalized Economy', *World Development*, vol. 26, pp. 145-154.

Ventara, J, (1996), 'A Survey of Macroeconomic Models at the World Bank', World Bank, Mimeo.

Whalley, J. (1984), 'A Review of Numerical Modelling Activity at the World Bank', World Bank Mimeo.

Wijnbergen, V.S. (1986), 'Macroeconomic Aspects of the Effectiveness of Foreign Aid: The Two-Gap Model', *Journal of International Economics*, vol. 21, pp. 123-36.

Williamson, J. (1990), *Latin American Adjustment; How Much has Happened?*, Washington DC: Institute for International Economics.

World Bank (1989), *Sub-Saharan Africa: From Crisis to Sustainable Growth*, Washington DC, New York.

World Bank (1994), *Adjustment in Africa: Reforms, Results, and the Road Ahead*, Oxford: Oxford University Press.

World Bank (1995), *RMSM-X Model Building Reference Guide*, World Bank, Washington DC.

World Bank (1996), *Uganda: The Challenge of Growth and Poverty Reduction*, World Bank, Washington DC, New York.

World Bank (1997), *Private Capital Flows to Developing Countries: The Road to Financial Integration*, New York, Oxford University Press.

World Bank (1997), *World Development Report*, Oxford University Press, New York.

World Bank (1998), *The Road to Recovery*, Washington D.C. New York.

World Bank (1998), *Lithuania: An Opportunity for Economic Success*, I and II, World Bank, Washington DC.

Chapter 2

Money, Credit, Asset Prices and Monetary Transmission Mechanism

Mansor H. Ibrahim

Introduction

The recent Asian financial crisis has placed banks at the central of attention. While the sharp devaluation of various currencies in East Asia and subsequent drastic fall in their stock prices are generally unanticipated at least in magnitudes, the role of the banking system in the propagation of financial and monetary shocks has been much emphasised. Prior to the crisis, domestic banks were able to lend aggressively because of excessive liquidity in the banking system. However, the financial turmoil that started with the devaluation of the Thai baht on July 2, 1997 led to a reversal of banks' lending behaviour resulting in massive contraction of bank loans. The subsequent reduction in real output in the affected countries is drastic, equally unexpected as the initial drastic fall in the exchange rates and stock prices. In 1997, the growth rates of Indonesia, Korea, Malaysia, the Philippines, and Thailand were respectively 4.7percent, 5.0percent, 7.3percent, 5.2percent, and -1.7percent. These growth rates drastically dropped to respectively -13.1percent, -6.7percent, -7.4percent, -0.6percent, and -10.2percent in 1998. Given this chain of events from currency devaluation to credit crunch to finally contraction in economic activity, bank credits may have played an important role in aggravating the economic downturn observed during the Asian crisis.

Indeed, the role of banks in accounting for economic fluctuations has received great interest in monetary transmission mechanism literature and the Asian crisis has only further strengthened the interest in the subject. Two views are generally discussed in this context, the "money view" and the "credit view". In the traditional framework of monetary transmission mechanism, termed the "money view", all bank assets are assumed to be perfect substitutes and as such there is no independent role for the banks' assets. The effects of monetary policy work only through the liability side of the banks' balance sheets, leading to changes in real interest rate and interest-sensitive components of spending. However, the recent "credit view" introduces an additional or complementary channel through which banks play a role in the propagation of monetary shocks. According to this view, due to asymmetric information and capital market imperfections, banks' assets (for example loans and securities) are not perfect substitutes and they are special to some types of borrowers. Accordingly, to the extent that some borrowers are dependent on banks for finance and that monetary policy can affect bank loan supply, the financial structure matters in amplifying the effects of monetary shocks on the economy.[1] Identifying the role of bank credits, thus, can help in determining the precise impacts of monetary policy action or financial shocks on real economic activity.

The present chapter seeks to contribute to this interest in the relations between money, credit and macroeconomic fluctuations by examining the case of Malaysia. Over the period 1990-1997, Malaysia recorded an average growth rate of about 8percent annually. The Asian crisis, however, halted this impressive growth path leading to a sharp contraction of real output by more than 7percent in 1998. The unbridled expansion of bank credit during the high growth period and its subsequent contraction may have played a key role in this wide swing of real economic activity. Employing market disequilibrium framework to quantify excess demands for loans in Malaysia, Gan and Soon (2001) note the period immediately after the devaluation of the Thai baht, i.e. from July 1997 to March 1998, to be the credit crunch period. Bacha (1998) further argues that a sudden tightening of policies (including monetary policies) in response to the sharp decline in the value of the Ringgit led to a credit crunch. These studies, thus, seem to be suggestive of the credit channel at work where the period of sharp reduction in bank loans precedes economic contraction. However, using data prior to the Asian crisis, Azali and Matthews (1999) provide empirical evidence supportive of the dominant role of money as opposed to bank credit in the Malaysian monetary transmission mechanism for the post-liberalisation period from 1979 to 1993. Further analysis may shed additional light on the issue.

In the analysis, we focus on the role of bank balance sheet variables in the monetary transmission mechanism and their dynamic interactions with real output. In light of the recent Asian crisis, we also consider other asset or financial prices such as exchange rate and equity prices in the relations between monetary variables and real activities. Apart from serving as additional channels through which monetary policy influences output, the inclusion of these variables enables us to gauge the additional role of banks in transmitting other financial shocks to real output. To this end, the analysis makes use of impulse-response functions and variance decompositions generated from unrestricted VAR models.

Background Information

The Central Bank of Malaysia (i.e. Bank Negara Malaysia) was established in January 1959 under the Central Bank of Malaysia Ordinance 1958 to perform an essential function of monetary management. The Bank is assigned with broad macroeconomic objectives including stable price level, stable exchange rate, sustainable output growth, low unemployment rate, and recently in light of the Asian financial crisis, stable financial markets. In its early stage of establishment, due to the lack of a well-developed financial market, the conduct of monetary policy was limited to the use of mainly statutory reserve and liquidity ratio requirements. As the Malaysian financial markets progress over the years, the range of monetary instruments available to the Central Bank broadens to include foreign exchange swap, open market operations, recycling government deposits, and others. Overall, the Central Bank is highly active in its role of stabilising the economy. Its monetary policy stance at a given point in time rests crucially on the economic conditions of the country. Monetary policy turns expansionary to stimulate real output, as in 1975, 1985-1986, and 1998-1999, and becomes contractionary to contain inflationary pressures and/or mop up excess liquidity in the market, as in 1969-1970, 1973-1974, 1981, and 1989-1992.

The active participation of the Central Bank in economic stabilisation naturally raises fundamental questions pertaining to monetary policy and its relations to the economic performance of the country. Namely, does monetary policy have real effects? And, if so, what are the main channels of monetary transmission mechanisms? Existing studies for the case of Malaysia generally provide affirmative answers to the first question. Monetary policy matters because it has real effects and because it is inflationary (see Ibrahim, 2002, for a review of the literature). However, the issue of monetary transmission mechanism and the role of banks remain largely unexplored. Recently, Azali and Matthews (1999) analysed patterns of the interactions between money and income and credit and income in an attempt to assess the "money view" and "credit view" of monetary transmission mechanism using quarterly data from 1971 to 1993. Their findings suggest that credit innovations possessed significant influences on aggregate demand variations during the pre-liberalisation period (1971-1978) while money innovations turned significant during the post-liberalisation period (1979-1993). However, Kwek (1992) provides supportive evidence for the predictive ability of credit aggregates during the 1970s as well as the 1980s. In the present analysis, we complement these works by updating the samples to more recent observations and by explicitly considering banks' balance sheet variables.

Since the 1970s, Malaysia has experienced significant developments in its financial markets. Important aspects of these developments include the liberalisation of interest rates, financial innovations, and rapid growth of the equity market.[2] The de-regulation of deposits and lending rates, where banks can set their own deposits and lending rates, began in 1978. In 1983, however, the government introduced the Base Lending Rate (BLR) of two leading banks, calculated based on the banks' cost of funds adjusted for the costs of statutory reserves, liquid assets requirements and overheads, to which all banks were required to peg their lending rates. Similarly, in 1985, all banks were required to peg interest rates on deposits of up to 12-month maturity to that of the two leading banks. This requirement on deposit rate pegging was lifted in 1987. Then, in February 1991, the BLR was liberalised in that each bank can set its own BLR. Despite an interrupted process of interest rate liberalisation, over time, market forces have been given more roles in the determination of the interest rate. Additionally, throughout the years, financial innovations bring a wider range of financial assets. The Malaysian stock market, the Kuala Lumpur Stock Exchange, has grown at an impressive rate interrupted only by the 1997 Asian crisis. The market capitalisation and turnovers witnessed high growth for over ten years since the recession of 1985. The market capitalisation increased by more than 9 times from RM74 billion in 1987 to RM807 billion in 1996. Meanwhile, the market turnovers increased by more than 45 times over the same period. This performance of the equity market had made the Malaysian equity market among one of the fast-growing stock markets not only in the East Asian region but also among emerging stock markets.

Financial developments such as those experienced by Malaysia have been noted to weaken the relations between money and output and led some researchers to evaluate other channels of transmission mechanism such as the credit channel (Garretsen and Swank, 1998). Ironically, however, these developments also raise doubts over the importance of bank lending in the transmission of monetary shocks. Namely, financial advancements reduce the extent of information asymmetry and, with wider range of financial assets, firms' dependency on bank loans (Agung, 1998). Moreover, as argued and evidenced by Azali and Matthews (1999), the liquidity channel of monetary transmission mechanism becomes effective with the liberalisation of the interest rate, an important aspect in the financial development of any country. The credit channel, on the other hand, is rendered less effective.

Despite these arguments, the role of banks in the propagation of monetary and financial shocks are still open to further empirical investigation. Although Malaysia has made important progress in its financial developments, the current state of its financial markets still lags behind those of the industrialised countries, especially in terms of information disclosures, supervisions and enforcement. In other words, asymmetric information is still a significant feature in the Malaysian financial scene. Moreover, the banking sector has not only progressed along side with other financial developments but has also continued to play a predominant role in providing sources of finance for Malaysian firms. Initially, the Malaysian banking sector was dominated by foreign commercial banks. The lending activities of the foreign banks, which concentrated mainly on trade financing and working capital financing of large firms, were generally viewed as not favourable to the needs of domestic firms. Accordingly, with emphasis by Bank Negara Malaysia on reforming the banking sector, domestic banks developed to play a major role in Malaysian financial markets.

According to Radiah (2000), the development of the domestic banking sector took about 35 years. In 1959, the year Bank Negara Malaysia was established, there were 18 foreign commercial banks with a total number of 99 branches operating in the country as opposed to only 8 domestic commercial banks with 12 branches. With restrictions on the establishments of new foreign banks and foreign banks' branches, domestic commercial banks' branches began to outnumber those of foreign banks in 1966. The number of domestic commercial banks began to surpass that of foreign banks ten years later in 1976. By 1994, all foreign banks were domestically incorporated and the number of domestic banks' branches far exceeded that of foreign banks. In parallel, since the inception of the New Economic Policy (NEP) in 1970, the Malaysian government has aimed at developing the nation into an industrialised-based economy. Bank Negara Malaysia has played its part in attaining this objective of successfully transforming the banking system by regulating the volume as well as the direction of bank lending to priority sectors. During 1990-1997, three sectors received more than 58percent of total bank loans. These are Manufacturing, Broad Property, and Finance, Insurance and Business Services.

The growth of the banking sector has been remarkable. Table 2.1 presents total assets (or liabilities) as well as loans and deposits of all Malaysian commercial banks, the core component of the Malaysian banking sector. Up until the recent 1997 Asian crisis, the growth rate of the commercial banks' assets, loans and deposits was well over the rate of Malaysian economic growth. The banks' assets (liabilities), loans and deposits increased more than two times every five years from 1970 to 1995, with the exception of only the period from 1985 to 1990. Note also that, while the ratio of loans to total assets seems to stabilise around 50percent to 65percent and the ratio of deposits to total liabilities declined initially and increased afterwards, the ratios of both loans and deposits to GDP posted an upward trend. The continuing growth and importance of the banking institutions together with prevalent asymmetric information in the markets led many firms to depend on bank loans as a source of finance. According to a survey conducted by Bank Negara Malaysia on 206 manufacturing companies in 1996, about 67percent of manufacturing companies in Malaysia depended on bank loans for their working capital. Additionally, 44percent of the 206 companies relied on bank financing for their export activities.[3] More importantly, reaffirming the central role of banks and probably the presence of asymmetric information, domestically owned companies depended more on bank loans as a source of financing than foreign-owned companies did. In short, the development of these banks' dependent sectors and firms suggest possible relevance of the bank loans, in addition to bank deposits, in monetary transmission mechanism.

Lastly, the recent episode of the Asian crisis is seen as indicating the central role of banks in the propagation of financial shocks. The Asian crisis, which was initiated by the devaluation of the Thai baht, resulted in the drastic fall of the Malaysian Ringgit and Stock Exchanges. The initial response of the Malaysian monetary authority was to tighten monetary policy in order to defend the exchange rate and stem inflationary pressures and capital outflows, which led to the increase in the interbank rate (see Figure 2.1). In 1996, a year prior to the crisis, the growth rate of the commercial banks' loans was over 20percent (Table 2.1). The eruption of the crisis in mid-1997 did not stall this rapid growth (i.e. more than 20percent) of the bank loans in 1997. Both bank assets and deposits recorded similar patterns of growth. The tight monetary policy implemented immediately after the eruption of the crisis was felt by the Banking sector in 1998. Deposit growth of the banking sector remained strong while loan growth slowed down drastically to only 3.4percent. Interestingly, total assets (liabilities) of the commercial banks witnessed a negative growth of 5.9percent. In late 1998, the Malaysian government reversed its policy stance toward easy monetary policy leading to a reduction in the interbank rate. Still, in 1999, the loan growth turned slightly negative while deposit growth slowed down to only 7.9percent. This pattern of growth in bank assets and loans and concurrent reduction in real GDP growth provides further ground for the present inquiry on the importance of bank balance sheets in

Malaysian economic fluctuations, an issue to be evaluated more formally in the next section.

Data and Empirical Approach

The analysis makes use of a reduced-form VAR framework. In line with other studies for developed countries (Bernanke and Blinder, 1992; Iturriaga, 2000) and developing countries (Agung, 1998), we use the short-term interest rate (i.e. the overnight interbank rate, INT) as our monetary policy variable. According to Domac (1999), the Central Bank of Malaysia directly influences the interbank rate through its intervention in the money market and thus makes it suitable as a monetary policy indicator. For the objective variables, we use real GDP (RGDP) and the consumer price index (CPI). These are the main variables that policy makers seek to influence. The banks' balance sheet variables are represented by total bank loans (BL) and bank deposits (BD) deflated by the CPI. The variables are key for the evaluation of monetary transmission mechanism, whether monetary policy shocks influence real output through bank loans or deposits or both.

Apart from these variables, we also consider the exchange rate and the stock price index. To represent the exchange rate, we use bilateral Ringgit rate vis-à-vis the U.S. dollar (EXC). Meanwhile, the Kuala Lumpur composite index represents the stock prices (KLCI). The inclusion of the exchange rate is justified on the basis that Malaysia is an open economy depending on both exports and imports for its development process. The shocks to the exchange rate can thus influence output and prices through their effects on international trade. More importantly, apart from this independent influence, the exchange rate can also serve as an additional channel through which monetary policy affects output. The equity prices may also be important in accounting for macroeconomic fluctuations via, for instance, wealth and balance sheet effects. Namely, a change in the stock prices affects consumers' wealth and accordingly their consumption plans. A rise in the stock prices also affects the balance sheets of the firms (or the Tobin's q) and, accordingly, raises their capacity to borrow. Accordingly, monetary policy may affect output through its potential effects on share prices.

Figure 1.1 provides time series plots of the data used, which are quarterly covering the period from 1978.Q1 to 1998.Q2. The main sources of the data are the *International Financial Statistics* (CD-ROM version) of the IMF and *Statistical Bulletin* of the Central Bank of Malaysia. We end the data in 1998.Q2 due to the implementation of capital controls and fixed Ringgit-USD exchange rate by the Malaysian government. At this juncture, two points are noteworthy. First, for the implementation of the VAR with all variables deemed necessary included, we need a sufficiently big sample size. Adding a variable to the VAR system with a rather limited sample size such as ours can quickly consume the degrees of freedom and lead to inefficient estimates. In other words, a limit needs to be placed on which variables should enter the VAR system. And second, our sample period runs through the Asian crisis, which started in July 1997. These additional four observations (1997.Q3-1998.Q2) can pose a problem to the estimation if they are statistical outliers. Yet, it remains interesting to see what effects these observations may have on the results.[4]

Taking note of these two points, we set our basic model to contain only six variables, namely *INT, EXC, BL, BD, RGDP,* and *CPI*. This system is in line with existing studies that incorporate the exchange rate in addition to basic variables in the transmission mechanism (Agung, 1998). We then attempt further analysis by incorporating the stock prices in the model, forming a 7-variable model. In each case, we run the regressions using the sample up to 1997.Q2 (i.e. excluding the crisis episode) as well as extending the sample to 1998.Q2. As it stands, the VAR model places minimal restrictions on the interactions among the variables and recognises potential endogeneity of all variables in the system. This feature of the VAR makes it suitable for the evaluation of the interactions between monetary policy and final objective variables, the subject that receives much attention but little agreement on how monetary impulses are transmitted to real economic activities.

More importantly, from the VAR estimation, we can generate forecast error variance decompositions and impulse response functions, which are useful for discerning dynamic interactions among the variables. Specifically, indicating the percentage of a variable's forecast error variance attributable to its own innovations and innovations in other variables, the variance decompositions provide natural measures of relative importance of various shocks in the monetary transmission mechanism. Accordingly, the importance of the bank balance sheet variables in accounting for economic fluctuations can be assessed by looking at the strength of the interactions between them as portrayed by the variance decompositions. Meanwhile, the impulse-response functions trace the directional responses of a variable to a one standard deviation shock in other variables, indicating whether the shock exerts a temporary or persistent effect on a variable of interest. In our context, the timing of the responses of bank balance sheet variables and macroeconomic variables to monetary policy shocks provides indication on specific channels of transmission mechanisms (Bernanke and Blinder, 1992).

In assessing monetary transmission mechanisms using the VAR, we need to address at least the following two issues: identification of monetary policy shocks and specification of the variables (in level or in first difference) in the VAR. As we have noted above, we employ the short term interest rate as a monetary policy variable and, as such, take its fluctuations as representing shifts in the stance of monetary policy. However, the policy variable may in part be endogenous due to the monetary authorities' reaction to non-policy variables. If this is the case, we need to identify exogenous and endogenous components of policy impulses since only the former is relevant for understanding monetary transmission mechanism. In the present chapter, we follow Sims' (1980, 1992) methodology by othogonalizing innovations of the variables in the VAR system using Choleski's decomposition of the residual covariance matrix. This amounts to imposing a recursive structure on the contemporaneous relationship among the variables. By placing the noted monetary policy variable first in the ordering, we impose non-contemporaneous responses of the policy variables to other variables in the VAR system.

Accordingly, its current shocks purified from its endogenous responses to lagged changes of other variables represent exogenous policy impulses.[5]

In addition to this identification problem, we also need to entertain an issue related to the specification of the variables in the VAR, whether they should be expressed in levels or in first differences. This issue arises due to the well-noted non-stationarity property of most macroeconomic variables and the possibility that a set of non-stationary variables shares a long run equilibrium or is cointegrated. Estimating the model using the variables in level runs the risk of being spurious if they are integrated series or are non-stationary (Phillips, 1986; Stock, 1987). Using the variables in first differences, however, entails the loss of long run information in the data in the case that the variables are cointegrated (Engle and Granger, 1987). Needless to state, a VAR in first difference is only valid when the variables are non stationary and are not cointegrated.

According to Engle and Granger (1987), the dynamics of the cointegrated variables can be represented using a vector error correction model, or restricted VAR model, which imposes long-run constraints among levels of the variables as implied by their cointegration. Further, they note that these long-run constraints are also satisfied asymptotically in a VAR in levels, or unrestricted VAR model. In other words, both approaches are appropriate for modelling dynamic interactions among time series. Estimating the unrestricted VAR model for the cointegrated variables seem to be a normal route taken by much of the literature on the topic. Ramaswamy and Slok (1998) outline the advantages of using the unrestricted VAR as opposed to using the restricted VAR. The most notable argument is the economic interpretation attached to impulse response functions of both models. While the impulse responses from the restricted VAR tend to imply that the impacts of monetary shocks are permanent, those from the unrestricted VAR allow history to decide on whether the effects of monetary shocks are permanent or not (Ramaswamy and Slok, 1998, p. 380). Accordingly, in line with the literature, we employ an unrestricted VAR model when the variables are cointegrated.

Estimation Results

Since a priori tests on the stochastic properties of the data are imperative, we first implemented the Augmented Dickey-Fuller (ADF) and Phillips-Perron (PP) unit root tests to establish the order of integration. Then, we conducted the Johansen-Juselius (1990) multivariate cointegration tests to assess whether the variables share a long run equilibrium relationship. The results of these tests are given in Table 2.2 The ADF and PP tests generally indicate that the variables are non-stationary and integrated of order 1. Namely, the PP test suggests non-stationarity in all variables considered as it fails to reject the null hypothesis of a unit root for the level variables while it rejects the unit root null when they are first-differenced. The ADF test further substantiates the I(1) process for *INT, KLCI, BD,* and *CPI*. Accordingly, we proceeded to cointegration tests taking all variables as being integrated of order 1. The results from the Johansen-Juselius cointegration tests suggest the presence of at least one cointegrating vector in the basic model (without stock prices) and the extended model (with stock prices). This allows us to estimate unrestricted VAR models for the purpose of assessing monetary transmission mechanisms for the case of Malaysia.[6]

This section estimates the basic 6-variable VAR model, excluding first the stock prices. Since we are interested in the role of banks in the propagation of monetary shocks, we report only the impulse-response functions of key variables (*BL, BD, RGDP, CPI*) to innovations in monetary policy impulses.[7] The pattern of these variables' responses, as in Bernanke and Blinder (1992), is then used to assess the relevance of the money and credit views. In addition, we present variance decompositions of these variables to innovations in other variables in the system to assess their dynamic interactions and gauge the importance of bank loan and deposit shocks to real economic activity. Figure 1.2 plots the impulse response functions while Table 2.3 provides their corresponding variance decompositions. Panel (a) of the figure and table refers to the sample period up to 1997.Q2. Meanwhile, panel (b) captures the results from the extended sample. Generally, the time path of the responses in macroeconomic variables and banks' balance sheet variables to monetary policy shocks accords well with our expectations and the variance decompositions indicate that monetary policy innovations explain a quite sizeable fraction of their error variances.

From Figure 2.2(a), consistent with the important role of monetary policy, real output contracts in response to a positive shock in the interbank rate, which occurs quite immediately and bottoms out after 10 quarters. Likewise, while it is not immediate, the price level response to the interest rate shock is also negative. Perhaps, a striking pattern that emerges from the figure is a quite persistent output response to monetary shocks, which remains negative even after 20 quarters.

A look at the figure indicates that bank deposits as well as bank loans may have played a role in this quite persistent decline in real activity. Focusing on the balance sheet variables, we note that both bank loans and deposits eventually decrease after monetary tightening and exhibit similar patterns of responses as documented by Bernanke and Blinder (1992) for the United States and Garretsen and Swank (1998) for the Netherlands. The timing of the responses seems to be in line with the money view and the credit view. Initially, in response to a positive shock in the interbank rate, bank deposits contract while bank loans increase. Bernanke and Blinder (1992) explains the lagged negative responses of bank loans in terms of contractual commitments that banks have with their customers. Accordingly, it seems that the initial contraction in real output comes from the money (liability) side of the bank balance sheet. As the horizon increases, the contraction in bank loans after 7 quarters of the policy shocks leads to a further decline in output until it reaches its bottom in quarter 10. The continuing decline in bank loans as well as bank deposits seem to keep the output response negative even after 20 quarters. In other words, both sides of the banks' balance sheet seem to be important.

Conforming to the impulse-response functions, we note the important role of the interest rate shocks to variations in bank loans, bank deposits and real output (see Table 2.3(a)). Namely, innovations in *INT* account for about 21percent of the bank loan forecast error variance and for about 14percent of the variations in bank deposits at 20-quarter horizon. Meanwhile, consistent with real effects of monetary policy, the monetary policy shocks explain a sizeable fraction of movements in real output, amounting to 17percent at 6-quarter horizon and increasing continuously to around 20percent after 20 quarters. The response of the price level seems sluggish and has noticeable fraction explained by interest rate innovations only after 20 quarters (i.e. about 9percent).

Another notable result is the presence of dynamic interactions between bank loans and real output as well as bank deposits and real output, suggesting the importance of the independent shocks in bank balance sheet variables to output fluctuations and vice versa. The impulse-response functions suggest positive response of real output to particularly bank deposit shocks while both bank loans and deposits react positively to output innovations. From variance decompositions (Table 2.3(a)), bank loan innovations explain more the variations in real output at shorter horizons, i.e. 3- to 12-quarter horizons. Meanwhile, the fraction of output forecast error variance attributable to bank deposit shocks increases steadily as the horizon increases, reaching 25percent after 20 quarters. Similarly, real output innovations account for about 20percent and 36percent for the error variances of, respectively, bank loans and bank deposits.

Note also that, while bank deposits seem to account, at least eventually, for significant fraction of the variations in bank loans, the reverse does not seem to be true. Apart from reacting positively to real output shocks, bank loans also seem to respond positively to shocks in the price level and bank deposits. The importance of bank deposits to bank loans fluctuations perhaps reflects the constraint faced by banks to raise funds from alternative sources in the face of adverse shocks in bank deposits. Moreover, an unexpected rise in bank deposits also exerts negative influences on the bank rate. Accordingly, reduction in transaction balances can have both "price" effect (money view) and "quantity" effect (credit view). For the present sample period, exchange rate innovations seem to play a minor role in accounting for fluctuations in other variables. Yet, it deserves mentioning that the exchange rate appreciates after positive shocks in real output and depreciates after positive innovations in bank loans.

The estimation from the extended sample (Figure 2.2(b) and Table 2.3(b)) provides several interesting insights in the interactions among the variables. Since many findings from the basic sample (i.e. 1978.Q1-1997.Q2) also hold true here, we note only distinct results from the extended sample. In particular, the responses of real output, bank loans and bank deposits to monetary innovations are more pronounced in the extended sample. Moreover, the timing of the responses seem to suggest that contraction in real GDP leads to the decline in both bank loans and bank deposits. The responses of real output reach its bottom after 6 quarters and then move toward zero afterwards. Meanwhile, both bank loans and deposits continue to fall and bottom out after about 11-14 quarters before they subside to zero as the horizon lengthens. A look at the variance decompositions further suggests that, by just adding only four observations from the crisis period, the role of the exchange rate seems prominent accounting for sizeable fractions of forecast error variance in other variables. The corresponding impulse-response functions (not shown) note a reduction in bank loans, bank deposits, real GDP and the price level at especially short horizons after depreciation shocks. The concurrent reduction in these variables to depreciation shocks suggests the vulnerability of the Malaysian economy and its banking sector to large exchange rate fluctuations.

If these results can be used to explain the crisis, they do not seem to support the contention that the credit crunch precedes economic contraction during the crisis. Yet, we believe that the evidence cannot be taken to nullify the money and credit channels of monetary transmission observed earlier. As we argued above, if the additional four observations are outliers, then the results are not reliable for inferences. Alternatively, the recent crisis may be taken as a unique experience due to the unusually pronounced role of the exchange rate fluctuations. It seems likely that the drastic devaluation of the Ringgit exerts independent adverse effects on both banks' balance sheets through, for example, capital outflows and on real economic activities through Malaysia's high dependence on imports. With the already noted interdependence between bank balance sheet variables and real activity, banks seem to be important in perhaps aggravating the adverse real effects of exchange rate shocks.

Stock Prices in VAR

The impulse-response functions we obtain from including the stock prices, presented in Figure 2.3, are qualitatively similar to those from the basic specification. To reiterate, for the sample up to 1997.Q2, negative responses of bank loans and bank deposits to monetary policy impulses tend to make the real effects of monetary policy more persistent. When the sample is extended to 1998.2, the output decline in response to unanticipated increase in the interest rate seems temporary and precedes the reduction in bank loans and bank deposits. However, their corresponding variance decompositions provided in Table 2.4, suggest a substantially reduced role, and to being non-existent in certain cases, of interest rate shocks on other variables except on bank loans.

Despite these results, it is comforting to note that other stated results from the basic model are largely unaffected by the inclusion of the stock prices. First, bank balance sheet variables and real output are dynamically interdependent in both samples, but interestingly, with less degree of interactions between them for the extended sample. Second, we also observe the dependence of bank loans to bank deposits and, similar to the previous results, shocks to bank deposits exert negative influence on the interbank rate. Third, the pronounced effects of exchange rate shocks on other variables when the sample is updated to 1998.Q2 also hold for this extended VAR model. More importantly, the fluctuations in the exchange rate are one key factor in driving all other variables. As in the basic models, with dynamic interactions between bank loans, bank deposits and real economic activity, negative responses of both bank loans and bank deposits to exchange rate depreciation may have aggravated the macroeconomic effects of depreciation shocks.

Adding to these findings, we uncover the importance of the stock prices in the Malaysian context.[8] We note positive responses by *BL, BD, RGDP*, and *CPI* to shocks in *KLCI*, regardless of the sample period. The variance decompositions suggest that innovations in *KLCI* explain significant fraction of the forecast error variance in these variables (see Table 2.4). While the fraction of real output and consumer price forecast error variances attributed to stock price shocks is roughly similar for both samples, the portion of bank loan and bank deposit variations explained by the stock price innovations seem to intensify in the extended sample. These results, conforming to the results for exchange rate innovations, seem to verify the importance of the balance sheet variables in the interactions between financial variables and real economic activity. At the same time, we also note the significant role of real output (basic sample) and exchange rate (extended sample) in accounting for fluctuations in stock prices. These results are in line with existing findings on the interactions between macroeconomic variables and stock prices (Habibullah and Baharumshah, 1996, Ibrahim, 2000, and Ibrahim and Aziz, 2003).

In sum, while the addition of stock prices has weakened the case for bank loans and bank deposits as channels of monetary transmission mechanism, the results are largely consistent with the significant role of bank balance sheet variables in the interactions among various key macroeconomic variables. The dynamic interdependence between bank balance sheet variables and real output and the importance of bank deposits to movements in bank loans as well as in interest rate remain robust across models and samples. Moreover, both balance sheet variables seem to react to fluctuations in such financial variables as the exchange rate and stock prices. In other words, the role of banks in accounting for macroeconomic fluctuations can hardly be dismissed.

Conclusion

Appealing to the developments in the financial sector particularly the banking system and the recent Asian crisis, the present chapter analyses the role of banks in the propagation of financial shocks and in macroeconomic fluctuations for the case of Malaysia. In the analysis, we made use of impulse-response functions and variance decompositions generated from VAR models to assess the relevance of money and credit views in monetary transmission mechanism and the dynamic interactions between bank balance sheet variables and macroeconomic variables. The temporal responses of the balance sheet variables and real output to policy shocks seem consistent with money and credit views in that, after monetary policy innovations, variations in both balance sheet variables tend to precede or aggravate the adverse effects of monetary tightening. However, this finding holds only for the model that excludes stock prices from the VAR specification and limits the sample to only the pre-crisis period.

Although the importance of banks in the propagation of monetary policy shocks receives only limited evidence, we find robust results on dynamic interactions between bank balance sheet variables and real output. Both impulse-response functions and variance decompositions suggest interdependence or bi-directional causality between them. Accordingly, independent shocks in bank loans and bank deposits can influence real output and vice versa. Moreover, we also note that shocks in bank deposits exert influence on bank loans and interest rate. The negative responses of bank loans, deposits, real output and prices to depreciation shocks and their positive responses to stock price innovations raise very notable points. Namely, they demonstrate the vulnerability of the Malaysian banking sector to financial shocks and the possible role of bank deposits and loans in the propagation of these shocks especially during the period of large fluctuations in asset prices. Lastly, while the exchange rate and stock prices do not seem to play a part in the transmission of monetary policy, both are important in accounting for fluctuations in the Malaysian macroeconomic variables.

Taking these findings together, the role of bank loans and bank deposits can hardly be ignored by policymakers. Still, it seems interesting to further assess the dynamic interactions among real, financial and monetary variables during the financial crisis. The results we obtained are only suggestive and may not be construed as demonstrating the effects of the crisis in the interactions since we added only four observations from the crisis episode. Evaluating the vulnerability of the banking sector to financial shocks and, in light of the recent emphasis on the construction of crisis indicators, measuring the degree of bank vulnerability may be an important avenue for future research.

It is appropriate to point out that our current analysis is only modest due to several caveats that we have. First, to be reliable, the use of the VAR model requires a large sample size. Given the limited sample size that we have, the issue of inefficient estimates may possibly arise. Moreover, we place both bank loans and bank deposits in the VAR model, raising the problem of assessing the relative importance of bank loans and bank deposits. Since these two variables are constrained by the condition of the bank balance sheets, they may be highly correlated. The presence of highly correlated variables, again, can generate inefficient estimates. Lastly, the conditions required for the identification of monetary policy shocks, especially the requirement that the policy variable (i.e. the interbank rate) does not react contemporaneously to other variables, may not be tenable. These caveats are noteworthy when interpreting our results.

Notes

1. Strictly speaking, this channel is referred to as the "bank lending" channel of monetary transmission mechanism. Another channel of monetary transmission as suggested by the credit view is the "balance sheet or net worth" channel. This refers to a situation where higher interest rate worsens households' and firms' financial positions and, accordingly, depresses their spending. This chapter only focuses on the former.
2. Singh (1993) and Ibrahim (2001) provide more detailed discussions on financial developments in Malaysia.
3. The survey is quoted in Public Bank's *Economic Review* (1998).
4. In the evaluation of the interactions between stock prices and macroeconomic variables, Ibrahim and Aziz (2003) note the irregularities in the interactions once observations from the crisis episode are incorporated.
5. According to Dale and Haldane (1995), in an economic sense, this requires that the monetary policy indicator be controllable by the Central Bank and it be responsive to other variables through solely the Bank's reaction function. The interbank interest rate seems to satisfy the controllability criterion (Domac, 1999). However, the use of quarterly data as well as the availability of asset prices without lags may make the second criterion untenable. While we appeal to possibly decision lags by monetary authorities, this point needs to be taken into consideration when interpreting our results.
6. We set the lag length of the VAR to 4 in all cases since we find it sufficient to render the error terms serially uncorrelated (Johansen, 1992).
7. As we have noted, we placed the interest first in the ordering. Following Dale and Haldane (1995), we ordered other variables in the VAR as follows: EXC, BL, BD, RGDP, and CPI. This ordering is in line with the purported transmissions of monetary policy shocks to final objectives.
8. To conserve space, the full results of the estimation are not given. However, they are available upon request from the author.

Table 2.1 Selected Assets and Liabilities of Malaysian Commercial Banks (in RM million)

		of which are					
	Total		percent of			percent of	
Year	Assets = Liabilities	Loans/ Advances	Total Assets	GDP	Deposits	Total Liabilities	GDP
1970	4460.2	2359.6	52.9	19.4	3391.8	76.0	27.9
1975	10881.2	6468.4	59.8	29.0	8099.5	74.9	36.3
1980	32186.1	21031.1	65.3	39.4	23326.3	72.5	43.8
1985	74233.0	48981.7	66.0	63.2	45853.2	61.8	59.1
1990	129284.6	80758.0	62.5	67.8	62259.1	48.2	52.3
1995	292211.9	175007.4	59.9	78.7	161992.7	55.4	72.8
1996	358083.8	217820.5	60.8	85.8	203941.5	56.9	80.4
1997	481114.1	276116.6	57.4	97.9	243810.8	50.7	86.5
1998	453492.0	285676.3	63.0	100.4	307439.6	67.8	108.1
1999	474681.7	283231.0	59.7	94.5	332598.6	70.1	111.0

Source: Bank Negara Malaysia's Statistical Bulletin (various issues).

Table 2.2 Unit Root and Cointegration Tests
(a) Unit Root Tests

	Level		First Difference	
Variables	ADF	PP	ADF	PP
INT	-2.957	-2.621	-6.303*	-7.382*
EXC	-1.410	-0.619	-2.225	-6.971*
KLCI	-1.653	-1.973	-5.725*	-8.776*
BL	-3.163***	-2.436	-3.899**	-6.338*
BD	-1.728	-1.823	-5.686*	-8.672*
RGDP	-2.260	-3.117	-2.098	-8.760*
CPI	-1.838	-1.825	-5.264*	-9.640*

(b) Cointegration Tests

Null Hypothesis	Trace	Max	Trace	Max
	A. INT, EXC, BL, BD, RGDP, CPI		*B. INT, EXC, KLCI, BL, BD, RGDP, CPI*	
r = 0	99.648**	36.463	149.64*	53.723*
r ≤ 1	63.246	28.366	95.985**	32.125
r ≤ 2	34.739	15.876	63.770	27.850
r ≤ 3	18.768	12.126	35.835	14.203
r ≤ 4	6.615	4.528	21.508	12.005
r ≤ 5	2.091	2.091	9.496	7.271
r ≤ 6			2.205	2.194

Notes: *, **, and *** denote significance at 1 percent, 5 percent, and 10 percent respectively. The critical values of the tests are from Osterwald-Lenum (1992).

Table 2.3 Variance Decompositions (Excluding Stock Prices)
(a) Sample: 1978Q1-1997Q2

	Innovations in					
Horizons	ΔINT	ΔEXC	ΔBL	ΔBD	ΔRGDP	ΔCPI
(i) Variance Decompositions of ΔBL						
3	20.11	0.69	73.22	1.80	1.07	3.10
6	15.16	1.83	68.04	3.51	1.99	9.47
12	18.53	6.00	44.28	9.53	11.44	10.22
20	21.31	4.06	22.67	25.58	19.71	6.65
(ii) Variance Decompositions of ΔBD						
3	7.17	2.20	3.79	80.94	4.19	1.71
6	5.87	6.31	2.90	72.56	10.91	1.45
12	6.31	6.73	6.11	49.81	29.72	1.33
20	14.06	4.33	8.17	35.21	35.76	2.47
(iii) Variance Decompositions of ΔRGDP						
3	4.27	0.71	10.00	4.16	80.56	0.29
6	17.13	1.00	11.83	6.03	63.12	0.89
12	20.02	3.65	9.13	19.49	44.15	3.30
20	19.52	6.88	5.15	25.40	36.50	6.54
(iv) Variance Decompositions of ΔCPI						
3	1.83	2.39	40.87	14.08	0.44	40.39
6	1.46	1.80	39.87	13.21	0.79	42.86
12	3.73	2.78	37.44	11.53	8.14	36.37
20	8.89	1.86	28.82	16.29	21.58	22.54

(b) Sample: 1978Q1-1998Q2

Horizons	Innovations in ΔINT	ΔEXC	ΔBL	ΔBD	ΔRGDP	ΔCPI
(i) Variance Decompositions of ΔBL						
3	10.03	4.46	78.03	2.11	2.00	3.36
6	5.70	12.46	59.56	4.20	5.77	12.30
12	20.35	14.54	29.89	3.36	15.72	16.14
20	14.64	25.91	18.91	14.34	11.83	14.37
(ii) Variance Decompositions of ΔBD						
3	6.12	5.34	2.67	81.26	2.28	2.34
6	5.86	13.07	2.80	66.23	10.43	1.62
12	12.40	34.13	4.94	20.31	23.07	5.14
20	14.78	33.00	9.15	14.99	22.19	5.89
(iii) Variance Decompositions of ΔRGDP						
3	8.89	20.91	1.74	1.71	66.51	0.24
6	26.40	21.19	3.02	1.25	44.95	3.20
12	24.11	22.20	7.45	7.10	35.60	3.53
20	12.11	33.77	6.20	14.43	19.45	14.04
(iv) Variance Decompositions of ΔCPI						
3	1.82	3.27	30.16	16.03	3.53	45.19
6	1.77	8.84	25.77	13.75	4.44	45.43
12	9.85	30.29	15.07	5.59	11.84	27.35
20	13.27	26.02	19.64	5.60	15.47	20.01

Table 2.4 Variance Decompositions (Including Stock Prices)
(a) Sample: 1978Q1-1997Q2

	Innovations in						
Horizons	ΔINT	ΔEXC	ΔKLCI	ΔBL	ΔBD	ΔRGDP	ΔCPI
(i) Variance Decompositions of ΔBL							
3	19.61	1.02	1.66	67.58	2.44	2.48	5.64
6	12.08	1.83	3.34	65.62	3.40	2.41	11.31
12	11.12	5.00	12.86	43.79	8.27	10.41	8.55
20	8.14	2.41	13.35	30.21	17.52	21.75	6.62
(ii) Variance Decompositions of ΔBD							
3	5.42	2.16	1.33	1.92	81.81	6.61	0.75
6	4.59	11.87	1.91	5.64	61.74	13.21	1.03
12	3.96	14.19	6.86	10.33	36.85	27.13	0.68
20	2.91	7.02	13.66	14.94	23.60	35.15	2.73
(iii) Variance Decompositions of ΔRGDP							
3	1.53	1.27	15.70	7.67	2.78	70.51	0.55
6	3.59	0.77	26.73	9.61	3.77	54.72	0.80
12	3.43	1.35	21.41	14.47	11.14	43.69	4.51
20	5.34	2.55	13.51	14.39	12.73	43.72	7.76
(iv) Variance Decompositions of ΔCPI							
3	3.55	5.31	21.86	26.15	9.67	1.54	31.93
6	5.57	3.36	46.88	15.47	6.29	1.95	20.47
12	6.62	2.64	55.54	9.85	6.60	6.43	12.32
20	4.72	2.20	40.82	14.90	9.20	19.45	8.72

(b) Sample: 1978Q1-1998Q2

	Innovations in						
Horizons	ΔINT	ΔEXC	ΔKLCI	ΔBL	ΔBD	ΔRGDP	ΔCPI
(i) Variance Decompositions of ΔBL							
3	9.30	5.57	0.50	74.71	2.28	3.37	4.27
6	4.48	15.93	1.22	60.17	3.37	4.90	9.91
12	5.45	21.30	25.04	29.27	3.17	10.37	7.42
20	3.02	27.19	19.32	23.81	9.88	9.13	7.64
(ii) Variance Decompositions of ΔBD							
3	4.85	7.09	1.22	1.87	78.74	5.32	0.90
6	3.87	22.34	1.09	6.08	51.45	13.20	1.97
12	2.89	41.28	15.95	7.30	14.77	16.56	1.45
20	1.56	34.39	22.75	13.24	10.41	14.67	2.99
(iii) Variance Decompositions of ΔRGDP							
3	1.75	22.09	15.03	1.97	1.87	56.84	0.42
6	5.27	27.19	27.35	3.34	1.46	34.36	1.02
12	3.16	20.68	29.06	13.00	4.89	26.70	1.59
20	1.47	44.10	18.15	7.98	6.01	13.82	8.46
(iv) Variance Decompositions of ΔCPI							
3	2.26	6.78	18.09	25.29	8.87	1.01	37.70
6	3.62	7.97	42.75	14.63	5.15	1.78	24.10
12	1.39	31.12	43.99	6.06	2.37	5.67	9.40
20	0.93	28.48	38.29	13.96	4.03	7.38	6.92

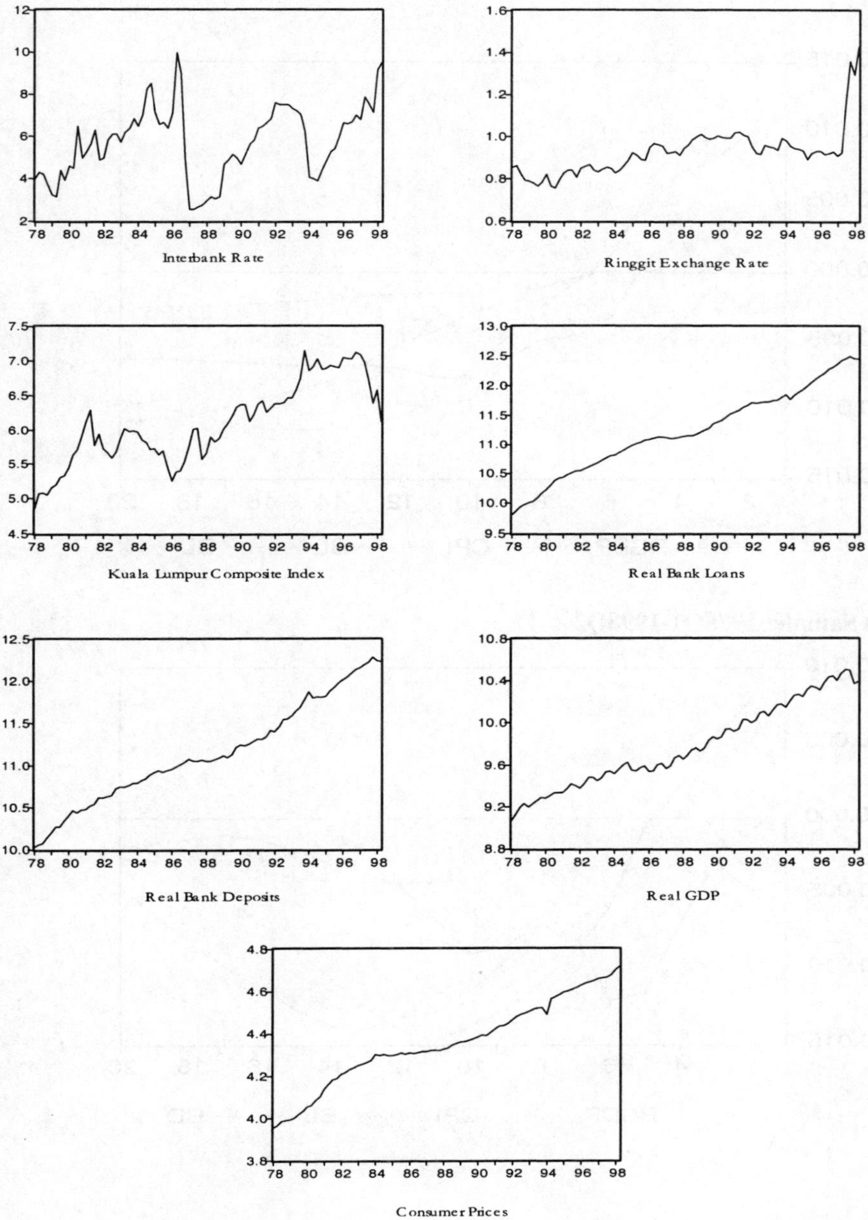

Figure 2.1 Time Series Plots

(a) Sample: 1978Q1-1997Q2

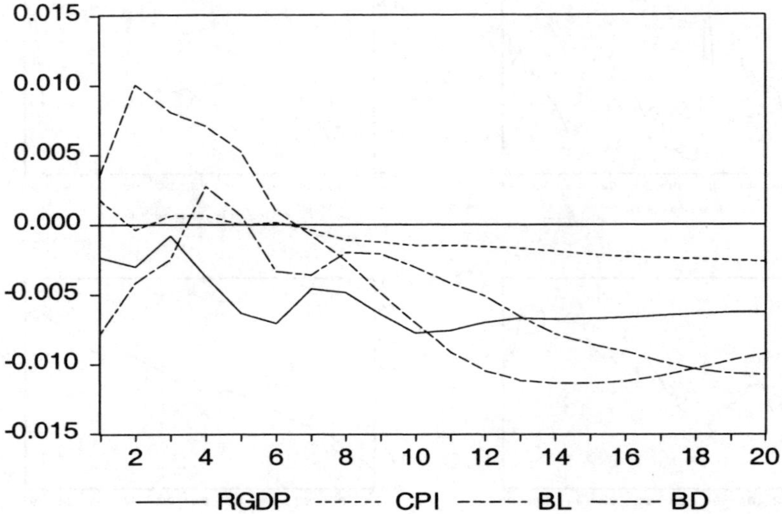

(b) Sample: 1978Q1-1998Q2

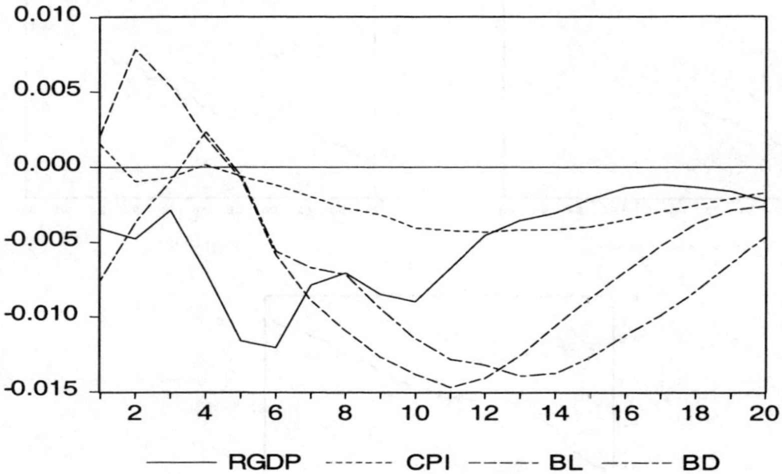

Figure 2.2 Responses to Interbank Rate Innovations (Excluding Stock Prices)

(a) Sample: 1978Q1-1997Q2

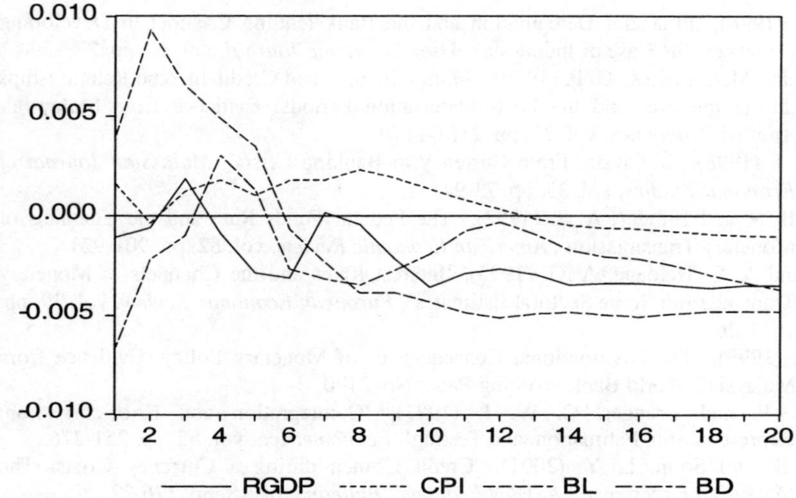

(b) Sample: 1978Q1-1998Q2

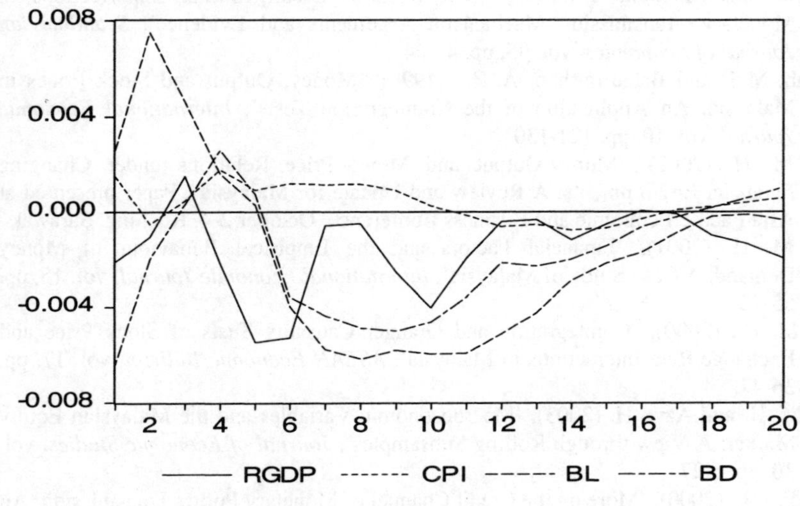

Figure 2.3 Responses to Interbank Rate Innovations (Including Stock Prices)

References

Agung, J. (1998), 'Financial Deregulation and the Bank lending Channel in Developing Countries: the Case of Indonesia', *Asian Economic Journal*, vol. 12, pp. 273-294.

Azali, M. and Matthews, K. G. P. (1999), 'Money-Income and Credit-Income Relationships during the Pre- and the Post-liberalisation Periods: Evidence from Malaysia', *Applied Economics*, vol. 31, pp. 1161-1170.

Bacha, O. I. (1998), 'Malaysia: From Currency to Banking Crisis', *Malaysian Journal of Economic Studies*, vol. 35, pp. 73-94.

Bernake, B. S. and Blinder, A. S. (1992), 'The Federal Funds Rate and the Channels of Monetary Transmission', *American Economic Review*, vol. 82, pp. 901-921.

Dale, S. and A. G. Haldane, A. G. (1995), 'Interest Rates and the Channels of Monetary Transmission: Some Sectoral Estimates', *European Economic Review*, vol. 39, pp. 1611-26.

Domac, I. (1999), 'The Distributional Consequences of Monetary Policy: Evidence from Malaysia', World Bank Working Paper No. 2170.

Engle, R. F. and Granger, C. W. J. (1987), 'Cointegration and Error-correction: Representation, Estimation, and Testing', *Econometrica*, vol. 55, pp. 251-276.

Gan, W. B. and Soon, L. Y. (2001), 'Credit Crunch during a Currency Crisis: The Malaysian Experience', *ASEAN Economic Bulletin*, vol. 18, pp. 176-92.

Garretsen, H. and Swank, J. (1998), 'The Transmission of Interest Rate Changes and the Role of Bank Balance Sheets: A VAR-Analysis for the Netherlands', *Journal of Macroeconomics*, vol.20, pp. 325-339.

Gertler, M. and Gilchrist, S. (1993), 'The Role of Credit Market Imperfections in Monetary Transmission Mechanism: Arguments and Evidence', *Scandinavian Journal of Economics*, vol. 95, pp. 43-64.

Habibullah, M.S. and Baharumshah, A. Z. (1996), 'Money, Output and Stock Prices in Malaysia: An Application of the Cointegration Tests', *International Economic Journal,* vol. 10, pp. 121-130.

Ibrahim, M. H. (2002), 'Money-Output and Money-Price Relations under Changing Financial Environments: A Review and Update for Malaysia', Paper presented at Asia Pacific Economic and Business Conference, October 2-4, Kuching, Sarawak.

Ibrahim, M. H. (2001), 'Financial Factors and the Empirical Behaviour of Money Demand: A Case Study of Malaysia', *International Economic Journal,* vol. 15, pp. 55-72.

Ibrahim, M. H., (2000), 'Cointegration and Granger Causality Tests of Stock Price and Exchange Rate Interactions in Malaysia', *ASEAN Economic Bulletin*, vol. 17, pp. 36-47.

Ibrahim, M. H. and Aziz, H. (2003), 'Macroeconomic Variables and the Malaysian Equity Market: A View through Rolling Subsamples', *Journal of Economic Studies*, vol. 30, pp. 6-27.

Iturriaga, F. J. L. (2000), 'More on the Credit Channel of Monetary Policy Transmission: An International Comparison', *Applied Financial Economics*, vol. 10, pp. 423-434.

Johansen, S. (1992), 'Testing Weak Exogeneity and the Order of Cointegration in UK Money Demand Data', *Journal of Policy Modeling*, vol. 14, pp. 313-334.

Johansen, S. and Juselius, K (1990), 'Maximum Likelihood Estimation and Inference on Cointegration - with Applications to the Demand for Money', *Oxford Bulletin of Economics and Statistics*, vol. 52, pp. 169-210.

Kashyap, A. K. and Stein, J. C., (1995), 'The Impact of Monetary Policy on Bank Balance Sheets', *Carnegie-Rochester Conference Series on Public Policy*, vol. 42, pp. 151-195.

Kwek, K. T. (1992), 'Financial Aggregates and Economic Activity: An Intermediate Targeting Framework for Malaysia', *Malaysian Journal of Economic Studies*, vol. 29, pp. 23-46.

Osterwald-Lenum, M. (1992), 'A Note with Quantiles of the Asymptotic Distribution of Maximum Likelihood Cointegration Rank Test Statistic', *Oxford Bulletin of Economics and Statistics,* vol. 54, pp. 461-472.

Phillips, P. C. B. (1986), 'Understanding Spurious Regressions in Econometrics', Journal of Econometrics, 33, 311-340.

Public Bank (1998), 'Direction and Impact of Bank Lending in Malaysia', *Economic Review,* January-February, pp. 1-4.

Radiah, A. K. (2000), 'Sektor Kewangan', in M. R. Mohamad and M. A. G. Hassan, (eds), *Pembangunan Ekonomi Malaysia Era Globalisasi*, Kuala Lumpur: University of Malaya Press, pp. 311-338. (in Malay Language).

Ramaswamy, R. and Slok, T. (1998), 'The Real Effects of Monetary Policy in the European Union: What are the Differences?', *IMF Staff Papers*, vol. 45, pp. 374-396.

Sims, C. A. (1992), 'Interpreting the Macroeconomic Facts: the Effects of Monetary Policy', European Economic Review, vol. 36, pp. 975-1000.

Sims, C. A. (1980), 'Comparison of Interwar and Postwar Cycles: Monetarism Considered', *American Economic Review*, vol. 70, pp. 250-257.

Singh, S. (1993), 'Monetary Policy in Malaysia: 1979-1989', in A. Talib (eds), *Monetary Policy in the SEACEN Countries: An Update*, Kuala Lumpur: SEACEN Center.

Stock, J. H. (1987), 'Asymptotic Properties of Lease-squares Estimators of Co-integrating Vectors', *Econometrica*, vol. 55, pp. 1035-1056.

Chapter 3

Output-Inflation Trade-Off in the Asian Countries

Chin-Hong Puah, Muzafar Shah Habibullah and Hway-Boon Ong

Introduction

Technological advancement in information technology, communication and transportation has made the world more connected than ever. The close connectivity between one country and another has promised better trading opportunities, as well as greater economic development and growth. However, economies today are also more vulnerable to economic shocks happening in other parts of the world. As such, the governing authorities in many countries strive to develop and implement effective policies in order to sustain their economies' growth and to cushion against any adverse economic shocks that might affect their economies.

The aim of economic policies is to tackle economic issues, mainly concerning national output, unemployment and inflation. However, for the past several decades, there have been many controversies among economists over the effectiveness of a stabilisation policy on output and employment. The main debate is whether to promote a non-activism or an activism stabilisation policy. Generally, there are two groups of macroeconomic theorists, who are of differing views. They are the new classical and the new Keynesian groups, both relying on the assumption of rational expectations.

The new classical theory, as pioneered by Lucas (1973), advocates that markets clear itself continuously. Although individuals and firms are assumed to possess imperfect information, the expectations of individuals and firms conform to the theory of rational expectations that the market operates efficiently and the economy's self-correcting mechanism works smoothly and quickly. Consequently, government intervention in the markets would be unnecessary. However, the short run trade-off between output and inflation arises because producers are unable to distinguish precisely between shocks affecting relative prices and aggregate prices, since these shocks are not directly observable and must be inferred from the behaviour of individual prices.

Hence, the relationship between output-inflation trade-off and variations in relative prices exists. The effect of a price change will be small when compared to a change in relative prices as well as the output if the aggregate prices fluctuate greatly. Therefore, the new classical economists believe that the short-run Phillips curve is rather steep, since inflation is more costly than unemployment. Correspondingly, Lucas (1973) suggests that there is a negative correlation between the output-inflation trade-off parameter and the variances of both nominal aggregate demand and the rate of inflation.

In contrast, the new Keynesian economists contend that the markets do not always equate quantity demanded to quantity supplied, either in the product or input markets. Instead, they believe if there is a sudden shift in demand or supply, price adjustments will not be quick enough to clear the markets. In their view, the economy can remain in a state of disequilibrium for many years due to price rigidity. "Menu costs" is one of the reasons that prices do not adjust immediately to clear markets because the price adjustment is costly. Staggering of prices is the other factor that makes the price level sluggish. Also, co-ordination failure and efficiency wages do contribute to the failure of market-clearing mechanisms.

The new Keynesian theory proposes that the intervention of government is crucial since the economy's self-correcting mechanism is slow and unreliable. Systematic fiscal or monetary policies will have substantial economic impact even with the rational expectation assumption imposed. When wages and prices tend to be sticky and inflexible, the total real output is not only affected by unanticipated or unexpected changes in economic variables, but also by the actual behaviour of these economic variables. As such, the real effects of a nominal shock depend on the speed of adjustment of individual prices. When price adjustment is fast, the real effects of a nominal shock would be small. Since price adjustment is slow, the short-run Phillips curve is relatively flat, which implies that unemployment is more costly than inflation.

The purpose of this chapter is to investigate whether the output-inflation trade-offs are negatively affected by the mean of inflation (as postulated by the new Keynesian theory) or by the variability of inflation (as postulated by the new classical model).

Literature Review

Lucas's (1973) discussion on output-inflation trade-off has led to numerous related studies, such as Koskela and Viren (1980), Attfield and Duck (1983), Hercowitz (1983), and Jung (1985), to name a few. However, some authors (Froyen and Waud, 1980, 1985; Katsimbris, 1990a, 1990b) have questioned the variance hypothesis proposed by Lucas and argued that the new classical model is less applicable as the analysis moves from cross-country to intertemporal analysis.

In a recent study, Ball, Mankiw and Romer (BMR) (1998) adopted a model of imperfect competition with aggregate-demand externality (menu costs) to propose an innovative attack on the existing tests of the new classical model. They challenged Lucas's (1973) approach as inappropriate for distinguishing between the new classical and the new Keynesian positions. They found that as the prices adjust relatively faster, the real effects on nominal shock of such an adjustment would be relatively smaller. The frequency of price adjustment depends on the variability of aggregate demand and the inflation rate. Furthermore, a higher inflation rate is found to increase the frequency of price adjustments and shorten the periodicity of these changes. Hence, there is a negative relationship between the output-inflation trade-off and the average rate of inflation. The work by BMR (1998) concluded that there is a negative correlation between the variance of aggregate demand and output-inflation trade-off, where the trade-off is inversely related to the mean of inflation.

By using the annual data from a sample of 43 countries, BMR (1988) examine the relationship between the output-inflation trade-off and the mean of inflation, after controlling for aggregate demand variability, in two stages. First, they estimated the standard Lucas aggregate supply curve by regressing real output on to its own lagged value, the rate of change in nominal GNP, and a time trend over the 1948-86 period. Subsequently, they estimated the cross-country linear and non-linear specifications of the estimated output-inflation trade-off coefficients on to the average inflation rate and the validity of aggregate demand and/or the variability of inflation rate. The time-series cross-section equations were also estimated by regressing the change in output in the output-inflation trade-off coefficients between two sub-periods of 1948 till 1972 and 1973 till 1986, on the respective changes of the average rate of inflation and of demand variability. Their results were robust and supported their hypotheses that there was negative correlation between the short-run output-inflation trade-off as well as the mean of inflation, the standard deviation and variance of normal income. That is to say, BMR's reject the new classical model in favour of the new Keynesian model.

Akerlof, Rose and Yellen (ARY, 1988), discovered that the model proposed by Ball, Mankiw and Romer (BMR, 1988) is unable to distinguish between the new Keynesian and the new classical positions. They pointed out that the BMR (1988) approach to the new Keynesian hypothesis is a weak test against the new classical theory because average inflation and the variability of nominal GNP are highly correlated. In view of this, they extended BMR model by adding the standard deviation and the variance of inflation in their model. The purpose for doing so was to test the hypothesis of a world with and without trade-off, where the output-inflation trade-off would then be influenced by the variability of inflation and nominal variable. By using a different non-linear specification on the same cross-country analysis, ARY (1998) conclude that there is no evidence for adherence to the new Keynesian model.

In line with this research, Katsimbris and Miller (1996) reconsidered the empirical tests of the new Keynesian and the new classical models proposed by BMR (1988) and ARY (1988) using both pooled and country-by-country regressions. The methodology adopted by Katsimbris and Miller (1996) mirrored the two-stage procedure of BMR (1988), except that for each country, the estimated output-inflation trade-off slope, the average inflation rate, and the variability of the inflation rate were allowed to vary over time. The time-varying variance of inflation rate was captured by the GARCH (generalized autoregressive conditional heteroscedasticity) model, but Katsimbris and Miller did not take into account the effect of unit root in real output. They found that there is no evidence supporting the new Keynesian hypothesis with the pooled data of 39 countries.

However, there is little evidence of consistency with either the new Keynesian or the new classical models when examining the issues on a multi-country basis.

However, when Asai (1999) employes a simple and straightforward testing procedure for each of BMR's (1988) and ARY's (1988) regressions with the cross-country data by considering the effects of a unit root in real output, and modelled the time-varying variance of inflation rate using the GARCH model, the empirical result indicated that there is strong evidence for the new Keynesian proposition in Canada, Germany, Japan and the US and only weak evidence in France and Italy. There is no supportive evidence for the new classical hypothesis that the output-inflation trade-off is negatively influenced by the variability of inflation.

Giorgioni (2001) added to the literature on the debate of the controversy between the new classical and the new Keynesian theories by looking at a sample of countries belonging to the Franc Zone from 1974-1992. The empirical results were consistent with those of Katsimbris and Miller's (1996), in the sense that there is no conclusive evidence on either theory. Both the BMR (1998) and ARY (1998) tests are unable to clearly distinguish between the two theories, as both the mean and the variability of inflation can inversely influence the output-inflation trade-offs. Keeping this previous research in mind, we undertook the task to investigate the output-inflation trade-offs through mean and variability of inflation.

Methodology

Following Asai (1999), we first estimated the time-varying variance of inflation rate by the GARCH (generalised ARCH) model, which was also the original motivation of Engle's (1982) work on ARCH (autoregressive conditional heteroskedasticity). This approach yields estimates of conditional variances, which also serves as a more convincing measure of perceived uncertainty than conventional measures that are based on unconditional variances. Prior to estimating the Lucas function for each country under study, the following equation was estimated in order to examine the existence of unit roots.

$$y_t = \alpha + \tau_t \Delta x_t + \sum_{i=1}^{p+m} \lambda_i y_{t-i} + \gamma_t + \varepsilon_{t,\dots t=1,\dots,T} \qquad (1)$$

where y is the log of real GDP, x is the log of nominal GDP, τ is the time-varying trade off coefficient, t is the time trend, Δ denotes the differencing operator, p denotes the lag length of which coefficient is significant, m is the number of unit roots in y, and T is the number of observations. Although Equation (1) contains an additional lag of y that might cause inefficiency as a result of the artificial lag length augmentation, the standard asymptotic theory is applicable.[1] The functional form that expresses the trade-off coefficient and inflation rate proposed by BMR (1988) is

$$\tau_t = a_1 + b_1 \pi_t + c_1 \sigma_t \qquad (2)$$

where τ_t is the trade-off coefficient, π_t is the inflation rate, and σ_t is the square root of time-varying variance of inflation rate. The stochastic properties of inflation volatility are estimated by the GARCH model. Substituting the time-varying trade-off coefficient in Equation (2) into Equation (1), we obtain

$$y_t = \alpha + a_1 \Delta x_t + b_1 \pi_t \Delta x_t + c_1 \sigma_t \Delta x_t + \sum_{i=1}^{p+m} \lambda_i y_{t-i} + \gamma_t + \varepsilon_t \quad (3)$$

Following Katsimbris and Miller (1996), the new Keynesian model is represented by a significantly negative coefficient on the inflation term and that the new classical model would be indicated by a significantly negative coefficient on the standard deviation of inflation and an insignificant negative coefficient of inflation.

As for ARY (1988), the functional form used by them to relate the trade-off coefficient and inflation rate is given by

$$1/\tau_t = a_2 + b_2 \pi_t + c_2 \sigma_t \quad (4)$$

Therefore, by substituting the inverse trade-off coefficient in Equation (4) into Equation (1), we came up with Equation (5).

$$y_t = \alpha + \frac{\Delta x_t}{(a_2 + b_2 \pi_t + c_2 \sigma_t)} + \sum_{i=1}^{p+m} \lambda_i y_{t-i} + \gamma_t + \varepsilon_t \quad (5)$$

ARY (1998) pointed out that a significantly positive coefficient on the inflation term supports the new Keynesian theory. However, if the coefficient on the standard deviation of inflation is significantly positive and the coefficient of inflation is insignificantly positive, then this is an indication of support for the new classical theory.

Sources of Data

In this chapter, we used quarterly data of nominal GDP, real GDP and CPI for the period from 1980:1 to 1999:4. Three countries were selected for this study, namely, Indonesia, the Philippines, and Singapore. All data were taken from various issues of the International Financial Statistics published by the International Monetary Fund (IMF).

Results and Discussions

In order to determine the number of unit roots in the real output, we employed the Phillips-Perron (Phillips and Perron, 1988) unit root tests to determine the order of integration of the time series. The unit root tests results are presented in Table 3.1. We cannot reject the null hypothesis of a unit root for nominal output as well as real output in their level form. However, all differenced series are stationary which imply that they are integrated at order one. Thus, the number of unit roots for real output, *m*, is one for all countries.

Following Asai's (1999) approach in conducting the two-step procedure of the BMR (1988) and ARY (1988) models, we allowed the variability of the inflation rate to change over time. As such, we estimated the time-varying variance of inflation rate by the GARCH model. Table 3.2 shows Lagrange Multiplier (LM) test statistics for several ARCH models. Engle's (1983) LM tests for ARCH reveal invariably strong evidence of temporal dependence in second moments. All the countries appeared to select the ARCH(1) model.

The estimated parameters of BMR's (1988) test regression in Equation (3) and ARY's (1988) test regression in Equation (5) are presented in Table 3.3. BMR (1988) uses the trade-off coefficient while ARY (1988) use its inverse. The nonlinear least squares method was employed in the estimation. Empirical results support the new Keynesian model when the trade-off coefficient is used in the BMR (1988) regression. All the estimated coefficients for inflation rate are significantly different from zero and carry a negative sign. The result is robust when we employed the ARY (1988) test regression. We found that all the coefficients on the inflation term are significantly different from zero and show positive sign. The inverse of the trade-off coefficient also shows support for the new Keynesian hypothesis for all the countries under study.

Conclusion

We utilised the non-linear least square estimation method proposed by Asai (1999) for each BMR (1988) and ARY (1988) regression to reconsider the empirical tests of the new Keynesian and the new classical models. The stationarity properties of the time series on real and nominal outputs were taken into account in the tests, and the GARCH model was employed to estimate the time-varying variance of inflation rate. The empirical findings in this chapter do not support the notion of the variability of inflation rate in explaining the output-inflation trade-off. In both tests, there are strong evidences in favour the new Keynesian model with the time series data in Indonesia, the Philippines, and Singapore.

Thus, the new Keynesian perspective that emphasises on government intervention and policy effectiveness on the output-inflation trade-off is probably more applicable in the case of these developing Asian economies. However, we would caution that the governing authority's action of trying to offset the inflationary impact of supply shocks might lead to a greater fluctuation in output and unemployment in the short run, while the stabilisation policy on output and unemployment would cause actual inflation to vary even more. As such, whether policymakers should intervene in practice is a subtle question that entails various political and economic judgements.

Note

1. This augmentation scheme is discussed in Stock (1995).

Table 3.1 Phillips-Perron Unit Root Tests

Country	x	Δx	y	Δy
Indonesia	-1.214 (3)	-4.973 (3)**	-2.188 (3)	-6.105 (3)**
Philippines	-1.801 (3)	-4.654 (3)**	-2.029 (3)	-6.218 (3)**
Singapore	-1.578 (3)	-3.188 (3)*	-1.644 (3)	-3.971 (3)**

Note: Asterisks (**) and (*) denote significance at 1percent and 5percent levels, respectively. x = log of nominal GDP, y = log of real GDP, Δ denotes the differencing operator. Figures in parentheses are the lag lengths.

Table 3.2 LM Test for Conditional Variance of Inflation Rate

Country	ARCH(1)	ARCH(2)	ARCH(3)	ARCH(4)	GARCH(1,1)
Indonesia	10.913*	8.731	9.076	0.504	8.931
Philippines	12.467*	3.058	3.461	2.826	2.558
Singapore	15.019*	2.008	3.165	0.761	0.697

Note: LM test denotes the test for ARCH. Asterisk (*) denotes significance at 5percent level.

Table 3.3 Nonlinear Least Squares Estimates for BMR and ARY Models

	BMR Model				ARY Model		
Country	*m*	*p*	b_1	c_1	*p*	b_2	c_2
Indonesia	1	1	-22.11**	45.57**	1	17.66**	-33.25**
			(-14.27)	(3.63)		(11.94)	(-3.33)
Philippines	1	2	-7.57**	-1.65	2	13.35**	3.34
			(-5.67)	(-0.46)		(5.66)	(0.70)
Singapore	1	1	-29.29**	20.41**	1	32.87**	-27.55**
			(-14.13)	(2.65)		(8.17)	(-2.42)

Note: Asterisks (**) denote significance at 1percent level. Figures in parentheses are *t*-statistics.

References

Akerlof, G.A. Rose, A. and Yellen, J. (1988), 'The New Keynesian Economics and the Output-Inflation Trade-off: Comment', *Brookings Papers on Economic Activity*, vol. 1, pp. 66-75.

Asai, M. (1999), 'Time Series Evidence on a New Keynesian Theory of the Output-Inflation Trade-off', *Applied Economics Letters*, vol. 6, pp. 539-41.

Attfield, C.L.F. and Duck, N.W. (1983), 'The Influence of Unanticipated Money Growth on Real Output: Some Cross-Country Estimates', *Journal of Money, Credit and Banking*, vol. 15, pp. 442-54.

Ball, L., Mankiw, N.G. and Romer, D. (1988), 'The New Keynesian Economics and the Output-Inflation Trade-off', *Brookings Papers on Economic Activity*, vol. 1, pp. 1-65.

Engle, R.F. (1982), 'Autoregressive Conditional Heteroskedasticity with Estimates of the Variances of United Kingdom Inflations', *Econometrica*, vol. 50, pp. 987-1007.

Engle, R.F. (1983), 'Estimates of the Variance of U.S. Inflation Based upon the ARCH Model', *Journal of Money, Credit and Banking*, vol. 15, pp. 266-301.

Froyen, R.T. and Waud, R.N. (1980), 'Further International Evidence on Output-Inflation Trade-offs', *American Economic Review*, vol. 70, pp. 407-21.

Froyen, R.T. and Waud, R.N. (1985), 'Demand Variability, Supply Shocks and the Output-Inflation Trade-off,' *Review of Economics and Statistics*, vol. 67, pp. 9-15.

Giorgioni, G. (2001), 'New Evidence on the Output-Inflation Trade-off from Developing Economies: The Case of the CFA France Zone,' *Applied Economics*, vol. 33, pp. 1077-1082.

Hercowitz, Z. (1983), 'Anticipated Inflation, the Frequency of Transactions, and the Slope of the Phillips Curve', *Journal of Money, Credit and Banking*, vol. 15, pp. 139-54.

Jung, W.S. (1985), 'Output-Inflation Trade-offs in Industrial and Developing Countries', *Journal of Macroeconomics*, vol. 7, pp. 101-13.

Katsimbris, G.M and Miller, S.M. (1996), 'The New Keynesian Economics and the Output-Inflation Trade-off', *Applied Economics Letter*, vol. 3, pp. 599-602.

Katsimbris, G.M. (1990a), 'Intracountry Evidence on the Lucas Variance Hypothesis', *Economic Inquiry*, vol. 28, pp. 756-73.

Katsimbris, G.M. (1990b), 'Output-Inflation Trade-offs in Industrial and Developing Countries: A Comment and Additional Evidence', *Journal of Macroeconomics*, vol. 12, pp. 483-99.

Koskela, E. and Viren, M. (1980), 'New International Evidence on Output-Inflation Trade-offs, A Note', *Economics Letters*, vol. 6, pp. 233-39.

Lucas, Jr., R.E. (1973), 'Some International Evidence on Output-Inflation Trade-offs', *American Economic Review*, 63, pp. 326-34.

Phillips, P.C.B. and Perron, P. (1988), 'Testing for a Unit Root in Time Series Regression', *Biometrika*, vol. 75, pp. 335-46.

Stock, J.H. (1995), 'Cointegration, Long-run Comovements, and Long-horizon Forecasting', presented at the Seventh World Congress of the Econometric Society, Tokyo.

PART II
EXCHANGE RATES

Chapter 4

Purchasing Power Parity

Venus Khim-Sen Liew and Ahmad Zubaidi Baharumshah

Introduction

The purchasing power parity (PPP) hypothesis postulates that the same basket of goods and services should cost the same amount in all countries when expressed in a common currency. PPP is expected to hold true in the long run, although deviation of exchange rate from PPP might occur in the short run, due to factors such as transaction costs, price rigidity, the differential composition of market baskets and price indices, and imperfect markets (as a result of subsidy, taxation, trade barriers, foreign exchange market interventions and the like). However, previous empirical studies have reported mixed results. For instance, the work of Lee (1976), Glens (1992), Lothian and Taylor (1996), Coakley and Fuertes (1997), Nagayasu (1998), Razzaghipour *et al.* (2001) and M. Azali *et al.* (2001) are all supportive of the long-run PPP hypothesis, whereas authors like Corbae and Outliaris (1988), Edison and Fisher (1991), Engel *et al.* (1997), O'Connell (1998), Baum *et al.* (1999) and Cuddington and Hong (2000) provide empirical evidence against PPP, even as a long run relationship. Meanwhile, Salehizadeh and Taylor (1999) produce mixed results, in the sense that only about one-half of 27 selected emerging economies under their investigation are supportive of PPP, while the other half are not.

One possible explanation for the contrasting empirical evidence on the PPP hypothesis is that earlier studies implicitly assumed that exchange rate behaviour is linear in nature. In fact, a number of recent studies have documented strong evidence that exchange rates do exhibit nonlinear behaviour (Mahajan and Wagner 1999; Coakley and Fuertes 1997), which is consistent with the observations made in earlier articles by Boothe and Glassman (1987) and Hsieh (1989). Since there is a possibility that exchange rate movements might be nonlinear in fashion, the study of exchange rate behaviour regardless of its linearity nature is inappropriate. Thus, conducting linearity tests in verifying the linearity of the exchange rate concerned is an important task in the study of exchange rate. Despite the importance of linearity tests, previous exchange rate studies in the Asian region had never included such tests, however. The purpose of this chapter is thus to investigate the linearity nature of the adjustment dynamic of the deviations of exchange rates from the long-run equilibrium level as suggested by the well-known purchasing power parity (PPP) hypothesis. To this end, we used data from 6

Asian countries and the commonly used third order auxiliary linearity test of Lukkonen *et al.* (1988) to accomplish this task. However, due to the constraint on sample size, the third order terms of this test have been omitted.

A Brief Review of Related Literature

The long-run PPP hypothesis has received much supportive empirical evidence in the past. For example, Lee (1976) examined the relationship between relative prices and exchange rates dating back to the year 1900 and concluded that the exchange rates of major currencies tended to assume the equilibrium PPP value in the long run. Glens (1992) in a study on the behaviour of exchange rates in the short, medium and long run using annual data of the European Monetary System (EMS) covering the period 1900 to 1987, also confirmed that PPP is a long run phenomenon. Lothian and Taylor (1996) used annual data spanning two centuries in another study for dollar-sterling and franc-sterling exchange rates, beginning in 1791 and ending in 1990. Their findings reinforced the mean reverting behaviour of exchange rate towards the long-run PPP value. The work of Nagayasu (1998) found support for a "semi-strong" version of the long-run PPP hypothesis in a sample of 16 African countries, whereas Coakley and Fuertes (1997) reported strong support for long-run PPP in the context of G-10 plus Switzerland. Salehizadeh and Taylor (1999) applied the standard Johansen cointegration approach to 27 emerging economies and claimed that they had found relatively strong evidence for 14 countries (including Korea and Thailand, but excluding Indonesia, Singapore, Philippines and Malaysia) in favour of long-run PPP. In a recent study, Razzaghipour *et al.* (2001) used statistical analysis to study the mean-reversion to PPP in the Asian currencies and obtained empirical support for PPP. Nevertheless, M. Azali *et al.* (2001) also found significant evidence that PPP holds during the recent floats between the Japanese and Asian economies by using the panel cointegration approach.

Even though many empirical findings are consistent with the PPP hypothesis, studies that provide counter empirical evidence against the validity of the PPP hypothesis are no less. For instance, the results of the standard unit root tests conducted by Corbae and Outliaris (1988) and Edison and Fisher (1991) were not supportive of the PPP hypothesis. Using a different approach, Baum *et al.* (1999) allowed for fractional integrated and structural breaks in testing the mean reversion in the CPI-based rates for seventeen countries and the WPI-based rates for twelve countries. Their evidence suggested a rejection of the absolute long run PPP during the post-Bretton Woods era. Cuddington and Hong (2000), on the other hand, reexamined the PPP hypothesis for the dollar-sterling and franc-sterling rate using the data from Lothian and Taylor (1996) and have rejected the long-run PPP hypothesis by fitting time trends or by considering longer lag length in the Augmented Dickey-Fuller (ADF) unit root tests. Other evidences against the PPP hypothesis are reported in, among others, Engel *et al.* (1997) and O'Connell (1998).

As we mentioned earlier, one possible explanation for the inconsistency in the empirical evidence on the PPP hypothesis is that most previous studies implicitly assumed that exchange rate behaviour is linear in nature. Taylor and Peel (2000) and Sarno (2000) amongst others illustrated that the adoption of linear stationarity tests is inappropriate in detecting mean reversion if the true data generating process of exchange rates is in fact a stationary nonlinear process. In fact, the importance of allowing for nonlinear adjustment of the exchange rates towards their long-run PPP equilibrium had been stressed in a number of past studies. For instance, Hsieh (1989) observed that exchange rate changes may be nonlinearly dependent. Boothe and Glassman (1987) pointed out that exchange rates are not linearly predictable. Sarno (2000) provided strong evidence that bilateral Turkish lira exchange rates against its major trading partners adjusted nonlinearly towards their long-run PPP equilibrium over the sample of 1980 to 1997. Mahajan and Wagner (1999) utilised the *BDS* statistic (see Mahajan and Wagner 1999 for a brief review) in the daily rates of eleven major countries and concluded that the behaviour of exchange rates are governed by nonlinear dynamics, and that innovations in real exchange rates are consistent with a PPP equilibrium. Using a nonparametric cointegration approach in testing the nonlinearities in exchange rates adjustment for 18 OECD economies indirectly Coakley and Fuertes (2001) also found significant nonlinearities in real exchange rates adjustment to PPP over the 1973 to 1998 period.

These findings of the existence of a nonlinear relationship between exchange rates and their fundamentals imply that exchange rate researchers could no longer take for granted that exchange rate movements are linearly dependent. In fact, the negligence of the presence of the nonlinearity nature of exchange rate adjustments has been regarded as a major explanation for the failure of previous linear exchange rate models in explaining the past or forecasting the future movements (Taylor and Peel 2000). It is argued in Taylor and Peel (2000) that deviations of exchange rate from the equilibrium level may be difficult to model using linear methods if they are governed by a nonlinear process.

Rationales for Nonlinear Exchange Rate Adjustments

There are few theoretical models that provide rationales for the existence of the nonlinear adjustment of exchange rate towards its fundamental equilibrium level; see Ma and Kanas (2000a) for a quick review. However, the most widely known model is the target zone model developed by Krugman (1991). Krugman (1991) argued that given a perfectly credible target zone, the relationship between exchange rate and its fundamentals will be nonlinear in nature. His rationale was that exchange rates adjust differently in magnitude within the zone, in accordance with the changes in fundamentals. For instance, when the exchange rate was near the upper bound of the target zone, a fall in the fundamentals will reduce the exchange rate more than a rise in the fundamentals would increase it. Although this model is appealing, there is no general consensus on which fundamentals are to be adopted in empirical studies. Moreover, Ma and Kanas (2000b) reported that most empirical studies have failed to reveal significant nonlinearities in this kind of exchange rate-fundamentals relationship.

Taking purchasing power parity as a specified fundamental of exchange rate, Dumas (1992) developed the no-arbitrage model to explain the nonlinear behaviour of exchange rate adjustments toward PPP. Dumas considered the existence of transaction costs to arrive at this model. The presence of transaction costs in international trade implies that deviations from PPP will only be arbitraged away by rational arbitrageurs if the price differentials exceed transaction costs. Thus, there is a band of inaction whereby the marginal profit due to price differential is unable to cover transaction costs. In other words, exchange rate is left unadjusted if its deviation from the parity is not big enough. As a result, the adjustment process tends to be discrete rather than continuous, enabling the modelling of exchange rate dynamics by using the nonlinear Threshold Autoregressive (TAR) model. Moreover, as the net arbitraging profit is larger, the larger the magnitude of deviation, the faster will the opportunity be arbitraged away. Thus, the speed of adjustment varies with respect to the size of deviation, thereby justifying the nonlinear adjustment of exchange rate towards PPP. A prominent nonlinear model that is capable of measuring the speed of adjustment is the Smooth Transition Autoregressive (STAR) model proposed by Granger and Teräsvirta (1993). Taylor and Peel (2000) argued that the STAR model is more appropriate than the TAR model in examining the movements of exchange rates based on national price indices involving a range of goods with different costs of arbitrage. Consistent with Taylor and Peel (2000), Baum *et al.* (2001) also postulated that based on observed aggregated process, regime changes may be smooth rather than discrete as long as economic agents do not act simultaneously.

The STAR Model

The origin of the nonlinear Smooth Transition Threshold Autoregressive or just Smooth Transition Autoregressive (STAR) model could be traced back to the Threshold Autoregressive (TAR) model first proposed by Howell Tong in 1977 (see Tong and Lim 1980). The TAR model assumes that a variable has different behaviours within different regimes. The basic idea underlying the TAR model is piecewise linearisation of nonlinear models over the state space by the introduction of the thresholds. An example of the TAR model is the Self-excited TAR (or SETAR) model, which assumes that a variable (say, exchange rate), z_t is a linear autoregression within a regime, but may move between regimes depending on the value taken by a lag of z_t, say z_{t-d} where d is known as a delay parameter. For the two-regime case ($q = 2$) where z_t follows an AR (p_1) process in the one regime and another AR (p_2) process in the other, the SETAR (2; p_1, p_2) representation of z_t can be written compactly as:

$$z_t = \beta_0 + \sum_{i=1}^{p_1} \beta_i z_{t-i} + \varepsilon_{1t} + I_{t-d}(r) \; [\beta_0^* + \sum_{i=1}^{p_2} \beta_i^* z_{t-i} + \varepsilon_{2t} - \varepsilon_{1t}] \qquad (1)$$

where $I_t(r) = 1$ if $z_t > r$ and 0 otherwise is the threshold. For $h = 1, 2$, $\varepsilon_{ht} \sim$ G (0, σ_h^2) where G (·) may be a Gaussian distribution but this is not necessarily the case. β_i for $i = 0, .., p_1$ and β_i^* for $i = 0, .., p_2$ are parameters to be estimated.

The introduction of nonlinear time series models such as the SETAR model is motivated by the fact that linear time series models should give place to a much wider class of models if we are to gain greater understanding of more complicated phenomena such as limit cycles, time irreversibility, amplitude-frequency dependency and jump resonance (Tong and Lim 1980). Since its introduction, few attempts have been made to apply and validate the SETAR model, and hence the usefulness of the model in empirical work is yet to be determined. For instance, Diebold and Nason (1990) pointed out that there is no guarantee that the SETAR model will perform better than the linear AR model. A similar view was expressed in Clements and Smith (1997), where they noted that neither the in-sample, nor the rejection of the null of linearity in a formal test in favour of nonlinearity guarantees that the SETAR model predicts more accurately than AR models.

The deficiency of the SETAR model is deemed to be due to the unrealistic fixed threshold in the model. The fixed threshold of the SETAR model was later replaced with a smooth function and thus led to the formation of the STAR model in the early 1990s. The STAR model allows the variable under study to alternate between two different regimes with a smooth transition function between these regimes, so that there can be a continuum of states between extreme regimes. This STAR representation is given by (Teräsvirta and Anderson 1993):

$$z_t = \beta_0 + \sum_{i=1}^{p} \beta_i z_{t-i} + [\beta_0^* + \sum_{i=1}^{p} \beta_i^* z_{t-i}] \, \mathrm{F}(z_{t-d}) + \varepsilon_t \qquad (2)$$

where z_t is mean-corrected, β_0, and β_0^* are constants, β_i and β_i^*, $i = 1, \ldots, p$ are autoregressive parameters, F(·) is the transition function depending on the lagged level, z_{t-d}, where d is known as the delay length or delay parameter, and ε_t is a white noise with zero mean and constant variance σ_{ε}^2.

For the application of the STAR model, Granger and Teräsvirta (1993) have proposed an exponential function as one of the plausible transition functions, thus resulting in the exponential STAR or ESTAR model. The exponential function is defined as:

$$F(z_{t-d}) = 1 - \exp[-\gamma^2 (z_{t-d} - u)^2 / \hat{\sigma}_{z_t}^2] \tag{3}$$

where γ is the scale-free transition parameter, which is standardised by $\hat{\sigma}_{z_t}^2$, the estimated variance of the mean-corrected deviation series, z_t. The γ^2 is the unstandardised transition parameter, u is the equilibrium or threshold value of the mean corrected z_t series and hence E(u) = 0, and $\hat{\sigma}_{z_t}^2$ is the estimated variance of z_t.

Note that the speed of transition between the two regimes is positively related to the value of the transition parameter γ^2. In other words, higher values of γ^2 imply a much faster speed of transition. Taylor and Peel (2000) used a version of the transition function, F(·) with $\hat{\sigma}_{z_t}^2 = 1$. Nevertheless, Granger and Teräsvirta (1993, p. 124) argued that scaling the exponential term by the sample variance speeds the convergence and improves the stability of the nonlinear least squares estimation algorithm. It also makes it possible to compare estimates of transition parameter across equations.

The exponential transition function is bounded between zero and one. Judging from Equation (3), when z_{t-d} equals its equilibrium value u or when $\gamma^2 / \hat{\sigma}_{z_t}^2$ goes to zero, F(·) = 0 and Equation 2 reverts to a standard linear AR(p) representation:

$$z_t = \beta_0 + \sum_{i=1}^{p} \beta_i z_{t-i} + \varepsilon_t \tag{4}$$

In such a case, the conventional restriction of $\sum_{i=1}^{p} \beta_i < 1$ applies so that z_t is mean-reverting. For extreme deviations from the fundamental equilibrium, F(·) = 1 (when $\gamma^2 / \hat{\sigma}^2_{z_t}$ approaches infinity), where Equation (2) becomes a nonlinear AR (*p*) model:

$$z_t = (\beta_0 + \beta_0^*) + \sum_{i=1}^{p}(\beta_i + \beta_i^*)z_{t-i} + \varepsilon_t \qquad (5)$$

If the nonlinear model as in Equation (5) is the correct specification, it is expected that $|\sum_{i=1}^{p}\beta_i| \leq 1$ such that z_t may exhibit unit root behaviour but the requirement for global stability is that $|\sum_{i=1}^{p}(\beta_i + \beta_i^*)| < 1$ must be met.

The exponential F(·) allows a smooth transition between a two regime symmetry adjustment for deviations above and below the fundamental equilibrium. This function is considered suitable for the nonlinear modelling of exchange rate as it has a number of attractive properties. For instance, it can capture the symmetrical response to positive and negative deviations from its fundamental equilibrium (Baum *et al.* 2001) by its inverted bell-shaped distribution around zero. Despite the potential usefulness of the ESTAR model in modelling the exchange rate specifically and other nonlinearities in general, much more empirical work has yet to be done to fill the gap in the related literature. There are only a few published articles on the STAR model. Most of them are theoretical in nature and the application is only for illustration purposes. Earlier works, for instance by Chan and Tong (1986), Luukonnen *et al.* (1988), Saikkonen and Luukkonen (1988), Teräsvirta (1994) and Eirtheim and Teräsvirta (1996), discuss the theoretical issues on the linearity tests and model specification of the STAR model. One notable exception is the work of Teräsvirta and Anderson (1993) that evaluated the forecast performance of the ESTAR model, in the context of the business cycle.

Linearity Tests

To determine the linearity nature of exchange rate, the commonly employed linearity test in empirical work is the third order test procedure of Lukkonen, Saikkonen and Teräsvirta (1988) which has an auxiliary regression of the general form (referred to as LST linearity test hereafter):

$$z_t = \alpha_0 + \sum_{i=1}^{p}\alpha_i z_{t-i} + \sum_{i=1}^{p}\sum_{j=1}^{p}(\beta_{ij} z_{t-i} z_{t-j} + \delta_{ij} z_{t-i} z_{t-j}^2 + \theta_{ij} z_{t-i} z_{t-j}^3) + \omega_t \quad (6)$$

where z_t is the series of interest; $\alpha_0, \alpha_i, \beta_{ij}$, δ_{ij} and θ_{ij} ; $i, j = 1, \ldots, p$ are parameters to be estimated and under the null hypothesis, ω_t is white noise with zero mean and constant variance.

Note that *p*, the autoregressive order of the linear component of Equation (6) is normally determined in advance by using selection criteria such as the Final Prediction Error (FPE), Schwarz Information Criterion (SIC) and Akaike's Information Criterion (AIC). However, these criteria are of course not without any shortcomings; see for instance, Liew and Shitan (2002) for a brief review of the properties of these selection criteria. In general, these information criteria tend to penalise high-order lags. On the other hand, if the selected *p* is too low, the estimated AR model may suffer from autocorrelated residuals. Teräsvirta and Anderson (1993) pointed out that neglecting the autocorrelation structure of the residuals may lead to false rejection of the linearity hypothesis in favour of the nonlinearities alternative, because often the test also has low power against serially correlated errors. As such, one may think that over-parameterisation of the linear AR (*p*) is preferable to under-parameterisation. However, selecting a maximum lag-length greater than the true order *p* may also weaken the power of the test compared to the case where the maximum lag is known (Teräsvirta and Anderson 1993). Thus it is important to select order *p* sufficient enough to eliminate autocorrelation.

In this chapter, the optimal lag length *p* of linear AR (*p*) model is selected based on Akaike's biased Corrected Information Criterion (AICC). This criterion selects the minimum AICC model, among a class of models with no serial correlation. Liew and Shitan (2002) examined the behaviour of AICC through a simulation study and found that it had little tendency to underestimate the true order *p*. Thus the use of AICC avoids the problem of a too parsimonious model being selected.

Referring to Equation (6), the null hypothesis of $\beta_{ij} = \delta_{ij} = \theta_{ij} = 0$ for all *i* and *j* holds under linearity assumption and may be tested by chi-squared (χ^2) distributed test statistic (see Lukkonen *et al.* 1988) or Lagrange Multiplier (LM) test statistic (see Teräsvirta, 1994). LST linearity test has the power against the STAR model, in which the rejection of the null hypothesis would imply the series under investigation follows a nonlinear STAR process rather than a linear AR process. In particular, two well-known specifications of the STAR model, namely the LSTAR or Logistic STAR and ESTAR or Exponential STAR (see Teräsvirta 1994; and Teräsvirta and Anderson 1993, among others, for a theoretical discussion of these specifications) are detectable by this LST linearity test. Briefly, conditioned on $\theta_{ij} \neq 0$, rejection of the null hypothesis of $\delta_{ij} = 0$ implies ESTAR is the correct specification, whereas conditioned on $\theta_{ij} \neq 0$ and $\delta_{ij} \neq 0$, rejection of the null hypothesis of $\beta_{ij} = 0$ indicates LSTAR is appropriate.

Nevertheless, this linearity test procedure is only practical if our sample size is relatively large when compared to the autoregressive order p. This is because both χ^2 and LM test statistics of this LST linearity test have $3p$ degrees of freedom if we assume that d is known (which is unrealistic). These degrees of freedom explode quadratically with respect to p in the case of unknown d (see Lukkonen *et al.* 1988). Considering the fact that our exchange rate deviation series have only 134 observations and that the order p can attain a relatively high value of 8 as in the case of the Indonesian rupiah – Japanese yen deviation series, we decided to omit the third order term of LST test as specified in Equation (6) in conducting our linearity test. Effectively, assuming p, the order of linear AR and the delay parameter d is known, the auxiliary model to be estimated is then

$$z_t = \alpha_0 + \sum_{i=1}^{p} (\alpha_i z_{t-i} + \beta_i z_{t-i} z_{t-d} + \delta_i z_{t-i} z_{t-d}^2) + \omega_t \tag{7}$$

where α_0, α_i, β_i and δ_i ; i = 1, ..., p are parameters to be estimated and other notations follow from Equation (6).

The linearity test as specified in Equation (7) actually has power against both the ESTAR (at least one $\delta_i \neq 0$) and LSTAR (at least one $\beta_i \neq 0$ given that all $\delta_i = 0$) specifications of the general STAR model. With this specification, both χ^2 and *LM* test statistics have $2p$ degrees of freedom for known d. Direct use of the linearity test as depicted in Equation (7) rather than Equation (6) is also adopted in Baum *et al.* (2001). It is argued in Baum *et al.* (2001) and many other related studies that the nonlinear adjustment process of exchange rate deviations is symmetrical in nature and ESTAR (rather than LSTAR) is deemed more appropriate in representing this process. Hence, this chapter follows Baum *et al.* (2001) in the sense that we do not narrow down our test [Equation (7)] to further detect the existence of the LSTAR model.

Similar to Equation (6) the optimum lag length p and delay parameter d in Equation (7) have to be determined from the data as they are normally unknown. In the current study, the optimal p of linear AR (p) model is selected from a class of models with no autocorrelation based on the minimum Akaike's biased corrected information criterion (AICC). In order to specify d, linearity tests are carried out for the range of values $1 \leq d \leq 12$. Optimal d is chosen from the one that minimises the marginal significance value of the implied test statistic.

Empirical Analysis

The data used in this chapter include 6 Japanese yen-based Asian currencies, namely the Indonesian rupiah, Korean won, Malaysian ringgit, Philippines peso, Singaporean dollar and Thai baht. All exchange rates are the end of period nominal bilateral exchange rate data series, taken from various issues of the International Monetary Funds' International Financial Statistics (IMF/IFS). Consumer price indices (CPI) from the same source are also taken to construct relative price (P_t) series. Our data spans from the first quarter of the year 1968 to the second quarter of the year 2001 (1968:1 to 2001:2).

Deviations of exchange rates from PPP are estimated by the standard Johansen procedure. These deviation series are mean-corrected before they are subjected to the two-step linearity test procedures. First, we estimated the optimum lag length p of the linear AR model for each deviation series, based on the minimum *AICC* criterion. The estimated results and residual diagnostics are depicted in Table 4.1. Table 4.1 shows that all linear AR models are free from autocorrelation and heteroscedasticity problems (except INR which does not pass the higher order heteroscedasticity test) at standard significance levels. However, with the exception of SGD, all linear AR models fail to capture the ARCH effects of the corresponding deviations. These preliminary results tend to suggest that linear AR processes are inadequate in characterising the adjustment dynamic of the exchange rate deviations.

Rejection of the linear process provides us with the motivation to determine whether the adjustment dynamic could be represented by a nonlinear autoregressive process. Thus, we proceed to the second step of our linearity test procedures, that is, to conduct the LST linearity test. The linearity test results are depicted in Table 4.2. It is obvious from Table 4.2 that in all cases, linearity can be rejected at 5 percent significance level for the deviation series in favour of the STAR model, on the basis of χ^2 statistic. This finding is strongly supported by the *LM* statistic. We also computed the *F* statistic (see Teräsvirta 1994), which is said to have superior small-sample performance. Our results show that although the *F* statistic has a smaller marginal significance value (as compared to the other two statistics) for each *d*, it does not lead to a different selection of the optimal *d* value. Hence, we found from this chapter that there is no significant gain in differentiating these three test statistics as they have the same power in determining the optimal delay parameter *d*.

To sum up, our formal linearity test results strongly suggest that the adjustment process of exchange rate deviations towards the PPP equilibrium follows a smooth transition autoregressive (STAR) process, which is nonlinear in nature. In particular, this chapter reveals that the adjustments of the rupiah followed a STAR process of order 8 and a delay lag length of 8 (or, conveniently denoted as the STAR (8, 8) process). By the same token, the won, ringgit, peso,

Singaporean dollar and baht followed the STAR (5, 11), STAR (5, 6), STAR (7, 8), STAR (3, 5) and STAR (3, 9) processes respectively.

As the null hypothesis of the linearity tests specified in Equation (7) is effectively in favour of the ESTAR specification, we estimated the transition function defined in Equation (3). This transition function F[z_{t-d}] is estimated for each series as it provides us information on the degree of mean-reversion, that is the speed of adjustment of the deviations towards the equilibrium level. The specification of F[z_{t-d}] in the current study differs from that of Granger and Teräsvirta (1993), which includes a threshold parameter (to reflect the mean equilibrium level) in the transition function. The threshold parameter in our case is assumed zero as we are using the mean-corrected series. The estimated scale-free transition parameters, γ, which may be compared across series, and the residual diagnostics results are summarised in Table 4.3.

All estimated transition parameters as depicted in Table 4.3 are significantly different from zero at standard significance levels. Moreover, the estimated variances of the nonlinear STAR specification are smaller than those of the linear AR specification in all cases. These two findings indicate that linear specification itself is sufficient to represent the exchange rate adjustments.

Residual diagnostics indicate that there is no autocorrelation (from the Q statistic) or heteroscedasticity (from the HET statistic) effect in the remaining residuals at 5 percent significance level. Moreover, the non-rejection of the Q statistics also suggests that the residuals are independently and identically distributed. ARCH effect or the 4th or higher order is also not detected in all cases at the same significance level with the exception of Indonesia. A comparison of Table 4.2 and Table 4.3 reveals that with the Exponential STAR specification, all the residual ARCH effects due to the linear AR specification has been eliminated (with one exception). All in all, the residual diagnostics demonstrate that the Exponential STAR specification is able to adequately capture the nonlinear adjustment process of all the six exchange rates except the rupiah (INR), whereby the ARCH effect is not fully accounted for. It is well known that the rupiah had experienced great instability during the 1997 Asian Financial Crisis and the remaining ARCH effect in its deviation series may be due to this extraordinary volatility (estimated variance over the sample period is as high as 1102982.64). It is interesting to know whether the Smooth Transition GARCH model (a variant of the STAR model) of Lundbergh and Teräsvirta (1998) is able to fully capture the ARCH effect in such a case. However, we leave this issue for future research.

The transition parameters of the rupiah, won, ringgit, peso, Singaporean dollar and baht are, in that order, 0.082, 0.751, 0.823, 0.167, 6.533 and 0.317, implying that the speeds of transition differ by exchange rates. Figure 1 shows the plots of the estimated transition functions, F[z_{t-d}] against the corresponding lagged values of the exchange rate deviations from the PPP equilibrium, z_{t-d}. As our series are mean-corrected, the PPP equilibrium level in each case is exactly represented by $z_{t-d} = 0$ in the horizontal axis of Figure 4.1. The inverted-bell shaped plots in Figure 1 show that the adjustment processes of the negative and positive deviations are acceptably symmetrical in nature. This finding is in accordance with most literature (Baum *et al.* 2001; Taylor and Peel 2000; Sarno 2000, among others). In each case, the slope of the transition function, F[z_{t-d}] indicates the speed of adjustment towards the long-run equilibrium (Sarno 2000). The approximate values of these slopes are, sorted in descending order, 1000.00 (for SGD), 53.33 (MYR), 10.00 (PHP), 8.00 (THB), 0.60 (KRW) and 0.12 (INR). Relatively, this means the speed of adjustment is the fastest for the deviations of the Singaporean dollar – yen rate and this is followed by deviations of the yen-based Malaysian ringgit and Philippines peso. The adjustment of the Indonesian rupiah – yen deviation towards the PPP equilibrium is found to be the slowest amongst all cases. Interestingly, this speed of adjustment seems to have a direct relationship with the degree of depreciation during the 1997 Asian Financial Crisis. Carbaugh (2000) reported that this crisis had minimal and the most negative impact on the Singaporean dollar and Indonesian rupiah respectively, with other currencies moderately affected. Specifically, we find that the Singaporean dollar recorded a drop of only nearly 15 percent (as in 1998:3) in value as measured in Japanese yen, whereas the Indonesian rupiah plunged more than double in value during the same period. Meanwhile, other currencies in this chapter dived by 34 percent to 47 percent. Our empirical results seem to postulate that an exchange rate with a higher speed of adjustment (visualised by steeper slope of transition function), tends to be more sustainable (less adversely affected) during crisis. One plausible explanation for this phenomenon is that an exchange rate with high speed of adjustment (as in Singapore dollar) tends to adjust faster with respect to its fundamentals and hence will be less affected by the market correction process such as the 1997 crisis, since not much deviation is left for further correction. On the other hand, for an exchange rate characterised by a low speed of adjustment (as in rupiah), most of the deviations will be left unadjusted or only partially adjusted because of the slow adjustment mechanism. This will reach a stage when the accumulated deviations are no longer sustainable, causing a tremendous market correction process to be taken place, leading to a tremendous plunge in value as we observed in the rupiah rate during the 1997 crisis.

Conclusion

The hypothesis that the adjustment dynamic of exchange rate deviations is nonlinear in nature has been widely accepted by most exchange rate researchers. Moreover, many published articles characterised this nonlinear adjustment process with the Smooth Transition Autoregressive (STAR) Model. Following these studies, we utilised the linearity test statistics devised by Lukkonen *et al.* (1988) and Teräsvirta (1994) to determine the linearity nature of the adjustment process, in the context of yen-based Asian exchange rates. We note here that linearity tests have been conducted in developed countries (Baum *et al.*, 2001) as well as in the Middle Eastern Countries (Sarno, 2000) but it is not until this current study that similar test have been applied in the context of Asian countries. Our test statistics verified that the adjustment process towards the purchasing power parity equilibrium is actually nonlinear in nature and could be characterised by a STAR process for each of the selected exchange rates. As such, any estimation of linear exchange rate models for the Asian economies may yield unreliable policy conclusion. Besides, we discovered that the STAR process has the ability to deal with the ARCH effects of the adjustment process, which the linear AR process had failed to do.

One implication of this discovery is that the nonlinear nature of the adjustment process of exchange rate deviations may be due to exchange rate volatility. Moreover, our empirical results postulate that exchange rates with high speeds of adjustment tended to be less adversely affected by the recent Asian Financial Crisis. Our explanation for this phenomenon is that exchange rates with high speeds of adjustment tend to adjust faster with respect to its fundamentals and hence will be less affected by market correction processes such as that of the 1997 crisis, since not much deviation is left to be corrected. On the other hand, exchange rates characterised by low speeds of adjustment will result in most of the deviations being left unadjusted or only partially adjusted due to the slow adjustment mechanisms leading to a stage where the accumulated deviations are no longer sustainable causing a tremendous market correction process to occur.

Table 4.1 Residual Diagnostics for Linear AR (*p*) Models

Series	Optimum *p*	Marginal Significance Values of Residual Diagnostics					
		Q_4	Q_{12}	HET_4	HET_{12}	$ARCH_4$	GARCH
INR	8	0.910	0.800	0.886	0.000	0.000	0.000
KRW	5	0.999	0.778	0.999	0.355	0.000	0.000
MYR	5	0.999	0.952	0.999	0.911	0.001	0.000
PHP	7	0.865	0.866	0.829	0.644	0.075	0.000
SGD	3	0.342	0.118	0.352	0.132	0.341	0.132
THB	3	0.947	0.768	0.951	0.160	0.012	0.000

Notes: Q_i and HET_i are, in that order, Ljung-Box Q statistics and Breusch-Pagan-Godfrey test statistics to ensure the absence of serial correlation and heteroscedasticity problems up to the order of i; where i = 4, 12. Q statistic also has the power against the alternative hypothesis that the residuals do not follow normal distribution. $ARCH_4$ and GARCH tests detect the ARCH effects up to 4th and higher order respectively.

Table 4.2 Marginal Significance Values of Linearity Tests

Tests	Delay Length, *d*											
	1	2	3	4	5	6	7	8	9	10	11	12
					Indonesian rupiah (*p*=8)							
χ^2	0.00	0.00	0.00	0.00	0.00	0.00	0.00	**0.00**	0.00	0.00	0.00	0.00
LM	0.00	0.00	0.00	0.00	0.00	0.00	0.00	**0.00**	0.00	0.00	0.00	0.00
F	0.00	0.00	0.00	0.00	0.00	0.00	0.00	**0.00**	0.00	0.00	0.00	0.00
					Korean won (*p*=5)							
χ^2	0.30	0.84	0.66	0.30	0.32	0.24	0.22	0.07	0.06	0.09	**0.02**	0.05
LM	0.45	0.93	0.81	0.46	0.48	0.38	0.36	0.14	0.12	0.18	**0.05**	0.27
F	0.19	0.67	0.47	0.19	0.20	0.15	0.36	0.04	0.04	0.06	**0.01**	0.09
					Malaysian ringgit (*p*=5)							
χ^2	0.00	0.00	0.00	0.00	0.00	**0.00**	0.00	0.00	0.00	0.00	0.01	0.00
LM	0.02	0.02	0.00	0.07	0.00	**0.00**	0.00	0.00	0.00	0.05	0.10	0.05
F	0.01	0.01	0.00	0.02	0.00	**0.00**	0.00	0.00	0.00	0.02	0.03	0.01
					Philippines peso (*p*=7)							
χ^2	0.00	0.00	0.00	0.00	0.00	0.00	0.00	**0.00**	0.00	0.00	0.00	0.00
LM	0.00	0.00	0.00	0.00	0.00	0.00	0.00	**0.00**	0.00	0.00	0.00	0.00
F	0.00	0.00	0.00	0.00	0.00	0.00	0.00	**0.00**	0.00	0.00	0.00	0.00
					Singaporean dollar (*p*=3)							
χ^2	0.00	0.00	0.00	0.00	**0.00**	0.00	0.00	0.00	0.00	0.00	0.00	0.00
LM	0.01	0.00	0.02	0.02	**0.00**	0.00	0.02	0.00	0.03	0.07	0.00	0.05
F	0.00	0.00	0.01	0.01	**0.00**	0.00	0.01	0.00	0.01	0.02	0.00	0.02
					Thai baht (*p*=3)							
χ^2	0.00	0.07	0.82	0.61	0.25	0.64	0.37	0.03	**0.00**	0.23	0.18	0.18
LM	0.02	0.20	0.96	0.84	0.51	0.87	0.65	0.11	**0.01**	0.48	0.41	0.41
F	0.00	0.06	0.70	0.48	0.19	0.51	0.28	0.03	**0.00**	0.17	0.14	0.14

Note: The optimal lag length *p* is determined by the AICC. Minimum marginal significance value for each linearity test is printed in bold.

Table 4.3 Estimated Transition Parameters (γ)

Series	γ (Standard Error)	VR	Marginal Significance Values of Residual Diagnostics					
			Q_4	Q_{12}	HET_4	HET_{12}	$ARCH_4$	GARCH
INR	0.082 (0.006)**	0.842	0.281	0.136	0.391	0.232	0.052	0.000
KRW	0.751 (0.203)*	0.810	0.461	0.964	0.451	0.955	0.994	0.969
MYR	0.823 (0.350)**	0.955	0.859	0.695	0.835	0.691	0.347	0.545
PHP	0.167 (0.057)**	0.695	0.713	0.302	0.744	0.275	0.115	0.987
SGD	6.533 (0.807)**	0.866	0.926	0.700	0.922	0.838	0.376	0.752
THB	0.317 (0.231)**	0.675	0.186	0.163	0.211	0.356	0.104	0.955

Notes: VR stands for variance ratio of the nonlinear Smooth Transition (STAR) model to the linear Autoregressive (AR) model.

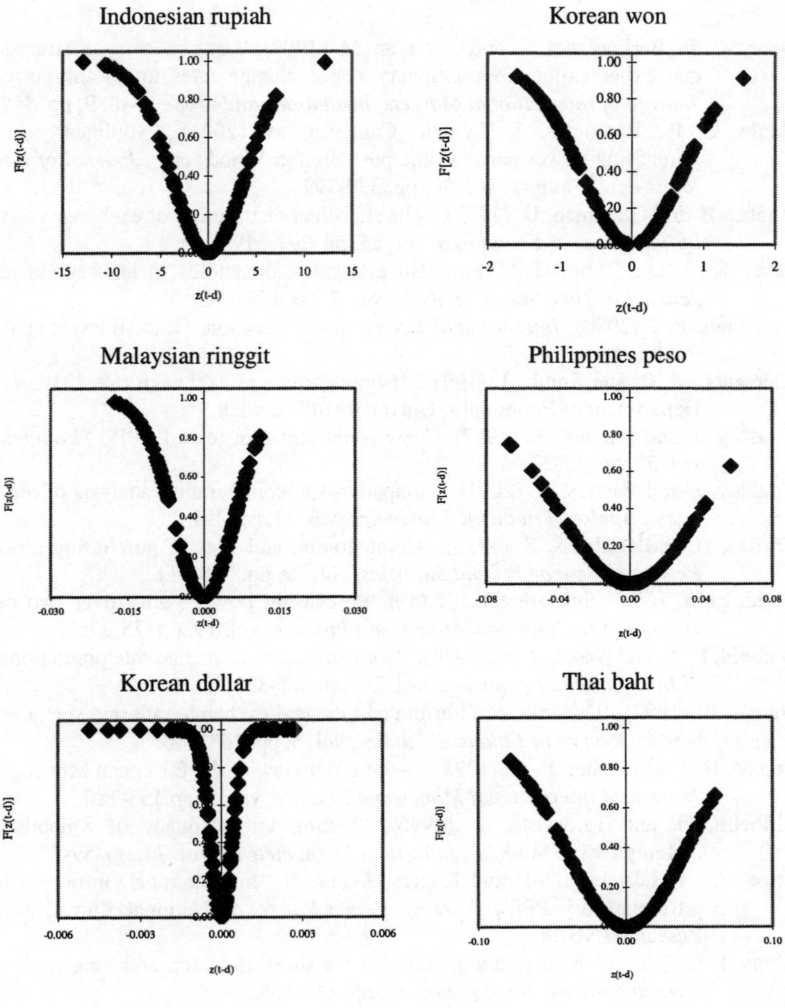

Figure 4.1 Estimated Transition Functions

References

Baum, C. F., Barkoulas, J. T. and Caglayan, M. (1999), 'Long memory or structural breaks: can either explain nonstationary real exchange rates under the current float?', *Journal of International Markets, Institutions and Money*, vol. 9, pp. 359-376.

Baum, C. F., Barkoulas, J. T. and Caglayan, M. (2001), 'Nonlinear adjustment to purchasing power parity in the post-Bretton Woods era', *Journal of International Money and Finance*, vol. 20, pp. 379-399.

Boothe, P. and Glassman, D. (1987), 'The statistical distribution of exchange rates', *Journal of International Economics*, vol. 25, pp. 297-319.

Chan, K. S. and Tong, H. (1986), 'On estimation thresholds in autoregressive models', *Journal of Time Series Analysis*, vol. 7, pp. 179-190.

Carbaugh, R. J (2000), *International Economics*, 7th edition, Ohio: International Thomson Publishing.

Clements, M. P. and Smith, J. (1998), 'Nonlinearities in exchange rates', *Working Paper*, Department of Economics, University of Warwick.

Coakley, J. and Fuertes, A. (1997), 'New panel unit root test of PPP', *Economics Letters*, vol. 57, pp. 17-22.

Coakley, J. and Fuertes, A. (2001), 'Nonparametric cointegration analysis of real exchange rates', *Applied Financial Economics*, vol. 11, pp. 1-8.

Corbae, D. and Outliaris, S. (1988), 'Cointegration and tests of purchasing power parity', *Review of Economics and Statistics*, vol. 70, pp. 508-511.

Cuddington, J. T. and Hong L. (2000), 'Purchasing power parity over two centuries?', *Journal of International Money and Finance*, vol. 19, pp. 753-757.

Diebold, F. X. and Nason, J. A. (1990), 'Non-parametric exchange rate predictions', *Journal of International Economics,* vol. 28, pp. 315-332.

Dumas, B. (1992), 'Dynamic equilibrium and the real exchange rate in a spatially separated world', *Review of Financial Studies*, vol. 5, pp. 153-180.

Edison, H. J. and Fisher, E. O. (1991), 'A long-run view of the European Monetary System', *Journal of International Money and Finance*, vol. 5, pp.153-180.

Eirtheim, Ø. and Teräsvirta, T. (1996), 'Testing the adequacy of Smooth Transition Autoregressive Models', *Journal of Econometrics*, vol. 74, pp. 59-75.

Engel, C., Hendrickson, M. and Rogers, J. (1997), 'Intra-national, intra-continental and intra-planetary PPP', *Working Paper No. 6069*, National Bureau of Economic Research (NBER).

Glens, J. D. (1992), 'Real exchange fates in the short, medium, and long run', *Journal of International Economics*, vol. 33, pp. 147-166.

Granger, C. W. J. and Teräsvirta, T. (1993), *Modelling Nonlinear Economic Relationships*, Oxford: Oxford University Press.

Hsieh, D. A. (1989), 'Testing for nonlinearity in daily foreign exchange rate changes', *Journal of Business*, vol. 62, pp. 339-368.

Krugman, P. (1991), 'Target zones and exchange rate dynamics', *Quarterly Journal of Economics*, vol. 106, pp. 669-682.

Lee, M. H. (1976), *Purchasing Power Parity*, New York: Dekker.

Liew, K. S. and Shitan, M. (2002), 'The performance of AICC as order determination criterion in the selection of ARMA time series models', *Pertanika Journal of Social Science*, vol. 10, pp. 25-33.

Lothian, J. R. and Taylor, M. P. (1996), 'Is a random walk the best exchange rate predictor?', *International Journal of Forecasting*, vol. 13, pp. 255-267.

Lundbergh, S. and Teräsvirta, T. (1998), 'Modelling economic high-frequency time series with STAR-STGARCH models', *Unpublished Paper*, Department of Economic Statistics, Stockholm, Sweden.

Luukkonen, R., P. Saikkonen and Teräsvirta, T. (1988), 'Testing linearity against Smooth Transition Autoregressive Models', *Biometrika*, vol. 75, pp. 491-499.

M. Azali., Habibullah, M. S. and Baharumshah, A. Z. (2001), 'Does PPP hold between Asian and the Japanese economies: Evidence using panel unit root and panel cointegration', *Japan and the World Economy*, vol. 13, pp. 35-50.

Ma, Y. and Kanas, A. (2000a), 'Testing for nonlinear Granger causality from fundamentals to exchange rates in the ERM', *Journal of International Financial Markets, Institutions and Money*, vol. 10, pp. 69-82.

Ma, Y. and Kanas, A. (2000b), 'Testing for a relationship among fundamentals and exchange rates in the ERM', *Journal of International Money and Finance*, vol. 19, pp. 135-152.

Mahajan, A. and Wagner, A. J. (1999), 'Nonlinear dynamics in foreign exchange rates', *Global Finance Journal*, vol. 10, pp. 1-23.

Nagayasu, J. (1998), 'Does the long run PPP hypothesis hold for Africa? Evidence from panel cointegration study', *IMF Working Paper No. 98.*

O'Connell, P. G. (1998), 'The overvaluation of purchasing power parity', *Journal of International Economics*, vol. 44, pp. 1-9.

Razzaghipour, A., Fleming, G. and Heaney, R. (2001), 'Deviations and mean reversion to purchasing power parity in the Asian Currency Crisis of 1997', *Applied Economics*, vol. 33, pp. 1093-1100.

Saikkonen, P. and Luukkonen, R. (1988), 'Lagrange multiplier tests for testing nonlinearities in time series models', *Scandinavian Journal of Statistics*, vol. **15**, pp. 55-68.

Salehizadeh, M. and Taylor, R. (1999), 'A test of purchasing power parity for emerging economies', *Journal of International Financial Markets, Institutions and Money*, vol. 9, pp. 183-193.

Sarno, L. (2000), 'Real exchange rate behaviour in high inflation countries: Empirical evidence from Turkey, 1980 – 1997', *Applied Economics Letters*, vol. 7, pp. 285-291.

Taylor, M. P. and Peel, D. A. (2000), 'Nonlinear adjustment, long-run equilibrium and exchange rate fundamentals', *Journal of International Money and Finance,* vol. 19, pp. 33-53.

Teräsvirta, T. (1994), 'Specification, estimation, and evaluation of Smooth Transition Autoregressive Models', *Journal of the American Statistical Association*, vol. 89, pp. 208-218.

Teräsvirta, T. and H. M. Anderson (1993), 'Characterizing nonlinearities in business cycles using Smooth Transition Autoregressive Models', in M. H. Pesaran and S. M. Potter (eds), *Nonlinear Dynamics, Chaos and Econometrics*, US: John Wiley, pp. 111-128.

Tong, H. and Lim, K. S. (1980), 'Threshold Autoregression, limit cycles and cyclical data', *Journal of Royal Statistical Society*, vol. 42, pp. 245-292.

Chapter 5

The Dynamics of Monetary Exchange Rate Model

Ahmad Zubaidi Baharumshah, Muzafar Shah Habibullah and M. Azali

Introduction

Interest in the determinants of long-run exchange rates has a long history. Lane (1999) explained why there is much interest on the long-run movements in exchange rates. First, explaining the long-run behavior of currencies is illuminating for those interested in tracing the evolution of the global economy.[1] Second, understanding of what determines long-run changes in nominal exchange rate is potentially helpful to investors comparing expected return on medium- or long-term nominal bonds in different currencies. Third, modelling the long-run behaviour of the exchange rate is the underpinning for useful understanding of the short-run behaviour of exchange rates: it is necessary to know the long-run behaviour in order to work out whether a given exchange rate movement is a deviation from its long-run path. Finally, long-run movements in exchange rate are less prone to the 'noise' that is present in higher-frequency exchange rate data and hence may more easily relate to the fundamental determinants indicated by theory.

The main purpose of this chapter is to investigate the role of economic fundamentals in explaining the ASEAN-5 exchange rates behaviour. More specifically, this chapter focuses on the usefulness[2] of the monetary model as a long run relationship in explaining the movements of the ASEAN currencies. The behaviours of these currencies have received very little attention in the literature. In view of the recent Asian financial crisis, it is also important to show that fundamentals have clear and significant roles in determining the behaviour of the ASEAN currencies. To this end, we focus on the ASEAN currencies against the US dollar and the Japanese Yen.

The study on the determinants of exchange rate in the ASEAN-5 is of interest for several reasons: First, most of these countries are characterised as managed floats, with frequent intervention by the respective central banks in the foreign market to maintain exchange rates that is in line with their governments' policies.[3] Their currencies are pegged within margin to a basket of currencies.[4] These economies have long-standing policies of open capital markets and it would be interesting to see if the monetary model is relevant to these economies. Secondly, given the increasing importance of trade and investment of the ASEAN countries and its trade dependency on the US and Japan, it is important to understand the movements of the currencies against the major trading partners. Moreover, Japan and the US are believed to have strong economic influence in the region. Not only are Japan and the US the two largest trading partners, but they are also the two largest foreign investors in the region. Finally, because several studies have found that purchasing power parity (PPP) does not hold in the ASEAN countries, we seek evidence to examine if the more complete monetary exchange model holds for these countries.[5]

Many researchers have undertaken empirical estimation of the monetary model for exchange rate determination in the industrial countries. Although the monetary model is theoretically appealing, its empirical validity is surrounded by controversy. In general, the data up to the end of 1978 tend to be supportive of the asset market approach to exchange rate determination. In contrast to the earlier work, studies using data beyond 1978 have produced results that are inconsistent with the model.[6] However, empirical studies in the 1990s by MacDonald and Taylor (1991, 1992, 1993, 1994a and 1994b), McNown and Wallace (1994), and Moosa (1994) that utilised a variety of econometric methods to deal with non-stationary data found that the monetary model is a valid framework to analyse movements in major currencies.[7] In addition, studies by Diamandis *et al.* (1996), Makrydakis (1998), Diamandis and Kouretas (1996), and Berg and Jayanetti (1993) that have focused on the less significant currencies showed that the monetary model works quite well in the recent float.[8] In other words, the monetary model produces sensible long-run equilibrium relationships and has the ability to track exchange rates for the smaller economies.[9] It is these favourable findings that have motivated us to apply the model to the ASEAN-5 countries.

ASEAN countries have received little attention in the exchange rate literature. The obvious reason that may impede major empirical works on these economies is probably due to some misunderstanding on the creditability of the exchange rate policy practices among these countries.[10] Our present task is to recollect a thorough empirical work on the monetary model for exchange rate determination among the ASEAN-5 economies. In doing so, this chapter attempts to answer the following policy question: Is monetary model of exchange rate determination valid in the long run for ASEAN countries? The monetary framework is employed to analyse the movements of ASEAN currencies vis-à-vis the US dollar (US) and the Japanese yen (JY). Following the current tradition, the Johansen-Juselius multivariate cointegration approach was utilised to analyse the long-run movements in exchange rate. The technique fully captures the underlying time series properties of the data, provides estimates of all the cointegrating vectors that exist within a vector of variables and offers a test statistic for the number of cointegrating vectors.[11]

The Monetary Model

The flexible-price monetary model approach relies on two building blocks and can be summarised by the following equations:[12]

$$e_t = \alpha + p_t - p_t^* \tag{1}$$
$$m_t - p_t = \beta_1 y_t - \beta_3 i_t \tag{2a}$$
$$m_t^* - p_t^* = \beta_2 y_t^* - \beta_4 i_t^* \tag{2b}$$
$$i_t - i_t^* = E_t[e_{t+1}] - e_t, \tag{3}$$

where e_t is the spot exchange rate (units of home currency per unit of foreign currency), p_t is the domestic price level, m_t is the domestic money supply, y_t is the domestic income and i_t is the domestic interest rates. Here, an asterisk denotes the corresponding foreign country variables. The term $E_t[e_{t+1}]$ denotes the expectation of the next period's level of the exchange rate, conditional on information available in period t.

Equation (1) represents the purchasing power parity (PPP), equation (2a) and (2b) are the home and foreign demands for money respectively and (3) is the uncovered interest parity (UIP) condition. The monetary model of exchange rate determination is an extension of the quantity theory of money in the case of an open economy. It assumes that (i) real income and money supply are determined exogenously; (ii) capital and goods are perfect substitutes; (iii) goods prices are fully flexible; and (iv) domestic money is demanded only by domestic residents and foreign money only by foreign residents. Under these assumptions a typical monetary approach model of exchange rate determination may be written by the following unrestricted reduced form equation:

$$e_t = \alpha_0 + \beta_1 m_t + \beta_2 m_t^* + \beta_3 y_t + \beta_4 y_t^* + \beta_5 i + \beta_6 i^* + u_t,$$

$$\beta_1, \beta_4, \beta_5 > 0, \qquad \beta_2, \beta_3, \beta_6 < 0 \tag{4}$$

where u_t is a residual term. For estimation purposes, all variables except for the domestic and foreign interest rates are expressed in natural logarithms.

The specification given by equation (4) considers the fundamental variables (money, real income and the interest rates) as determinants of exchange rates. As pointed out by Makrydakis (1998) this reduced-form model nests both the flexible version (Frenkel, 1976; Bilson, 1978) as well as the sticky-price variant of the monetary model (Dornbusch, 1976). The former is based on continuous purchasing power parity (PPP) and stable money demand functions for the domestic and foreign economies. The latter relaxes the unrealistic continuous PPP hypothesis, which implies a fixed real exchange rate and permits instead overshooting of both nominal and the real exchange rates over their long-run equilibrium (PPP) levels in the short-run. Furthermore, MacDonald and Taylor (1992) argued that between the two versions of the theory, the Dornbusch's version provides a more useful description of the recent floating exchange regime, which is characterised by wide fluctuations of real exchange rates.

The monetary model also implies a set of coefficient restrictions on the reduced form equation. The most important of these restrictions is the existence of proportionality between exchange rate and relative money (β_1=-β_2=1). Less important for the validity of the monetary model, yet also frequently imposed and tested in the empirical work, are equal and opposite coefficients on relative incomes (β_3 = -β_4) and interest rates (β_5 = -β_6). This implies that the domestic demand is equal to their counterparts in foreign demand function (See Moosa, 1994; MacDonald and Taylor, 1991, 1994b).

Data and Methodology

Data Description

Quarterly data spanning 1976:1 to 1997:2 were used in this chapter. The sampling period ended with 1997:2 which is the last quarter prior to the Asian financial crisis. They were bilateral exchange rates of the Malaysia ringgit (RM), Singapore Dollar (SD), Indonesian Rupiah (IR), Thai Baht (TB) and Philippines Peso (PP) all against the US dollar (US) and Japanese yen (JY). The quarterly data were chosen since a high frequency data would preclude the use of macroeconomic data such as money and income, available on quarterly frequency for most of the sample countries. We used three-month treasury bill rates as interest rates for Malaysia, Singapore, Japan and the US. For the other countries, we picked a similar rate. The rates are: Indonesia, interbank call rate; the Philippines, interbank call rate and Thailand, discount rate. The money supply is narrow money (M1), and real GDP as output measurement. In most cases, quarterly GDP figures are not available for the estimation period. They are interpolated from annual GDP using the procedure suggested by Gandolfo (1981). The data utilised in this chapter were collected from various issues of the International Financial Statistic published by IMF. All the series are expressed in natural logarithms except interest rates and they are all seasonally unadjusted.

The development of cointegration analysis has allowed for another approach to examine the relationship between fundamental variables (money, interest rate, GDP) and exchange rate. A set of variables are said to be cointegrated if they are integrated of the same order and a linear combination of them is stationary. Such a linear combination would then posit to the existence of a long-term relationship among the variables (Johansen and Juselius, 1990). The first step in the cointegration analysis is to verify the order of integration of the variables. So we test the variable for unit roots to verify their stationary. Schwert (1987) and DeJong *et al.* (1992), for instance, have noted that the Augmented Dickey-Fuller (ADF) (Dickey and Fuller, 1981) statistics may reject the null hypothesis of unit root too often in the presence of the first order moving average process. However, Campbell and Perron (1991) have shown that the ADF statistics has better small-sample properties. To ensure robustness and overcome the criticisms of any individual testing technique, both the ADF and the Phillips-Perron (PP) (Phillips and Perron, 1988; Phillips, 1987) procedures are considered in the analysis to determine the order of integration. Since these tests are now well known, we do not explain them here.

Cointegration Analysis

Once we have determined the order of integration of each series, the next step is to test for cointegration relationships between exchange rate and the fundamental variables. We employ the maximum-likelihood cointegration test due to Johansen and Juselius (1990). The Johansen procedure provides more robust results than other methods when there are more than two variables (Gonzalo, 1994).[13] The Johansen approach sets up the nonstationary time series (Y) as a vector autoregression (VAR):

$$\Delta Y_t = \mu_0 + \sum_{i=1}^{k-1} \Gamma_i \Delta Y_{t-i} + \prod Y_{t-k} + \varepsilon_t \tag{5}$$

where $\Gamma_i = -(I - \Pi_1 - \dots - \Pi_i)$ for $i = 1, \dots, k-1$
$\Pi_i = -(I - \Pi_1 - \dots - \Pi_k)$

Y_t is a vector of p variables, μ_0 is a constant and ε_t is a vector of Gaussian random variables. Γ and Π represent coefficient matrices, Δ is the difference operator, and k denotes the lag length.

The model is estimated by regressing the ΔY_t matrix against the lagged differences of ΔY_t and $Y_{t=k}$. The number of cointegrating vectors is determined by the rank (r) of Π, which indicates the number of cointegrating vectors. If Π is of full rank, or r=p, no cointegration is present as all series are themselves stationary. On the other hand, if Π is a null matrix, or r = 0 then no long run relationship is present as equation (5) is the usual VAR model in first differences. In the case when $0 < r < p$, then there exists one or more cointegrating relationships among the variables. The Π matrix can be decomposed as $\Pi = \alpha\beta'$, where the elements of the α matrix are the adjustment coefficients and the β matrix contains the cointegrating vectors. The procedure uses two likelihood ratio statistics to test for cointegration vectors, namely the trace and maximum eigenvalue (λ-max) statistics. The trace test for the null of r or fewer cointegrating vectors (versus more than) r is

$$TR_r = -T \sum_{i=r+1}^{p} \ln\left(1 - \hat{\lambda}_i\right) \tag{6}$$

This is a function of the squared canonical correlations ($\hat{\lambda}_i$) between the first difference and the levels of the variables, having factored out the dynamic and deterministic factors. The $\hat{\lambda}_i$ are the solutions to a certain eigenvalue problem. An alternative maximal eigenvalue test statistic of the null that there is r cointegrating vectors against the alternative that there are r+1 is

$$\lambda - \max_r = TR_r - TR_{r+1} \tag{7}$$

Both test statistics can then be compared with their respective critical values provided by Osterwald-Lenum (1992).[14]

Empirical Results

For testing of the number of cointegrating vectors, the Johansen procedure requires that all variables are not to be I(2), but the procedure can handle both I(1) and a mixture of I(1) and I(0). To verify the univariate properties of the variables concerned, we relied on two-unit root testing procedure-the ADF, PP and KPSS testing principles. Unlike the ADF and the PP tests, the KPSS procedure tests for level (η_{μ}) or trend stationary (η_{τ}) against the alternative of a unit root. In applying these tests, the optimal lag structure is determined using the Akaike Information criteria (AIC) and the Schwartz criteria (SBC). In addition, insignificant lags were dropped from the regression based on the conventional *F*-test. However, if the elimination of lags produced serial correlation then the lags were added back on. Overwhelmingly, this array of tests provides strong support that both exchange rate and the fundamental variables contain a unit root in level or *I(1)* series for all the countries.

Next, we proceeded with the Johansen-Juselius procedure to determine the number of cointegration relation in the seven-dimensional vector [e, m, m*, y, y*, i, i*] for the bilateral ASEAN currencies against the US and Japanese counterparts. To implement the methodology, a lag length must be chosen for each of the VAR systems.[15] To this end, we employed the Akaike Information Criterion (AIC) and the Schwerz Bayesian Criterion (SBC) that is commonly used in the literature to determine the optimal lag length. Table 5.1 shows the AIC and SBC to select the lag length required for the VAR model. Lags up to 4 periods were calculated in both the AIC and SBC. The SBC criterion suggests a lag of one period but the AIC implies longer lag length in the VAR model. We preferred to stick to the lower order of VAR model where the chosen lag length for each equation in the model shows no evidence of serial correlation. The resulting VAR orders based on these strategies are 1 for RM/US, SD/US, PP/JP and IR/JP and 2 for IR/US, TB/US, PP/US, RM/JP, SD/JP and TB/JP.

Despite the relatively short lag-length, the VAR system passes a series of diagnostic tests. Box-Pierce test shows that no equations contain serial correlation. The results for Hosking's (1980) multivariate portmanteau test show that serial cross-correlation is not significant at conventional significant levels when ten lags are considered. There is no evidence of dynamic heteroskedastic errors in the equations. However, the LM statistics of the Jarque-Bera (1980) normality test reveal that most equations have non-normal residuals. Finally, we used the LM test proposed by Engle (1982) to test for autoregressive conditional heteroscedasticity (ARCH) up to the 4th order. The equations in the VAR show no evidence of ARCH effect except in few cases. Since the Johansen procedure does not strictly depend on normality assumptions, we employed the stated lag-length in the rest of the analysis (Lutkepohl, 1991).[16] Note that a constant term is included in all the VAR models used to generate the Johansen results in Table 5.2. Indeed, the likelihood ratio statistic indicated that the constant was significant. Thus, the trace and λ-max statistics are computed with a constant term in the cointegrating relationship.

Results of using the optimal lag structure for cointegration tests are summarised in Table 5.2. In some cases we find conflicting results between the maximum eigenvalue and the trace statistics. To choose the number of cointegrating vectors, we followed the approach taken by McNown and Wallace (1994) where the vectors revealed to be significant in both tests are considered. The results indicate that using the US as the base country, Indonesia and the Philippines exhibit 3 cointegrating vectors and Singapore has 4 vectors. For Malaysia and Thailand, at least two significant vectors represent the long-run relationship between exchange rate and fundamental variables at conventional significance level (Panel A). On the other hand, when Japan is used as the base country two significant vectors are identified in all of the ASEAN countries, except for only Thailand. As shown in Table 5.2 Panel B we found three vectors for the baht-yen bilateral rate. Hence, the results may be interpreted to mean that the stochastic trend in exchange rates of the ASEAN countries is related to the stochastic trend in fundamental variables. Hence, an important conclusion that can be drawn here is that the Asian currencies are all driven by fundamental variables at least prior to the 1997 Asian financial crisis.

Having determined the cointegrating rank, we proceeded to the test of weak exogeneity. This test is important for at least two reasons. First, evidence pointing to the exogeneity of exchange rates would be inconsistent with the monetary model. Second, so far we have treated all the seven variables as endogenous variables. The weak exogeneity test will reveal if the variables are weakly exogenous with respect to the cointegrating vector (see Johansen, 1992 and Urbain, 1992) and this allows for model reduction. Testing the null hypothesis that a variable is weakly exogenous is equivalent to the hypothesis that this variable is not error correcting and the test can easily be conducted within the vector error correction framework using either the conventional t-test or the Wald test. In this chapter, we utilised Wald tests and the results are reported in Table 5.3. They suggest the followings: First, all the evidence point to the endogeneity of the exchange rate and this is consistent with the monetary model (except for the RM-US dollar rate). In most cases, the exchange rate adjusts to clear any disequilibrium from its long-run PPP. Second, the US interest rate appears weakly exogenous in all cases except for Thailand, whereas the Japanese interest rate is weakly exogenous in the case of Singapore and Malaysia. Third, most of the other fundamental variables appear to be endogenous except for domestic income (Baht-US dollar rate and Peso-US Dollar rate) and foreign income (Baht-US dollar rate).

The exogeneity of some of the fundamental variables allows for further reduction of the VAR model by including the exogenous variable into the conditioning set. For example, in the case of the dollar rates domestic and foreign interest rates in most of the systems appear exogenous. The reduced models contain five endogenous variables (m, m_{US}, y and y_{US}) and two exogenous variables (i and i_{US}).[17] We re-estimated the VAR model and conducted the cointegration tests to identify the significant vector(s) in the system.[18] In general, the findings suggest that there are stationary long-run equilibrium relationships between exchange rates and the fundamental variables. For all bilateral exchange rates, we have evidence of stationary relationships between exchange rate, money supply, income, and interest rates. In other words, exchange rate shares a long-term equilibrium relation with the set of macroeconomic variables. In addition, the exogeneity test reveals that the adjustment towards equilibrium is carried out by the exchange rate. Generally, the results so far are similar to that of Diamandis and Kouretas (1996), Diamandis *et al.* (1996), Moosa (1994) and Berg and Jayanetti (1993), among others who found at least a single cointegrating vector in the system of the monetary variables. However, these results contrast sharply with Baillie and Pecchenino (1991), Sarantis (1994) and McNown and Wallace (1994) who have shown that the monetary model does not provide an adequate representation of the behaviour of exchange rates.

In interpreting these results one must bear in mind two important points: First, a cointegrating vector implies a long-run stable relationship among jointly endogenous variables arising from constraints implied by the economic structure on the long-run relationship.[19] Second, evidence of multiple cointegration vectors is found for all country-pairs. In general, the more the number of cointegrating vectors, the more stable will be the system of non-stationary cointegrated variables (Johansen and Juselius, 1990 and Dickey *et al.*, 1991).[20] However, multiple cointegrating vectors lead to the problem of identifying the relationship that represents the process whereby exchange rate is determined.

The estimated parameters of the cointegrating vectors (βs) are reported in Table 5.4. Normalising the equations by the exchange rate allows us to directly compare the hypothesized values of the βs in equation 4. Results on the ASEAN bilateral exchange rates for the US are presented in Panel A whereas results on using Japan as the base country is reported in Panel B. Considering the most likely vector to represent the exchange rate relationship, the first-vector in the RM/US case produced 2 incorrect signs and for the TB/US case, the second-vector has only 2 signs that is consistent with theory. For the case of the PP/US the third vector has all the right signs. For the four-vector cases, the IR/US (second-vector) has all the signs as predicted by theory and the SD/US (first- and second- vectors) has three out of six variables with the right signs.

For the IR/JP, the first vector produces all signs that are consistent with the monetary model. However, the second vector shows four wrong signs (see Table 5.3, Panel B). For the SD/JY, the second vector has all the signs as anticipated but the first vector has one wrong sign. For Thailand (TB/JP), there are two wrong signs in the third and fourth vectors. For the three-vector cases (RM/JP and PP/JP), none of these vectors has all the signs that are consistent with the theory. In any event, the second vector has at least four out of six coefficients as anticipated. It seems that in the Japanese yen based bilateral exchange rates there is a much higher proportion of correctly signed coefficients compared with the US bilaterals. This perhaps reflects the increasing role of the Japanese Yen in the region. Aggarwal and Mougoul (1996) also found that the Japanese Yen is much more influential in the Asian region than the US dollar in the recent years.

We view that our results provide some support for equation 4. A comparison can be made between the findings in this chapter and those reported in Makrydakis (1998) and Moosa (1994). Makrydakis (1998) found that except for interest rates, the signs of all the other variables are consistent with theory for the Korean-won-US dollar rate. On the other hand, Moosa (1994) showed that the magnitudes of the coefficient are in many cases excessively high and the signs are inconsistent with those predicted in theory. Previous studies on demand for money also encountered similar problems. Specifically, the equations obtained by normalising cointegrating vectors on real money demand balances look like money demand functions, money supply functions or some complicated interaction that appear not to make "economic sense" (see Johansen and Juselius, 1990; Dickey *et al.*, 1991; Moosa, 1994).

To test for the most popular restrictions on the estimated parameters, we compute the log-likehood ratio (LR) statistics described in Johansen and Juselius (1990: p. 176-80). The LR tests are computed on the full set of cointegrating vectors and Table 5.5 reports the results. The restrictions are overwhelmingly rejected in all cases at the five-percent significance level, except for the following cases: IR/US (H_{1us}), RM/US (H_{3JY}), TB/JY (H_{3JY}) and RM/JY (H_{3JY}). The finding that the above hypotheses are generally rejected is in accordance with Kanas (1997), Moosa (1994), and MacDonald and Taylor (1991, 1994b). For instance, MacDonald and Taylor (1994b) found that all the restrictions are rejected at the conventional significance level for the sterling-dollar exchange rate. In applying the same model to Korea, Makrydakis (1998) found at least three cointegrating vectors for the Korean won-US dollar rate. However, all the parameter restrictions implied by the model are easily rejected by the data.

Lane (1991) pointed out that these restrictions are partly responsible for the failure of the restricted version of the monetary model. Our results may suggest that the restricted version of the monetary model that assumes the equality of coefficients may not be appropriate to model the long run exchange rates behaviour in the ASEAN-5 economies. The rejection of the monetary restrictions may indicate that the long-run relationship may not be that implied by the monetary model. However, Alogoskoufis and Smith (1991, 1992) argued that the coefficients of a long-run equation, such as the monetary model, could be a combination of adjustment, expectation and structural variables. Following this line of argument suggests that rejection of the monetary restrictions may be due to omission of these variables. Since our model does not reflect such variables, the estimated parameters may not be given structural interpretation (Dickey *et al.*, 1991). Of course this issue needs further research. Nevertheless, an important empirical result obtained from this chapter is that the ASEAN currencies shared a common stochastic trend with the fundamental variables.

Conclusions

This chapter examined the monetary model of exchange rate using quarterly frequency data that ends in 1997:2 for the ASEAN currency in terms of the US dollar and the Japanese yen. Specifically, this chapter shows a stable long run relationship between fundamental variables and the ASEAN currencies. The findings of this chapter may be summarised as follows. First, cointegration between the fundamental variables and the exchange rate for all the bilateral exchange rates may be interpreted as evidence of a long-run relationship between the exchange rate and the fundamental variables for the country-pairs considered. The empirical results have shown that a common set of variables can explain the behaviour of the ASEAN currencies. Second, as in most other studies we found multiple cointegrating vectors. The existence of multiple vectors causes interpretation problems but it is indicative of a more stable long-run relationship between the exchange rate and the fundamental variables. Third, with perhaps few exceptions, the restrictions imposed on the model were easily rejected by the data, indicating that the long-run relationship may not be consistent with the assumptions of the monetary model. The findings regarding the rejection of these assumptions should be taken as a signal of directions for future research rather than an outright rejection of the monetary approach to exchange rate. Fourth, in most of the models we found that the error correction term enters significantly in the exchange rate equations, implying that the bilateral rates adjust to clear any long run disequilibrium.

Finally, the results of this chapter suggest that an unrestricted monetary model can account for the long-run movements of Asian currencies vis-à-vis the US dollar and the Japanese yen. The estimates show that the monetary model appears to work for certain currencies and the results could be used as an important reference by the respective monetary authorities in setting up their monetary policy reaction functions. Our mixed results imply that, there could be a possibility that several factors such as volatility and balance of payment issues are impeding the usefulness of the monetary model for the ASEAN countries i.e., Malaysia, the Philippines, Indonesia, Thailand and Singapore. Moreover, understanding the exchange rate determinants by narrowing down on the monetary model may not fully work for these countries. Hence, it is interesting to have further work carried out to deal with this line of research. In conclusion, we have established some empirical evidence that could be used for future research works for the ASEAN-5 economies.

Notes

1. Recent studies found that on the basis of covered and/or uncovered interest rate parity, there is substantial integration between ASEAN and the world financial markets. See for example, Faruqee (1992), Phylaktis (1997) and Zhou (1996), among others.
2. Most of the existing studies on the usefulness of the monetary approach to exchange rate determinations have been mainly on the major industriliased countries.
3. The currency of the Philippines have been independently floated since 1992. Prior to this period it was a managed rate tied largely to the US dollar.
4. The Singapore dollar, Malaysian ringgit, Indonesian rupiah, and Thai baht are heavily weighted to the US dollar and the Japanese yen.
5. Earlier studies by Gan (1991), Bahmani-Oskooee (1993) and Baharumshah and Ariff (1997) showed that the data rejected the PPP condition. However, Manzur and Ariff (1995) showed that the PPP relationship holds in the long-run for the ASEAN as a whole. Evidence from Phylaktis and Kassimatis (1994) also support long-run PPP.
6. The models for the period beyond 1978 produced poor results in terms of the signs and significance of the coefficients as well as the within-sample predictive power, not to mention the poor out-of-sample predicting performance.
7. The Johansen methodology generally provides stronger support for the monetary model especially when the distinction between traded and non-traded goods is introduced. Using the Johansen procedure on three exchange rates (sterling, mark and yen against the dollar), MacDonald and Taylor found evidence in favour of long-run relationships for the three exchange rates. This led them to conclude that the monetary model does provide a valid explanation of the long-run exchange rate.
8. Diamandis and Kouretas (1996) applied the monetary model to four Greek drachma bilateral rates (drachma-Deutschemark, drachma-US dollar, drachma-sterling and drachma-french franc) using data for the recent float. Other studies by Phylaktis (1997) shows that interest rates of the Pacific countries have been moving together since the 1970s both versus the US and Japan.
9. In this chapter the term fudamental variables refer to money, interest rate and income. Both Flood *et al.* (1991) and Kanas (1997) adopted the same term for these three variables.
10. These countries peg their exchange rates to a major currency or a basket of currencies. However, their effective exchange rates will vary as long as major currencies vary.
11. See Gonzalo (1994) and Campbell and Perron (1991) for a more detailed discussion on the advantages of the Johansen-Juselius approach.
12. See Baillie and MacMahon (1989), MacDonald and Taylor (1992), amongst others, for a more comprehensive discussion.
13. The procedure is useful since: (i) it uses maximum likelihood techniques; (ii) it can detect and estimate multiple cointegration; and (iii) it allows us to test restrictions on the cointegrating vector(s). Gonzalo (1994) provides evidence that the Johansen and Juselius (1990) method performs better than the single equation methods and alternative multivariate methods (for example Stock and Watson, 1989).
14. To adjust for the finite sample inference problem of the Johansen technique, we used the degree-of-freedom suggested by Reinsel and Ahn (1992). The correction

factor suggested by Reinsel and Ahn is to multiply the test statistics in both (6) and (7) by *(T-pk)/T*, where *p* corresponds to the number of variables in the VAR model and k is the number of lags employed.

15. The appropriate lag length must be determined because the results of the Johansen cointegration test are known to be sensitive to lag length. Some authors prefer to use the likelihood ratio test suggested by Sims (1980) to determine the appropriate lag length. We conducted the test starting with lag of four and compared the LR statistics of lag length 4 vs. 3, 3 vs. 2 and 2 vs. 1. These tests indicated a lag length of one or two is adequate to capture the dynamic of the systems.

16. The Jarque-Bera statistics is computed as $[(T-m)/6]\ (SK^2 + EK^2/4)$, where m is the number of regressors, SK is skewness and EK is excess kurtosis. This statistics is distributed as $\chi^2_{(2)}$. A detailed description of the ARCH effect and heteroskedasticity is made in Engle (1982) and White (1980) respectively. These results are not reported here to conserve space but are available from the authors upon request.

17. The exceptions are the domestic interest rates for the dollar rates for Indonesia, Singapore and Thailand. The US interest rate in the dollar rate also appears to be endogenous.

18. We re-run the cointegration tests on the reduced model and the results with respect to the number of cointegrating vectors are quite similar to those presented earlier. The details are available upon request from the first author.

19. MacDonald and Taylor (1994b, p. 283) argued that evidence in favor of the long-run monetary model implies indirect evidence in favor of PPP.

20. The finding of more than one cointegrating vector leads to the problem of identifying the single long-run relation of interest, in this case it is the monetary equation that supposedly represents the process whereby the exchange rate is determined in the long-run.

Table 5.1 Choice of Lag Length

	Indonesia	Malaysia	Philippines	Singapore	Thailand
A. Base Country: US					
			AIC		
1	574.11	815.98	458.97	750.75	804.54
2	604.62	852.06	466.89	758.46	838.68
3	600.77	840.88	481.84	783.39	850.22
4	602.03*	849.19*	540.95*	787.42*	868.25*
			SBC		
1	516.68*	758.55*	401.55*	693.33*	747.12*
2	489.77	737.21	352.04	643.61	723.84
3	428.50	668.61	309.57	611.12	677.95
4	372.48	619.49	311.25	557.73	638.56
B. Base Country: Japan					
	Indonesia	**Malaysia**	**Philippines**	**Singapore**	**Thailand**
			AIC		
1	559.64	754.76	463.27	687.55	750.29
2	559.71	781.60	470.79*	689.70	774.53
3	540.69	757.28	469.27	681.86	795.78
4	563.19*	788.03*	465.32	697.98*	804.15*
			SBC		
1	502.21*	697.33*	404.01*	630.13*	692.86*
2	448.76	666.76	352.27	574.85	659.68
3	368.42	585.01	292.06	509.59	623.51
4	333.19	558.33	259.32	468.29	574.45

Notes: AIC = Akaike Information Criterion; SBC= Schwarz Bayesian Criterion. SBC(j) = $\ln \left|\left|\sum\right|\right| + (9j \ln(T)) / T$, j= 1,2,3 and T is the size sample . AIC(j) = $\ln \left|\left|\sum\right|\right| + (18j)/T$, j= 1,2,3 and T is the size sample. The asterisk (*) indicates the optimal lag.

Table 5.2 Johansen and Juselius Cointegration Results

Tests H_0	H_A	Indonesia	Malaysia	Philippines	Singapore	Thailand
A. Base Country: US						
				λ-max		
r = 0	= 1	87.02**	211.0**	54.31**	216.2**	93.90**
r ≤ 1	= 2	63.21**	46.11**	42.59*	68.27**	52.83**
r ≤ 2	= 3	36.91*	31.54	35.92*	49.77**	32.25
r ≤ 3	= 4	25.77	18.56	26.21	28.58*	21.78
r ≤ 4	= 5	15.36	14.90	19.33	14.42	13.31
r ≤ 5	= 6	5.952	10.64	14.16	11.11	9.502
r ≤ 6	= 7	1.992	4.464	7.342	3.869	3.738
				Trace		
r = 0	= 1	236.2**	337.2**	199.9**	392.2**	227.3**
r ≤ 1	= 2	149.2**	126.2**	145.5**	176.0**	133.4**
r ≤ 2	= 3	85.98**	80.11*	103.0**	107.8**	80.58*
r ≤ 3	= 4	49.07	48.57	67.04**	57.99*	48.33
r ≤ 4	= 5	23.30	30.01	40.83**	29.41	26.55
r ≤ 5	= 6	7.944	15.11	21.50*	14.98	13.24
r ≤ 6	= 7	1.992	4.464	7.342	3.869	3.738
B. Base Country: Japan						
				λ-max		
r = 0	= 1	203.8**	52.44**	125.2**	60.16**	299.4**
r ≤ 1	= 2	52.28**	40.49*	62.80**	50.09**	70.33**
r ≤ 2	= 3	29.96	36.50*	39.39*	28.71	62.21**
r ≤ 3	= 4	15.21	16.62	18.16	23.32	30.20*
r ≤ 4	= 5	12.54	12.96	8.247	20.36	10.63
r ≤ 5	= 6	4.647	5.549	4.174	9.590	9.106
r ≤ 6	= 7	3.814	3.672	1.634	4.855	3.099
				Trace		
r = 0	= 1	322.3**	168.2**	259.6**	197.1**	485.0**
r ≤ 1	= 2	118.5**	115.8**	134.4**	136.9**	185.6**
r ≤ 2	= 3	66.17	75.30	71.61	86.84**	115.2**
r ≤ 3	= 4	36.21	38.80	32.22	58.13*	53.03
r ≤ 4	= 5	21.00	22.19	14.05	34.81	22.84
r ≤ 5	= 6	8.461	9.222	5.807	14.45	12.21
r ≤ 6	= 7	3.814	3.672	1.634	4.855	3.099

Notes: Asterisks (**) and (*) denote statistically significant at the 5 percent and 10 percent levels respectively (see Osterwald-Lenum, 1992).

Table 5.3 Weak Exogeneity Tests

Country and Series	e_{US}	m	m_{US}	y	y_{US}	i	i_{US}
	A. Base Country: US						
Indonesia	18.32 (0.00)*	10.57 (0.01)*	18.93 (0.00)*	50.68 (0.00)*	27.69 (0.00)*	12.43 (0.00)*	1.41 (0.70)
Malaysia	2.50 (0.29)	54.60 (0.00)*	35.59 (0.00)*	116.39 (0.00)*	141.25 (0.00)*	0.16 (0.93)	0.56 (0.76)
Philippines	13.22 (0.00)*	10.04 (0.02)*	18.86 (0.00)*	5.51 (0.14)	12.84 (0.01)*	3.96 (0.27)	2.32 (0.51)
Singapore	16.80 (0.00)*	48.03 (0.00)*	42.86 (0.00)*	173.41 0.00)*	137.18 (0.00)*	13.37 (0.01)*	3.16 (0.53)
Thailand	5.56 (0.06)*	40.18 (0.00)*	35.65 (0.00)*	0.63 (0.73)	2.55 (0.28)	16.12 (0.00)*	8.43 (0.01)*
	B. Base Country: Japan						
	e_{JP}	m	m_{JP}	y	y_{JP}	i	i_{JP}
Indonesia	7.86 (0.02)*	63.91 (0.00)*	10.55 (0.01)*	154.56 (0.00)*	105.51 (0.00)*	9.11 (0.01)*	8.25 (0.02)*
Malaysia	8.47 (0.04)*	9.36 (0.02)*	17.57 (0.00)*	21.83 (0.00)*	31.51 (0.00)*	6.09 (0.11)	2.77 (0.43)
Philippines	18.77 (0.00)*	39.79 (0.00)*	34.00 (0.00)*	78.53 (0.00)*	80.00 (0.00)*	9.04 (0.03)*	9.24 (0.03)*
Singapore	8.20 (0.02)*	20.46 (0.00)*	9.12 (0.01)*	19.00 (0.00)*	10.62 (0.00)*	2.74 (0.25)	0.27 (0.87)
Thailand	10.18 (0.04)*	59.23 (0.00)*	49.18 (0.00)*	254.14 (0.00)*	131.9 (0.00)*	1.49 (0.83)	9.25 (0.04)*

Notes: Figures in parentheses are p-values. Asterisk (*) denotes statistically significant at the 5 percent level.

Table 5.4 Estimated Cointegrated Vectors in the Johansen Estimation

Country and Series	e_{US}	m	m_{US}	y	y_{US}	i	i_{US}	Constant
	A. Base Country: US							
Indonesia	-1.00	-3.20	6.08	0.40	6.72	0.16	0.43	-50.23
	-1.00	0.65	-0.44	-1.37	2.99	0.06	-0.10	-11.67
	-1.00	0.94	0.41	-2.90	5.79	-0.02	0.06	-29.46
	-1.00	-2.12	0.50	1.45	2.22	0.02	0.00	4.91
Malaysia	-1.00	0.42	0.38	-0.66	-0.23	0.02	-0.02	1.48
	-1.00	-0.99	-2.28	0.68	2.67	-0.01	-0.05	-5.45
Philippines	-1.00	-2.49	1.67	2.14	3.19	-0.02	0.21	-21.32
	-1.00	-1.50	0.00	2.02	0.25	-0.01	-0.03	7.06
	-1.00	11.79	-77.96	-34.88	102.88	0.05	-2.21	-283.66
Singapore	-1.00	-967.78	-638.98	660.62	861.73	-47.50	-0.64	-378.32
	-1.00	-44.44	-45.09	29.17	48.68	-1.13	-1.23	37.99
	-1.00	-3.19	2.22	2.18	-1.48	0.01	0.01	7.54
	-1.00	-0.44	0.69	-0.35	0.01	-0.06	0.03	3.48
Thailand	-1.00	-1.38	0.11	1.43	-0.28	-0.04	0.01	3.65
	-1.00	-0.08	-0.13	0.17	0.18	-0.04	0.02	2.29
	B. Base Country: Japan							
	e_{JP}	m	m_{JP}	y	y_{JP}	i	i_{JP}	Constant
Indonesia	-1.00	1.18	-3.96	-0.50	4.95	0.01	-0.19	-30.09
	-1.00	-4.09	9.11	0.28	4.89	0.15	0.05	-103.41
Malaysia	-1.00	1.14	-35.79	14.93	13.70	0.00	-0.60	-177.74
	-1.00	13.04	0.20	-17.15	5.20	0.09	-0.11	-56.01
	-1.00	0.36	4.57	-1.74	-0.69	-0.07	0.10	-43.85
Philippines	-1.00	-0.95	-3.23	2.30	3.18	-0.03	-0.08	-7.02
	-1.00	0.28	-8.02	3.29	1.54	-0.04	-0.10	51.53
	-1.00	-7.50	10.65	2.63	6.80	0.00	0.05	-144.38
Singapore	-1.00	6.71	0.51	-6.79	1.87	0.04	0.04	-32.71
	-1.00	3.58	-2.02	-1.75	0.52	0.09	-0.08	-5.17
Thailand	-1.00	-0.74	1.15	0.31	0.86	-0.07	0.05	-25.39
	-1.00	-0.04	11.53	-4.27	-0.73	0.14	-0.01	-100.37
	-1.00	7.71	-4.99	-7.92	7.87	-0.13	0.08	-35.73
	-1.00	0.30	-2.22	0.43	1.24	-0.05	-0.03	4.33

Table 5.5 Tests of Monetary Restrictions

A: Base Country: US					
	Indonesia	**Malaysia**	**Philippines**	**Singapore**	**Thailand**
	k=2 r=4	**k= 1 r= 1**	**k =2 r =3**	**k= 1 r =4**	**k=2 r=2**
$H_{1\,US}$	4.00(0.41)	26.45(0.00)	14.33(0.00)	49.09(0.00)	30.19(0.00)
$H_{2\,US}$	17.03(0.00)	30.59(0.00)	14.70(0.00)	48.80(0.00)	21.66(0.00)
$H_{3\,US}$	33.34(0.00)	5.73(0.06)	27.31(0.00)	56.54(0.00)	29.82(0.00)
$H_{4\,US}$	39.35(0.00)	33.97(0.00)	24.85(0.00)	61.17(0.00)	31.73(0.00)
$H_{5\,US}$	52.99(0.00)	31.11(0.00)	43.35(0.00)	81.43(0.00)	45.12(0.00)
$H_{6\,US}$	54.67(0.00)	36.10(0.00)	45.29(0.00)	81.06(0.00)	36.27(0.00)
$H_{7\,US}$	92.91(0.00)	37.14(0.00)	46.55(0.00)	94.81(0.00)	46.41(0.00)
B. Base Country: Japan					
	Indonesia	**Malaysia**	**Philippines**	**Singapore**	**Thailand**
	k= 1 r= 2	**k= 2 r= 3**	**k= 1 r= 3**	**k =3 r =2**	**k=1 r= 4**
$H_{1\,JP}$	10.28(0.01)	23.91(0.00)	52.43(0.00)	35.27(0.00)	52.37(0.00)
$H_{2\,JP}$	9.01(0.01)	22.60(0.00)	22.33(0.00)	30.54(0.00)	37.45(0.00)
$H_{3\,JP}$	24.36(0.00)	2.57(0.05)	15.91(0.00)	9.15(0.00)	9.88(0.04)
$H_{4\,JP}$	23.71(0.00)	34.30(0.00)	64.60(0.00)	38.49(0.00)	93.00(0.00)
$H_{5\,JP}$	26.05(0.00)	28.12(0.00)	54.46(0.00)	35.49(0.00)	61.16(0.00)
$H_{6\,JP}$	32.93(0.00)	26.37(0.00)	32.58(0.00)	30.65(0.00)	42.05(0.00)
$H_{7\,JP}$	39.42(0.00)	41.34(0.00)	71.08(0.00)	39.26(0.00)	100.19(0.0 0)

Notes: H_1: $\beta_1 = -\beta_2 = 1$; H_2: $\beta_3 + \beta_4 = 0$; H_3: $\beta_5 + \beta_6 = 0$; H_4: $H_1 \cap H_2$; H_5: $H_1 \cap H_3$; H_6: $H_2 \cap H_3$ and H_7: $H_1 \cap H_2 \cap H_3$. The second and third subscripts identify the country: US is United States; JP is Japan. The numbers not in parenthesis are the χ^2 statistics with the degree of freedom r×s, where r= the number of cointegrating vectors and s is the number of restrictions.

References

Aggarwal, R. and Mougoue, M. (1996), 'Cointegration Among Asian currencies: Evidence of Increasing Influence of the Japanese yen', *Japan and the World Economy*, vol. 8, pp. 291-308.

Alogoskoufis, G. and Smith, R. (1991), 'On Error Correction Models: Specification, Interpretation and Estimation', *Journal of Economic Surveys*, vol. 5, pp. 97-128.

Alogoskoufis, G. and Smith, R. (1992), 'Monetary Accommodation, Exchange Rate Regimes and Inflation Persistence', *The Economic Journal*, vol. 102, pp. 461-480.

Baillie, R.T. and MacMahon, P.C. (1989), *Foreign Exchange Market: Theory and Econometric Evidence*, Cambridge University Press, Cambridge.

Baillie, R.T. and Pecchenino, R.A. (1991), 'The Search for Equilibrium Relationships in International Finance: The Case of Monetary Model', *Journal of International Money and Finance*, vol. 10, pp. 582-593.

Berg, H. and Jayanetti, S.C. (1993), 'A Novel Test of the Monetary Approach using Black Market Exchange Rates and the Johansen-Juselius Cointegration Method', *Economics Letters*, vol. 41, pp. 413-418.

Bilson, J.F.O. (1978), 'Rational Expectations and the Exchange Rate', in J.A. Frenkel and H.G. Johnson (eds), *The Economics of Exchange Rates*, Addison-Wesley, Reading, MA, pp. 75-96.

Campbell, J. Y. and Perron, P. (1991), 'Pitfalls and Opportunities: What Macroeconomists Should Know About Unit Roots', in O.J. Blanchard and S. Fischer (eds), *National Bureau of Economic Research Macroeconomics Annual*, MIT Press, Cambridge, pp. 144-201.

DeJong, D.N., Nankervis, J.C., Savin, N.E. and Whiteman, C.H. (1992), 'The Power Problems of Unit Root Tests in Time Series with Autoregressive Errors', *Journal of Econometrics*, vol. 53, pp. 323-44.

Diamandis, P.F. and Kouretas, G.P. (1996), 'The Monetary Approach to the Exchange Rate: Long-Run Relationships, Coefficient Restrictions and Temporal Stability of the Greek Drachma', *Applied Financial Economics*, vol. 6, pp.351-362.

Diamandis, P.F., Georgoutsos, D.A. and Kouretas, G.P. (1996), 'Cointegration Tests for the Monetary Exchange Rate Model: The Canadian-US dollar, 1970-1994', *International Economic Journal*, vol. 10, pp.83-97.

Dickey, D.A. and Fuller, W.A. (1981), 'The Likelihood Ratio Statistics for Autoregressive Time Series With a Unit Root', *Econometrica*, vol. 49, pp. 1057-72.

Dickey, D.A., Jansen, D.W. and Thornton, D.L. (1991), 'A Primer on Cointegration with an Application to Money and Income', *Federal Reserve Bank of St. Louis Economic Review*, vol. 73, pp. 58-78.

Dornbusch, R. (1976), 'Expectations and Exchange Rate Dynamics', *Journal of Political Economy*, vol. 84, pp. 1161-76.

Engle, R.F. (1982), 'Autoregressive Conditional Heteroskedasticity with Estimates of the Variance of United Kingdom Inflation', *Econometrica*, vol. 50, pp. 987-1007.

Faruqee, H. (1992), 'Dynamic Capital Mobility in Pacific-Basin Developing Countries', IMF Staff Papers, vol. 39, pp. 706-717.

Flood, R.P., Rose, A.K. and Mathieson, D.J. (1991), 'An Empirical Exploration of Exchange-Rate Target-Zones', *Carnegie Rochester Conference Series on Public Policy*, vol. 35, pp. 7-77.

Frenkel, J.A. (1976), 'A Monetary Approach to the Exchange Rate: Doctrinal Aspects and Empirical Evidence', *Scandinavian Journal of Economics*, vol. 78, pp. 200-24.

Gan, W.B. (1991), 'On the Deviation from Purchasing Power Parity: The Case of the Ringgit Effective Exchange Rate', *Applied Economics*, vol. 23, pp. 1461-71.

Gandolfo, G. (1981), *Quantitative Analysis and Econometric Estimation of Continuous Time Dynamic*, North-Holland Publishing Company Amsterdam.

Gonzalo, J. (1994), 'Five Alternative Methods of Estimating Long-Run Equilibrium Relationship', *Journal of Econometrics*, vol. 60, pp. 203-233.

Hosking, J.R.M. (1980), 'The Multivariate Portmanteau Statistics', *Journal of American Statistical Association*, vol. 75, pp. 602-608.

Jarque C.M and Bera, A.K. (1980), 'Efficient Tests for Normality, Homescedasticity and Serial Interdependence of Regression Residuals', *Economics Letters*, vol. 6, pp. 225-259.

Johansen, S. (1988), 'Statistical Analysis of Cointegration Vectors', *Journal of Economic Dynamics and Control*, vol. 12, pp. 231-254.

Johansen, S. (1992), 'Cointegration in Partial Systems and the Efficiency of Single Equation Analysis', *Journal of Econometrics*, vol. 52, pp. 389-402.

Johansen, S. and Juselius, K. (1990), 'Maximum Likelihood Estimation and Inference on Cointegration with Applications to the Demand for Money', *Oxford Bulletin of Economics and Statistics*, vol. 52, pp. 169-210.

Kanas, A. (1997), 'The Monetary Exchange Rate Model within the ERM: Cointegration Tests and Implication Concerning the Germany Dominance Hypothesis', *Applied Financial Economics*, vol. 7, pp. 587-598.

Kwiatkowski, D., Phillips, P.C.B. Schmidt, P. and Shin, Y. (1992), 'Testing the Null Hypothesis of Stationarity Against the Alternative of a Unit Root. How Sure Are We that Economic Time Series Have a Unit Root?', *Journal of Econometrics,* vol. 54, pp. 159-178.

Lane, T.D. (1991), 'Empirical models of Exchange Rate Determination: Picking up the Pieces, *Economia Internazionale*, vol. 44, pp. 210-26.

Lane, P.R. (1999), 'What Determines the Nominal Exchange Rate? Some Cross-Sectional Evidence', *Canadian Journal of Economics*, vol. 32, pp. 118-38.

Lutkepohl, H. (1991), *Introduction to Multiple Time Series Analysis*, Heidelberg: Springer Verlag.

MacDonald, R. and Taylor, M.P. (1991), 'The Monetary Approach to the Exchange Rate: Long-Run Relationships and Coefficient Restrictions', *Economics Letters*, vol. 37, pp. 179-85.

MacDonald, R. and Taylor, M.P (1992), 'Exchange Rate Economics: A Survey', *IMF Staff Papers*, vol. 39, pp. 1-57.

MacDonald, R. and Taylor, M.P (1993), 'The Monetary Approach to the Exchange Rate: Rational Expectations, Long-Run Equilibrium, and Forecasting', *IMF Staff Papers*, 40, 89-107.

MacDonald, R. and Taylor, M.P. (1994a), 'The Monetary Model of the Exchange Rate: Long-Run Relationships, Short-Run Dynamics, and how to beat a Random Walk', *Journal of International Money and Finance*, vol. 13, pp. 276-90.

MacDonald, R. and Taylor, M.P. (1994b), 'Re-examining the Monetary Approach to the Exchange Rate: The Dollar-Franc, 1976-90', *Applied Financial Economics*, vol. 12, pp. 167-76.

Makrydakis, S. (1998), 'Testing the Long-Run Validity of the Monetary Approach to the Exchange Rate: The Won-US Dollar Case', *Applied Economics Letters*, vol. 5, pp. 507-511.

Manzur, M. and Ariff, M. (1995), 'Purchasing Power Parity: New Methods and Extensions, *Applied Financial Economics*, vol. 5, pp. 19-26.

McNown, R. and Myles, W. (1989), 'Cointegration Tests for Long-Run Equilibrium in the Monetary Exchange Rate Model', *Economics Letters*, vol. 31, pp. 263-267.

McNown, R. and Wallace, M. S. (1994), 'Cointegration Tests of the Monetary Exchange Rate Model for Three High Inflation Economies', *Journal of Money, Credit and Banking*, vol. 26, pp. 396-411.

Moosa, I.A. (1994), 'The Monetary Model of Exchange Rates Revisited', *Applied Financial Economics*, vol. 4, pp. 279-287.

Osterwald-Lenum, M. (1992), 'A Note with Quantiles of the Asymptotic Distribution of Maximum Likelihood Cointegration Rank Test Statistic', *Oxford Bulletin of Economics and Statistics*, vol. 54, pp. 461-472.

Phillips, P.C.B. (1987), 'Time Series Regression with Unit Roots', *Econometrica*, vol. 55, pp. 277-302.

Phillips, P.C.B. and Perron, P. (1988), 'Testing for a Unit Root in Time Series Regression', *Biometrika*, vol. 75, pp. 335-46.

Phylaktis, K. and Kassimatis, Y. (1994), 'Does the Real Exchange Rate Follow a Random Walk? The Pacific Basin Perspective', *Journal of International Money and Finance*, vol. 13, pp. 476-495.

Phylaktis, K. (1997), 'Capital Market Integration in the Pacific-Basin Region: An Analysis of Real Interest Rate Linkages, *Pacific-Basin Finance Journal*, vol. 5, pp. 195-213.

Reimers, H.E. (1992), 'Comparisons of Tests for Multivariate Cointegration', *Statistical Papers*, vol. 33, pp. 335-359.

Reinsel, G.C. and Ahn, S.K. (1992), 'Vector Autoregressive Models with Unit Roots and Reduced Rank Structure: Estimation, Likelihood Ratio Tests, and Forecasting', *Journal of Time Series Analysis*, vol. 13, pp. 353-375.

Sarantis N. (1994), 'The Monetary Exchange Rate Model in the Long-Run: An Empirical Investigation', *Weltwirtschaftliches Archic*, vol. 130, pp. 698-710.

Schwert, G.W. (1987), 'Effects of Model Specification on Tests for Unit Roots in Macroeconomic Data', *Journal of Monetary Economics*, vol. 20, pp. 73-103.

Sims, C.A. (1980), 'Macroeconomics and Reality', *Econometrica*, vol. 48, pp. 1-48.

Stock, J.H. and Watson, M.W. (1989), 'Interpreting the Evidence on Money-Income Causality', Journal of Econometrics, vol. 40, pp. 161-182.

Taylor, M.P. (1988), 'An Empirical Examination of Long Run Purchasing Power Parity using Cointegration Techniques', *Applied Economics*, vol. 20, pp. 1369-81.

Urbain, J.P. (1992), 'On Weak Exogeneity in Error Correction Models', *Oxford Bulletin of Economics and Statistics*, vol. 54, pp. 187-207.

White, H. (1980), 'A Heteroskedastic-Consistent Covariance Matrix Estimator and Direct Test for Heteroskedasticity', *Econometrica*, vol. 48, pp. 817-838.

Zhou, S. (1996), 'Trade Connections and Interest Rate Linkages Among ASEAN, Japan, and the USA: An Empirical Analysis', *Applied Economics*, vol. 28, pp. 617-30.

Chapter 6

Forecasting the Exchange Rates

Ahmad Zubaidi Baharumshah, Venus Khim-Sen Liew and Kian-Ping Lim

Introduction

Most exchange rate markets in the floating exchange rate regime have experienced continuous and sometimes dramatic fluctuations and volatility. Mussa (1996) has summarized the broad features of exchange rate behaviour. Mussa noted that (i) exchange rates are extremely volatile, with deviation of about 3 percent per month for the US dollar-Japanese yen and US dollar-Deutschemark rates; (ii) changes in exchange rates are very persistent, and the exchange rates closely approximate a random walk; (iii) there is correlation of almost unity between real and nominal exchange rates on high frequency data; and (iv) the variability of real exchange rates increases dramatically when a country moves from fixed to floating exchange rates. All these suggest that exchange rates can be much more volatile than the apparent fundamentals, and in practice deviation from equilibrium value can be persistent. Thus, researches of exchange rate behaviour and exchange rate forecasting have become perennial topics in international economics since the floating exchange rate regime was established in March 1973. As a result, many theories and models were developed.

The existing models of foreign exchange rates were developed using the linear and nonlinear frameworks. Models based on the linear framework include the simple efficiency market approach (Fama 1965; Cornell 1977), the simple random walk approach (Giddy and Duffey 1975; Hakkio and Rush 1986), the linear fundamentals approach (for example, Dornbusch 1976; Frankel 1979; Meese and Rogoff 1983; Mark 1995; Clark and MacDonald 1998; Baharumshah *et al.* 2002), the time series approach (for instance, Keller 1989; Cheung 1993; Palma and Chan, 1997; Brooks 1997; Parikh and Williams 1998; Baharumshah *et al.* 2002) and the conditional heteroscedasticity approach (Engle 1982; Bollerslev 1986), among others.

There is a growing consensus among researchers that exchange rates and other financial variables are nonlinear in nature (Brooks 1996; Taylor and Peel 2000) and they are linearly unpredictable (Boothe and Glassman 1987; Plasmans *et al.* 1998). Hence the nonlinear structural models are regarded as more relevant in modelling these variables. Models in conjunction with this more recent view are commonly estimated through the nonlinear fundamentals approach (see for example, Meese and Rose 1991; Lin and Chen 1998; Ma and Kanas 2000; and

Coakley and Fuertes 2001), the Exponential GARCH approach (Nelson 1991), the SETAR approach (Kräger and Kugler 1993), and the neural networks approach (Franses and Homelen 1998; Plasmans *et al.* 1998), among others.

Nevertheless, after three decades of research, exchange rate theory that provides a satisfactory and empirically consistent theory of the exchange rate remains to be uncovered (Hallwood and MacDonald 1994, p. 22). Like any other financial variables, exchange rates are difficult to forecast with any precision. The bulk of evidence has so far been proven illusive (Berkowitz and Giorgianni 1997; Lin and Chen 1998). In their survey of empirical works on exchange rate, Frankel and Rose (1994) made the following remark: '*We, like much of the profession, are doubtful of the value of further time series modelling of exchange rates at high or medium frequencies using macroeconomic models.*' This observation has motivated us to search for an alternative approach to model exchange rates.

This chapter attempts to model exchange rates and the focus is on the ability of the model to yield reliable forecasts in the short and intermediate run. The main focus is to construct a model that can capture the dynamics of exchange rates in the emerging economies well. The model that we considered is one that has a linear combination of long and short run functions. The long run component of the model is set to represent the relationship between any exchange rate and its fundamental variables (e.g. relative price, interest differential and money supply), whereas the short-run equation is based on a time series model and is used to capture the deviations of the exchange rate from its long-run path.[1] Thus, the estimation procedure involves two stages: first, the long-run model is fitted to the data, and this is followed by the short-run function. To this end, we relied on the widely used linear structural model (purchasing power parity, PPP) hypothesis to trace the long-run relationship between exchange rate and its determinants.[2] To account for the inadequacy of the pure PPP model, we augmented the short-run component of the model based on the statistical properties of the data.[3] In this article, our focus is on the PPP and interest differential models (IRD). We have no intention of identifying a set of fundamental variables that is most appropriate to trace the movements of the exchange rates but simply to show that information contain in both domestic and foreign macroeconomic variables (prices and term structures of interest rates) may not be sufficient to trace the movement of exchange rates. Intuitively, one may expect to gain efficiency in the forecasts, by adding more information to the model. For this purpose, we compare the performance of the simple PPP model with that of the interest rate differential (IRD) model.[4]

Derivation of the Model

The estimation of the model is based on a two-step procedure. First, the long-run component of the model is considered and second, the deviation of the actual observations from its long-run equilibrium path is considered to model the short-run component of the model. In this way, our forecasting model will not only be capable of tracing the long-run movement, but it will also be capable of capturing misalignments in the exchange rate series that may occur in the short-run. This strategy is also in line with the argument that exchange rates can be more volatile than the fundamentals; in our case it is the relative price and/or interest rate differential.

Consider the model

$$X_t = f_t(l_1, l_2, ..., l_l) + g_t(s_1, s_2, ..., s_s) \quad (1)$$

where X_t is the exchange rate defined as domestic currency, per unit of foreign currency; $f_t(l_1, l_2, ..., l_l)$ is a set of long-run determinants $\{l_1, l_2, ..., l_l\}$ that explains the long-run movement of the exchange rate; and $g_t(s_1, s_2, ..., s_s)$ is a function of a set of short-run determinants $\{s_1, s_2, ..., s_s\}$ that may cause exchange rate to deviate from its long-run equilibrium path.

Let the expected value of f_t be given by $\hat{X}_t$, which is determined by the fundamental variables. By subtracting the value of $\hat{X}_t$ on both sides of (1) we obtained

$$X_t - \hat{X}_t = f_t - \hat{X}_t + g_t \quad (2)$$

If $\hat{X}_t$ is an unbiased predictor of f_t, then the term (f_t - $\hat{X}_t$) on the RHS of (2) vanishes to random error term, ε_t with mean zero and variance σ_ε^2. Thus, we have

$$X_t - \hat{X}_t = \varepsilon_t + g_t \qquad \text{where } \varepsilon_t \sim \text{WN}(0, \sigma_\varepsilon^2) \quad (3)$$

or equivalently

$$X_t = \hat{X}_t + g_t + \varepsilon_t \quad (4)$$

Modelling the short-run function g_t is even more complicated as the subsets of short-run determinants may change over time due to either internal or external events (e.g. policy change, capital reversal and regional financial crises). One way out of this dilemma is to think of g_t as generated by time series mechanism, whatever the underlying macroeconomic determinants may be. For instance, one may think of g_t as represented by the ARIMA, ARFIMA or GARCH processes. It is worth noting that the GARCH process involves modelling the square of residuals, and in our case, g_t. However, authors like McKenzie (1999) have pointed out that by squaring the residuals one effectively imposes a structure on the data, which has the potential of reducing the forecasting performance of the model. In the present chapter, we assume that it is sufficient to regard g_t as proportionate to its most recent available value, g_{t-1}, to avoid the problem of complexity. That is

$$g_t = \alpha\, g_{t-1} + v_t \qquad \text{where } v_t \sim \text{WN}(0, \sigma_v^2) \quad (5)$$

with $\alpha < 1$ if g_t is stationary and $\alpha \geq 1$ if g_t is non-stationary.

By simply substituting (5) into (4) and upon simplification, we obtained the final model that is

$$X_t = \hat{X}_t + \alpha(X_{t-1} - \hat{X}_{t-1}) + \mu_t \text{ where } \mu_t = \varepsilon_t + \nu_t \qquad (6)$$

Clearly that estimation of Equation (6) involves procedures for solving $\hat{X}_t$ and for searching for the optimal value of α.

Methodology

In this chapter we attempt to model the Malaysian ringgit (MYR), the Singapore dollar (SGD), and Thai baht (THB) against the US dollar (USD) and Japanese yen (JPY), all of which have received little attention in the exchange rate literature. The base currencies are chosen based on the importance of trade to these ASEAN countries. According to the International Monetary Fund (IMF)'s classification, these countries pegged their currencies to a basket of currencies (the US dollar received the highest weight). Our sample period covers from the first quarter of the year 1980 to the fourth quarter of the year 2000 (1980:1 to 2000:4). Bilateral rates used in the analysis are the end of period market rate specified as line *ae* in *International Financial Statistics* published by the IMF, except for the MYR/USD rate. For the case of the MYR/USD rate, we chose the series from line *aa*, which is calculated on the basis of the SDR rate. This is to avoid the problem of zero denominators that may arise during the assessment of the performance of the forecasting exercises.

Besides the bilateral exchange rate series, data on relative price and interest differential are also utilized in this chapter. The price variable is constructed as the ratio of domestic price to foreign price. We use consumer price indices (CPI 1995 = 100) as the proxy of prices. Interest rate differential is computed by dividing the domestic market rate over the foreign market rate. All the data series are taken from various monthly issues of IMF/IFS. The full sample period is divided into two portions. The first sub-period that begins in 1980:1 and ends in 1997:2 is used for the purpose of estimation and the remaining observations (1997:2-2000:4) are kept for assessing the out-of-sample forecast performance of the model. Following the work of García-Ferrer *et al.* (1997), our data were purposely treated in such a way that they showed a break in the trend (due to the 1997 Asian financial crisis) during the forecasting period, making the prediction exercise more difficult. Specifically, the large depreciation in the post currency crisis period makes the post-sample prediction more stringent.[5]

For each country, we first examined the time series properties of three variables used in the analysis. Overwhelmingly, we found that the variables contain the unit root or *I(1)*.Since exchange rates, relative price and interest rate differential exhibit the same order of integration, this allows us to proceed with the cointegration test. To this end we utilized the Johansen and Juselius (1990) multivariate cointegration test that is based on the statistics: trace test and the maximum eigenvalue test.

For each country we ran the vector autoregressive (VAR) system in levels with one to five lags. The primary goal was to eliminate serial correlation while avoiding power-draining due to the presence of too many lags. We also checked for serial correlation using the Bruesch-Godfrey asymptotic test before deciding on the optimal lag for the VAR model. The results of the Johansen-Juselius cointegration test are tabulated in Table 6.1. Table 6.1 reveals that all the exchange rates (except THB/USD) are cointegrated with their corresponding relative prices at 5 percent significance level or better. This finding suggests that a long-run relationship between exchange rate and relative price exists in the countries studied. Hence, the cointegration test results are consistent with the PPP hypothesis at least for the five exchange rates (MYR/USD, SGD/USD, MYR/JPY, THB/JPY and SGD/JPY).

Similarly, we found that for all the countries under study, exchange rates, relative prices and interest differential variables (except SGD/JPY and THB/USD) are cointegrated (see Table 6.1). All in all, there exists at least one cointegrating vector in the exchange rates based on conventional significance levels.

Our next task was to proceed with the forecasting model as given in Equation (6). The estimation involved two steps. In step one, we estimated the PPP model by regressing the exchange rate (X_t) on CPI (or IPI) ratios (P_t). For the case of SGD/USD, for instance, the PPP model was estimated by running SGD/USD on PS/PU, where PS and PU are CPI (1995=100) of Singapore and CPI (1995=100) of the US respectively. Then we computed the values of $\hat{X}_t$, which is the predictor of the spot exchange rate, X_t . The deviation from the long-run model, g_t was obtained as

$$g_t = X_t - \hat{X}_t \tag{7}$$

In step two, we estimated the function g_t as suggested in Equation (5). In this chapter, we employed a search algorithm to determine the optimum value of α such that the in-sample forecasting error is the minimum with respect to the selected criteria (e.g. Mean Square Forecast Error (*MSE*) and the Mean Square Percentage Error (*MSPE*), Mean Absolute Percentage Error (*MAPE*) and Theils' *U*). We chose to minimise the *MAPE* of the in-sample forecasts as we found that it was more reliable in the sense that the selected optimum α for the in-sample period was a better estimator for the optimum α value of the out-of-sample period (results are not shown here).

The optimum model was then subjected to a battery of diagnostic tests. We emphasized on two important aspects, namely the efficiency of the forecasts and the stationarity of the residuals, μ_t . If the model was capable of capturing the long run and short run movements of the actual exchange rate behaviour, the residuals had to be random errors and hence stationary. Besides that, since we were utilizing time series data it was important that we eliminated serial correlation. We checked for serial correlation by using the standard Durbin-Watson (*d*) and Bruesch-Godfrey Lagrange Multiplier (LM) test for autocorrelation.

To sum up, the selection process for the "optimum" model can be summarized as by the following steps:

Step One: (1) Regress sample exchange rate, X_t on sample relative price, P_t ; (2) Obtain $\hat{X}_t$ from the regression; and (3) Compute $g_t = X_t - \hat{X}_t$.
Step Two: (1) Search for the optimum α based on selected criteria; (2) Check for (i) serial correlation on the residuals and (ii) efficiency of model; and (3) proceed with forecasting.

In order to forecast X_{t+n} where the number of quarter, n = 1, …, 14 for the out-of-sample period (1997:3 to 2000:4), we needed to have the values of P_{t+n}. As P_{t+n} was also not available, the fastest way of obtaining a reliable estimator for it was to forecast using the ARIMA methodology. The reason why we chose not to forecast X_{t+n} directly using the ARIMA methodology was that although this method could provide better forecasts (see for examples, Montogomery *et al.* 1990; Lupoletti and Webb 1986 and Litterman 1986), it is not capable of outperforming the simple naïve model of the ASEAN countries' exchange rates (Baharumshah and Liew, 2000).

The performance of our forecasting models over the forecast horizon of n =1, then n = 2 and so forth until n =14 quarters was evaluated by taking the naïve models of predicting no change as the benchmark. The criteria involved are the minimum of the Mean Square Forecast Error (*MSE*) and the Mean Square Percentage Error (*MSPE*) and the Mean Absolute Percentage Error (*MAPE*) ratios of the two competing models, with the appropriate error criterion of the naïve model as denominator. If the ratio is greater than one, it implies the naïve model is better. If the ratio is less than one, it means the forecasting model has defeated the naïve model and the researchers' effort has at least paid-off. It is worth noting that the closer the ratio to zero, the better is the forecast. We also provide the statistical significance of the *MSE* ratio using the Meese and Rogoff (1988) (*MR*) test statistics defined as:

$$MR = \frac{\bar{s}_{UV}}{\sqrt{\frac{1}{n^2}\sum_{j=1}^{n} u_j^2 v_j^2}} \overset{asy}{\sim} N(0,1) \tag{8}$$

where $\bar{s}_{UV}$ is the sample covariance of means of U and V (transformed functions of forecast errors of two rival models) and is approximated by $\frac{1}{n}\sum_{j=1}^{n}(u_j - \bar{u})(v_j - \bar{v})$ where $\bar{u} = \frac{1}{n}\sum_{j=1}^{n} u_j$ and $\bar{v} = \frac{1}{n}\sum_{j=1}^{n} v_j$ with $u_j = e_{1j} - e_{2j}$ and $v_j = e_{1j} + e_{2j}$ in which e_{ij} , i = 1, 2 is the jth forecast error of model i; and n is the number of forecasts.

Following Wu and Chen (2001), we also applied the Fisher Sign test (*FS*). Briefly, the *FS* test compares the forecast accuracy of two competing models term by term on the basis of loss differential, whereby the accuracy criterion could be based on the *MSE*, *MSPE*, *MAPE*, among others. The Fisher Sign test is the total number of negative loss differential (d_j) observations in a sample size *n*. Under the null hypothesis of "equal accuracy of two competing forecasts", *FS* has a binomial distribution with parameter *n* and 0.5. The significance of the test is assessed using a table of the cumulative binomial distribution.

In this chapter we also estimated our model by using the same procedure as described above but with a different long-run fundamental model, the interest rate differential (IRD) model. This is achieved by adding the interest rate differential to the pure PPP model as an additional explanatory variable. The purpose is to study whether by adding extra information the forecasting performance of the model can be improved or not.

Results and Interpretation

The empirical results from the estimated PPP model and its adapted form are summarized in Table 6.2. As expected, the true PPP model only managed to capture the long-run movement of the actual exchange rate, but the adapted model had been adapted (or trained) to trace the short-run deviation of the actual exchange rate from the long-run course (Figure 6.1). The R^2 suggests that relative price, P_t could account for 58.52 percent to 68.35 percent of the variation in bilateral rates of the ASEAN currencies (Table 6.2). The adapted model for the five ASEAN currencies tabulated in the table is selected based on the MAPE criterion. Notice that the R^2 value for the Singapore dollar-yen rate (SGD/JPY) is unacceptably low (17.96)! Because of the poor model performance based on the R^2, we did not pursue it any further and dropped it from the analysis.[6]

We subjected the selected model to a battery of diagnostic checking before it was used to generate the in-sample and post-sample forecasts. Results of diagnostic tests performed on both the pure and adapted models' are depicted in Table 6.3. A striking feature of the results shown in Table 6.3 is that the pure PPP model proved impossible for completely attaining the serial correlation free standard. The PPP model is contaminated with a series correlation problem (positively correlated) as it has low Durbin-Watson *d* statistic.[7] This finding is further supported by the large values of Breusch-Godfrey Lagrange Multiplier (*LM*) statistics, which indicate that there exists serial correlation up to 12-lag length. On the other hand, the adapted PPP model easily passed the serial correlation tests. We consider these results as indication that the standard PPP model may not be adequate to explain the changes in exchange rates of the ASEAN countries.[8]

Another point worth mentioning here is that the residuals generated from the PPP model follow a nonstationary process [$\varepsilon_t \sim I(1)$] whereas the adapted form yields residuals that are stationary in level [$\mu_t \sim \mathrm{I}(0)$]. As reported in Table 6.3, the R^2 values between the spot exchange rate and the pure PPP model's predicted values are 79.30 percent, 75.23 percent, 42.33 percent and 66.44 percent for MYR/USD, SGD/USD, MYR/JPY and THB/JPY respectively. In the case of the adapted model, the R^2 values, in the same order, are 93.17 percent, 97.10 percent, 90.50 percent and 95.33 percent. It is obvious that the adapted model has significantly improved the explanatory power of the pure PPP model.[9]

Next, we compared the forecasts generated from the PPP and the adapted PPP model on the basis of efficiency criteria; see, for example, Lin and Chen (1998) and McKenzie (1999). Briefly, the efficiency criterion in its strong form requires that the forecast and actual series (spot rates) be cointegrated with a cointegrating vector of (1, –1). Meanwhile the weak form of the efficiency criterion requires only the slope coefficient from the regression of spot rate on the forecast exchange rate to be unity (β_1=1). The exchange rate forecasts are generated from the two exchange rate models and the results are given in Table 6.3. We found that the generated forecasts from the adapted models pass the strong form of the efficiency criterion fairly easily based on the Wald test. The results from the standard PPP model also satisfied this criterion. The in-sample forecasts of the standard model and adapted model for the four exchange rate series are plotted in Figure 6.1. It is obvious from these plots that while the true PPP model predicts the long-run movement, the adapted PPP model follows the exchange rate behaviour much more closely.

This improvement in the forecasting performance of our proposed model is also revealed by the Fisher Sign (*FS*) test. The results of comparing the in-sample forecast performances of the two models term by term using the FS test are shown in Table 6.4. We used the *MSE*, *MSPE* and *MAPE* to measure the performance. However, only the result from the first criterion is reported as the other two criteria produced the same outcome qualitatively. It appears that adapting the PPP model increased the total loss differentials from 15, 9, 7 and 10 to 32, 24, 24 and 33 out of a total of 65 forecasts for MYR/USD, SGD/USD, MYR/JPY and THB/JPY correspondingly. This finding implies that the adapted model is at least twice as good as the original PPP model. It is worth mentioning that the improvement is realised not only in the in-sample but also in the out-of-sample forecasts. We will discuss the out-of-sample forecasts in greater detail later.

A consensus has emerged among economists that exchange rate misalignments over extended periods of time may trigger a currency or economic crisis. Indeed, a number of studies have provided the evidence that overvaluation is a key factor in predicting forthcoming financial crises; see Kaminsky and Reinhart (1999) and Goldfajn and Valdes (1999), among others. We used the adapted PPP model to compute the equilibrium exchange rates and compare these values with the actual or observed rates. The period chosen is 8 quarters just prior to the outbreak of the Asian Financial Crisis. To accomplish this task, we calculated the mean deviation (*MD*) of the observed rate from its equilibrium value. A negative *MD* by definition implies overvaluation while a positive value means otherwise. Meanwhile, *MD*=0 means no deviation and the observed rate is effectively in equilibrium. Mean percentage error (*MPE*) was also constructed so that the magnitude of overvaluation (or undervaluation) can easily be compared across currencies. Interpretation of the sign of the *MPE* is similar to that of the

MD. Simply reporting the point estimates may not provide a complete picture of the misalignment experienced by the crisis-affected countries. We supplemented the point estimates by the Fisher Sign (*FS*) test to observe whether the point estimates are statistically significant. These test results are presented in Table 6.5.

It is obvious from Table 6.5 that both the *MD* and *MPE* values are all in the negative range for the four exchange rates. This suggests that all four currencies were overvalued several quarters prior to the crisis. In addition, the *MPE* values revealed that the baht-yen rate (THB/JPY, –7.6889 percent) was the most overvalued currency, followed by the MYR/JPY (–4.9811 percent), SGD/USD (–0.6966 percent) and MYR/USD (–0.1348 percent). It appears that the most overvalued currency (Thai baht) was the most susceptible currency to crisis. This result coincides with the historical events surrounding the recent financial crisis. The baht, which was initially pegged to the US dollar, was the first currency in the region that was forced to devalue. The pressures then quickly spread to neighbouring countries. Another interesting observation present in Table 6.5 is that the values of the *FS* statistic suggest that the overvaluation is statistically significant at the 5 percent level in the yen-based currencies (MYR and THB) but not for the dollar-based currencies (MYR and SGD). In a nutshell, although the *FS* test indicates not that all the currencies were statistically significantly misaligned, the model offers some support for the notion that the Asian Financial Crisis may be due to overvaluation of some of the regional currencies.

The estimated IRD models together with their adapted versions are tabulated in Table 6.2, and the related diagnostic tests results are given in Table 6.6. Several interesting observations emerge from these tables. The Wald (χ_2^2) statistics in Table 6.6 suggests that both models meet the strongly efficient criteria since β_0 and β_1 are not significantly different from zero and one respectively for each of the models. As previously observed in the PPP models, the standard IRD model is contaminated with autocorrelation problems as indicated by both the Durbin-Watson and Lagrange Multiplier tests results. The problem, however, disappeared in the adapted IRD models. Notice that the R^2 values of the adapted IRD models are generally lower than the corresponding adapted PPP models (Table 6.2). This comes as a surprise since we expect the adapted IRD models to have higher explanatory powers given that we have added interest rate differential to the adapted PPP model.

Both the adapted PPP and IRD models are used to generate the forecasted values of the exchange rate in the out-of-sample period. The out-of-sample forecasts from these models are compared with the simple random walk model based on the *MSE*, *MSPE* and *MAPE* ratios. Our preliminary results show that all the three criteria yield almost the same conclusion. Given the unanimity of the results across the three criteria, and to conserve space, we only report the criterion based on the *MSE* in Table 6.7. For the adapted PPP model, all the *MSE* ratios were found to be less than unity (Table 6.7A), implying that all the forecasting models estimated based on the adapted PPP model outperformed the random walk model, for the entire forecasting horizon ranging from one to fourteen quarters. In particular, the forecasting models for the SGD/USD and the THB/JPY rates statistically outperformed the random walk model at the 1 percent significance level regardless of whether we were comparing on the basis of one forecast value, two forecast values or more. Meanwhile, the ratio for the MYR/USD and MYR/JPY rates are statistically significant at 10 percent or better, up to at least 6 quarters. It is interesting to note that our forecasting models have defeated the competing random walk model, even in the presence of a more stringent forecasting period and over the short forecasting horizon.

Turning to the adapted IRD model, all the *MSE* ratios for the MYR/USD (significant up to 9 quarters), SGD/USD (significant up to 7 quarters) and THB/JPY (significant for all 14 quarters) rates are less than one (Table 6.7B). Hence, the adapted IRD model could also outperform the random walk for these three rates. The ratio for the MYR/JPY rate shows mixed results but the *MR* statistics suggest that the adapted IRD is only comparable with the random walk with the minor exception of the former being significantly beaten.

The forecast accuracy of the adapted PPP and IRD models are compared and the results are also depicted in Table 6.7C. On balance, the weight of the evidence is against the adapted IRD model: The adapted PPP model has smaller *MSE* values when compared to the adapted IRD model. As shown in the table, the ratios are smaller than one for the MYR/USD, SGD/USD and MYR/JPY rates across all forecasting horizons. Statistically, the adapted PPP model is better than the adapted IRD model up to all the 14 quarters in MYR/USD, 2 quarters in SGD/USD and 6 quarters in MYR/JPY. However, the adapted PPP model for the SGD/USD rate is statistically better than the adapted IRD model only up to 2 quarters ahead forecasting horizon. For the rest of the forecasting horizon, the latter is statistically better. Generally, these results suggest that the adapted IRD model, which is incorporated with more information, does not necessarily out-perform the adapted PPP model. Thus, we have shown that the simple PPP model can adequately represent the movements in exchange rate series by adapting the model to include information on the deviation from equilibrium value.

Conclusion

Numerous studies have compared the forecasting performance of the exchange rates models against the random walk model. The consensus that emerged from these studies is that it is extremely difficult to out-predict a random walk model using structural or non-structural models. In this article, we consider alternative procedures to model exchange rates in the ASEAN countries. Specifically, the proposed model is a linear combination of long run and short-run functions. We exploited the long-run information from the well-known PPP hypothesis in estimating the model, whereas the time series properties of the temporary deviations from equilibrium PPP is incorporated in our estimating procedure to capture the unusual feature of the data generating process. Our results show that even if the model includes the right set of fundamentals, they still cannot explain movements of exchange rates well. Meese (1990) and Frankel and Rose (1994), among others have highlighted this point.

To make the task much more difficult, our forecasting models are purposely set to allow the model to forecast in the post-crisis period. Our empirical results based on the bilateral exchange rates of the three ASEAN countries suggest that our approach has improved significantly the explanatory power of the pure PPP model. In other words, we found that the adapted model is more suited to capturing the salient features of currencies that experienced speculative attacks and severe depreciation. Furthermore, the out-of-sample forecasts of our model out-predicted the simple random walk model, even during the post-crisis period. The adapted PPP model outperformed the rarely beaten naïve model, for the forecast horizons ranging from one to fourteen quarters.

Giddy and Duffey (1975) pointed out that successful forecasting is premised on the satisfaction of at least one of the following criteria: (a) used of a superior forecasting model; (b) consistent access to information; (c) ability to exploit small, temporary deviations from equilibrium; and (d) ability to predict the nature of government intervention in the foreign exchange market. Based on the empirical results, we have shown that our procedure is capable of producing a model, which satisfies the above criteria. Specifically, the model is able to incorporate the long-run information based on macroeconomic theory, and the procedure is able to exploit small and temporary deviations from equilibrium and thereby yield a forecasting model much superior to the naïve model. Therefore, a reasonable conclusion that can be drawn from this chapter is that it provides us with some hope of achieving a reasonable forecast for the ASEAN currencies.

Given the sharp movements in the exchange rates of the East Asian countries, a natural question to ask is whether or not the exchange rates of these countries were out of line with economic fundamentals (equilibrium value) prior to the crash. There is a significant difference between the actual and fitted values just several quarters (4) before the crisis occurred suggesting that these currencies were misaligned. All these currencies appear to be persistently overvalued prior to the ASEAN crisis. Finally, the model can easily include other determinants as suggested by the monetary model and may be used to forecast other financial variables and we reserve this for future research.

Notes

1. Many theoretical models suggest that exchange rates should be jointly determined with macroeconomic variables such as foreign and domestic money supplies, real growth rates, interest rates, price levels, and balance of payments. However, as mentioned earlier the empirical performance of these models has been very poor. In fact, Meese (1990) concludes that "*the proportions of (monthly or quarterly) exchange rate changes that current models can explain is essentially zero.*"
2. A hallmark of the conventional model of real exchange rate is that it follows a PPP benchmark in the long run. Briefly, the PPP doctrine states that the price of a basket of goods should equate across countries when evaluated in common currency. For the empirical work on PPP, see Baharumshah and Ariff (1997) Nagayasu (1998), Coakley and Fuertes (1997), and M. Azali *et al.* (2001), to name a few. The work by Nagayasu found support for a "semi-strong" version of the long-run PPP hypothesis in a sample of 16 African countries. M. Azali *et al.* also found evidence that PPP holds between the developing Asian countries and Japan.
3. This is in line with the view that PPP is a long run relationship and over time prices adjust and PPP is re-established.
4. The literature has not provided conclusive evidence on the long-run determinants of exchange rate. Frankel (1979) sets the long-run determinants as the relative interest rates. Dornbusch (1976) and Chinn and Meese (1995) identify the long-run determinants based on the standard monetary model (money supply, income and inflation rate). Clark and MacDonald (1998) include interest rates, government debt ratio, terms of trade, price levels and net foreign assets to model the exchange rates.
5. Visual inspection of the data reveals that up to the middle of 1997 volatility is less pronounced, whilst thereafter it rises substantially.
6. We found that the optimum model selected through this criterion (and in fact, other criteria e.g. *MSE* and Theil-*U*) may not necessarily pass all the diagnostic tests.
7. In our study, we had 70 in-sample observations and hence the actual decision region for the Durbin-Watson autocorrelation test of no autocorrelation in our model is $1.485 \leq d \leq 2.571$, at 1 percent significance level.
8. The residuals diagnostic tests suggest that by adapting the PPP model, we can implicitly remove the serial correlation problem and produce residuals that are stationary. This comes as no surprise since we have indirectly introduced the lagged value of the exchange rate as an explanatory variable during the second step of our modelling process; see Equation (6). We view this as one of the merits of our adapting the PPP model.
9. A word of caution about comparing the R^2 from the two competing models. The R^2 from the standard PPP model should be interpreted with care because of the problem of autocorrelation (the R^2 values would be smaller; see Gujarati 1995, pp. 411).

Table 6.1 Cointegration Test Results

Pairwise Variables		Exchange Rate and Relative Price		Exchange Rate, Relative Price and Interest Differential			
		Likelihood Ratio			Likelihood Ratio		
Countries	Lag	r = 0	r ≤ 1	Lag	r = 0	r ≤ 1	r ≤ 2
Based Country: United States							
Malaysia	8	21.646#	8.189	6	3.576#	1.412	1.363
Thailand	10	12.573	4.765	3	8.346	3.435	4.066
Singapore	12	8.982*	8.871	2	3.610#	0.058	0.568
Based Country: Japan							
Malaysia	10	24.369#	5 061	12	89.299*	21.391*	1.359
Thailand	11	23.884#	9.080	12	36.579*	13.122	2.106
Singapore	12	24.559#	2.817	--	--	--	--
Critical Values							
5 percent		19.90	9.24		29.68	15.41	3.76
1 percent		24.60	12.97		36.65	20.04	6.65

Notes: * and # denote rejection of hypothesis at 1 percent and 5 percent significance levels respectively.

Table 6.2 Estimated Models

Exchange Rates	Estimated Coefficients[a] Intercept	Relative Price	Interest Differential	R^2 Values	Optimal α Values[b]
PPP Model[c]					
MYR/USD	12.283	–8.881	--	0.585	0.929
	(13.54)*	(–9.94)*			
SGD/USD	–0.529	2.177	--	0.678	0.900
	(–2.62)#	(11.96)*			
MYR/JPY	–0.010	0.028	--	0.451	0.935
	(–3.12)*	(7.467)*			
THB/JPY	–0.178	0.448	--	0.684	0.940
	(–6.14)*	(12.12)*			
SGD/JPY	0.020	–0.011	--	0.180	--
	(6.97)*	(3.564)*			
IRD Model					
MYR/USD	12.030	–8.669	0.038	0.352	0.929
	(11.17)*	(8.51)*	(0.44)		
SGD/USD	–1.468	3.113	–0.048	0.755	0.900
	(–5.52)*	(13.24)*	(–0.40)		
MYR/JPY	–0.029	0.054	–0.001	0.549	0.995
	(–5.55)*	(8.38)*	(–4.66)*		
THB/JPY	–0.295	0.659	–0.022	0.729	0.700
	(–6.69)*	(9.12)*	(–3.35)*		

Notes: *t*–statistics are given in parenthesis. * and # stand for significantly different from zero at 1 percent and 5 percent levels respectively. The adapted model is of the form $\hat{\hat{X}}_t = \hat{X}_t + \alpha\,(X_{t-1} - \hat{X}_{t-1})$ where $\hat{\hat{X}}_t$ and $\hat{X}_t$ denote exchange rate (X_t) predicted by the adapted model and PPP Model or IRD Model respectively, and the optimal α value for each adapted model is obtained by a computer search algorithm.

Table 6.3 Diagnostic Tests for the Models

PPP Model		Adapted PPP Model	
1. MYR/USD			
$X_t = -0.163 + 1.032\,\hat{X}_t + \varepsilon_t$ (0.217) (0.064)		$X_t = 0.039 + 0.987\,\hat{\hat{X}}_t + \mu_t$ (0.108) (0.033)	
$R^2 = 0.793$ $d = 0.361$	$\varepsilon_t \sim I(1)$	$R^2 = 0.932$ $d = 2.385$	$\mu_t \sim I(0)$
$\chi_2^2 = 4.039$	$\chi_1^2 = 0.250$	$\chi_2^2 = 0.200$	$\chi_1^2 = 0.154$
LM (12) = 48.226		LM (12) =11.839	
2. SGD/USD			
$X_t = -0.761 + 1.446\,\hat{X}_t + \varepsilon_t$ (0.200) (0.116)		$X_t = -0.204 + 1.115\,\hat{\hat{X}}_t + \mu_t$ (0.047) (0.026)	
$R^2 = 0.752$ $d = 0.141$	$\varepsilon_t \sim I(1)$	$R^2 = 0.971$ $d = 2.23$	$\mu_t \sim I(0)$
$\chi_2^2 = 0.951$	$\chi_1^2 = 0.358$	$\chi_2^2 = 4.389$	$\chi_1^2 = 3.402$
LM (12) = 60.232		LM (12) =11.655	
3. MYR/JPY			
$X_t = 0.000 + 0.977\,\hat{X}_t + \varepsilon_t$ (0.001) (0.144)		$X_t = 0.001 + 0.933\,\hat{\hat{X}}_t + \mu_t$ (0.006) (0.037)	
$R^2 = 0.423$ $d = 0.145$	$\varepsilon_t \sim I(1)$	$R^2 = 0.905$ $d = 1.728$	$\mu_t \sim I(0)$
$\chi_2^2 = 5.516$	$\chi_1^2 = 5.160$	$\chi_2^2 = 3.913$	$\chi_1^2 = 3.242$
LM (12) = 0.767		LM (12) =13.821	
4. THB/JPY			
$X_t = 0.002 + 0.989\,\hat{X}_t + \varepsilon_t$ (0.013) (0.085)		$X_t = 0.006 + 0.959\,\hat{\hat{X}}_t + \mu_t$ (0.005) (0.026)	
$R^2 = 0.664$ $d = 0.145$	$\varepsilon_t \sim I(1)$	$R^2 = 0.953$ $d = 1.706$	$\mu_t \sim I(0)$
$\chi_2^2 = 0.023$	$\chi_1^2 = 2.868$	$\chi_2^2 = 2.877$	$\chi_1^2 = 2.528$
LM (12) = 60.414		LM (12) =13.965	

Notes: X_t is the actual exchange rate, $\hat{X}_t$ and $\hat{\hat{X}}_t$ are obtained from the PPP model and the adapted model. The standard error for each estimated coefficient is given in parenthesis. The Wald tests for the null hypotheses of strong (β_0=0 and β_1=1) and weak (β_1=1) forms' efficiency of the predictors are reported as χ_2^2 and χ_1^2 respectively. The 5 percent critical values for the chi-square concerned are, in that order, 5.99 and 3.84. The 5 percent critical value for $LM(12)$ statistic (chi-squared distributed) is 21.03.

Table 6.4 Forecasting Performance of PPP Models and Adapted PPP Models by Fisher's Sign (*FS*) Test

PPP Model Vs. Random Walk			
MYR/USD	SGD/USD	MYR/JPY	THB/JPY
In-sample (Forecast Horizon = 65 Quarters			
15 (0.000)	9 (0.000)	7 (0.000)	10 (0.000)
Out-of-sample (Forecast Horizon = 14 Quarters			
0 (0.000)	3 (0.022)	4 (0.061)	5 (0.122)
Adapted PPP Model Vs. Random Walk			
In-sample (Forecast Horizon = 65 Quarters)			
32 (0.098)	24 (0.011)	24 (0.010)	33 (0.098)
Out-of-sample (Forecast Horizon = 14 Quarters)			
8 (0.183)	10 (0.061)	8 (0.183)	6 (0.183)

Notes: Total number of negative lost differential is reported with marginal significance value (msv) given in parenthesis. The null hypothesis of the *FS* test is 2 forecasting models have equal accuracy.

Table 6.5 Evaluation of the Exchange Rates before the Crisis

For 8 Quarterly Forecasted Values				
CRITERIA	MYR/USD	SGD/USD	MYR/JPY	THB/JPY
MD	–0.0079	–0.0097	–0.0008	–0.0177
MPE	–0.1348	–0.6966	–4.9811	–7.6889
FS	5 (0.2188)	5(0.2188)	7 (0.0313)	7 (0.0313)

Notes: *MD* = Mean deviation. *MPE* = Mean percentage error. *FS* = Fisher's sign test. Total number of overvaluation is reported with marginal significance value (msv) given in parenthesis. The null hypothesis of *FS* test is the exchange rate is in equilibrium before the crisis. Negative value implies overvaluation is detected.

Table 6.6 Diagnostic Test for IRD and Adapted Models

IRD Model		Adapted IRD Model	
1. MYR/USD			
$X_t = 0.038 + 0.987\,\hat{X}_t + \varepsilon_t$		$X_t = 0.035 + 0.988\,\hat{\hat{X}}_t + \mu_t$	
(0.106) (0.033)		(0.109) (0.033)	
$R^2 = 0.790$	$\varepsilon_t \sim I(1)$	$R^2 = 0.933$	$\mu_t \sim I(0)$
$d = 0.350$	$LM\ (12) = 49.290$	$d = 2.370$	$LM\ (12) = 13.036$
$\chi_2^2 = 3.975$	$\chi_1^2 = 0.223$	$\chi_2^2 = 0.189$	$\chi_1^2 = 0.132$
2. SGD/USD			
$X_t = -0.019 + 1.009\,\hat{X}_t + \varepsilon_t$		$X_t = -0.050 + 1.027\,\hat{\hat{X}}_t + \mu_t$	
(0.146) (0.075)		(0.051) (0.028)	
$R^2 = 0.754$	$\varepsilon_t \sim I(1)$	$R^2 = 0.961$	$\mu_t \sim I(0)$
$d = 0.150$	$LM\ (12) = 47.362$	$d = 2.142$	$LM\ (12) = 10.623$
$\chi_2^2 = 1.558$	$\chi_1^2 = 1.426$	$\chi_2^2 = 3.117$	$\chi_1^2 = 3.053$
3. MYR/JPY			
$X_t = 0.0003 + 0.977\,\hat{X}_t + \varepsilon_t$		$X_t = 0.001 + 0.960\,\hat{\hat{X}}_t + \mu_t$	
(0.002) (0.144)		(0.001) (0.025)	
$R^2 = 0.564$	$\varepsilon_t \sim I(1)$	$R^2 = 0.837$	$\mu_t \sim I(0)$
$d = 0.434$	$LM\ (12) = 48.831$	$d = 1.924$	$LM\ (12) = 22.484$
$\chi_2^2 = 0.026$	$\chi_1^2 = 0.245$	$\chi_2^2 = 2.249$	$\chi_1^2 = 2.186$
4. THB/JPY			
$X_t = -0.001 + 1.003\,\hat{X}_t + \varepsilon_t$		$X_t = 0.004 + 0.973\,\hat{\hat{X}}_t + \mu_t$	
(0.020) (0.060)		(0.006) (0.033)	
$R^2 = 0.712$	$\varepsilon_t \sim I(1)$	$R^2 = 0.931$	$\mu_t \sim I(0)$
$d = 0.248$	$LM\ (12) = 56.423$	$d = 1.820$	$LM\ (12) = 17.596$
$\chi_2^2 = 0.002$	$\chi_1^2 = 0.016$	$\chi_2^2 = 1.816$	$\chi_1^2 = 1.547$

Notes: X_t is the actual exchange rate, $\hat{X}_t$ and $\hat{\hat{X}}_t$ are obtained from the IRD model and the latter from the adapted model. The standard error for each estimated coefficient is given in parenthesis. The Wald tests for the null hypotheses of strong (β_0=0 and β_1=1) and weak (β_1=1) forms' efficiency of the predictors are reported as χ_2^2 and χ_1^2 respectively. The 5 percent critical values for the chi-square concerned are, in that order, 5.99 and 3.84. The 5 percent critical value for $LM\,(12)$ statistic (chi-squared distributed) is 21.03.

Table 6.7 Out-of-sample Forecasting Performances
(a) Adapted PPP Model Vs Random Walk

n^c	MYR/USD	SGD/USD	MYR/USD	THB/JPY
1	0.878***	0.709***	0.799***	0.246***
2	0.982**	0.872***	0.861***	0.456***
3	0.935***	0.863***	0.890***	0.708***
4	0.974	0.895***	0.887**	0.711***
5	0.955**	0.890***	0.912**	0.729***
6	0.966**	0.887***	0.913	0.714***
7	0.957***	0.895***	0.914	0.723***
8	0.955***	0.898***	0.913	0.728***
9	0.967	0.895***	0.915	0.754***
10	0.967	0.895***	0.915	0.764***
11	0.964	0.895***	0.916	0.770***
12	0.964*	0.895***	0.916	0.767***
13	0.959*	0.895***	0.916	0.763***
14	0.961	0.895***	0.948	0.948***

(b) Adapted IRD Model Vs Random Walk

n^c	MYR/JPY	THB/JPY	MYR/JPY	THB/JPY
1	0.890***	0.761***	0.962	0.451***
2	0.987***	0.924***	1.022**	0.541***
3	0.939***	0.899***	1.026	0.609***
4	0.977	0.957***	1.017	0.629***
5	0.958**	0.928**	1.023	0.650***
6	0.968*	0.924*	1.005	0.624***
7	0.960*	0.932*	1.006	0.635***
8	0.958**	0.936	1.005	0.678***
9	0.970**	0.933	0.999	0.670***
10	0.969	0.933	0.997	0.664***
11	0.966	0.931	0.997	0.668***
12	0.966	0.929	0.997	0.669***
13	0.961	0.928	0.997	0.669***
14	0.963	0.928	0.995	0.665***

(c) Adapted PPP Model Vs Adapted IRD Model

n^c	MYR/USD	SGD/USD	MYR/JPY	THB/JPY
1	0.986***	0.932**	0.831***	0.546***
2	0.996***	0.944***	0.842***	0.844***
3	0.996***	0.959	0.868***	1.163***
4	0.997***	0.958	0.873***	1.131***
5	0.997***	0.959	0.892***	1.121***
6	0.997***	0.959	0.909*	1.144***
7	0.997***	0.960	0.909	1.140***
8	0.997***	0.959	0.909	1.089***
9	0.997***	0.960	0.916	1.125***
10	0.997***	0.960	0.918	1.150***
11	0.997***	0.961	0.919	1.153***
12	0.997***	0.964	0.919	1.145***
13	0.997***	0.965	0.919	1.141***
14	0.997***	0.965	0.953	1.169***

Notes: *n* denotes number of quarters forecasted. *, ** and *** denotes statistically significant at 10 percent, 5 percent and 1 percent level as suggested by Meese-Rogoff (*MR*) statistics .

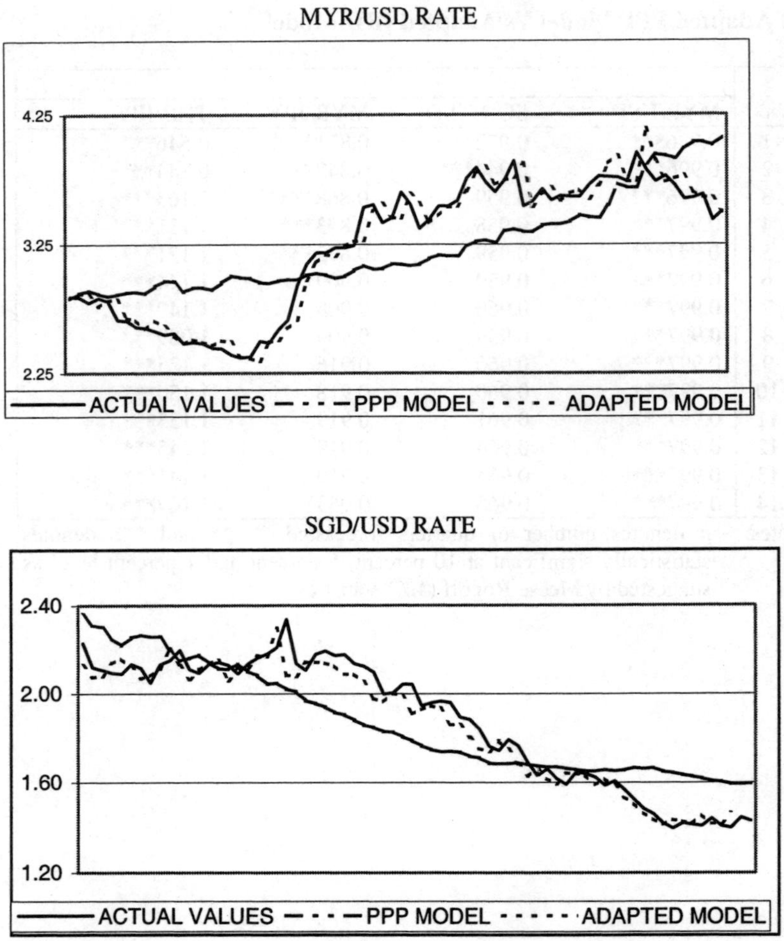

Figure 6.1 Graphs of In-sample Forecasts

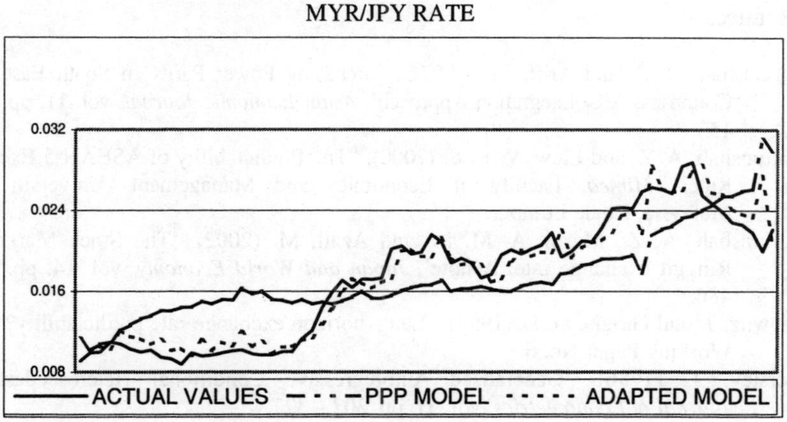

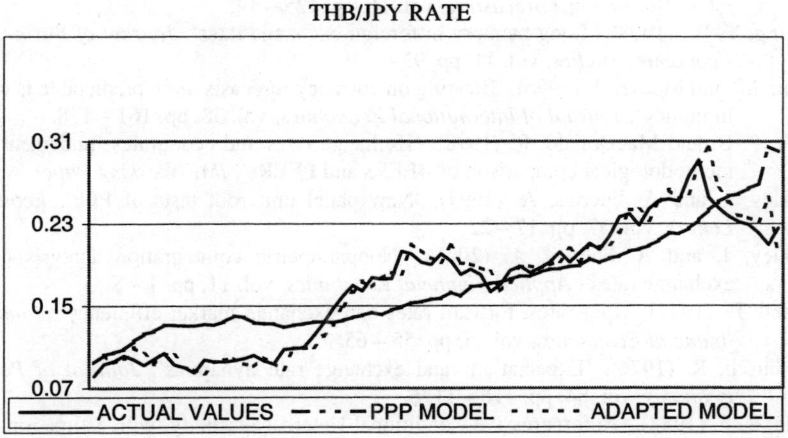

Figure 6.1 (continued)

References

Baharumshah, A. Z. and Ariff, M. (1997), 'Purchasing Power Parity in South East Asian Countries: A Cointegration Approach', *Asian Economic Journal,* vol. 11, pp. 141 – 153.

Baharumshah, A. Z. and Liew, V. K. S. (2000), "The Predictability of ASEAN-5 Exchange Rates, *Mimeo,* Faculty of Economics and Management, Universiti Putra Malaysia, Kuala Lumpur.

Baharumshah, A. Z., Masih, A. M. M. and Azali, M. (2002), 'The Stock Market and Ringgit exchange rate: A note', *Japan and World Economy,* vol. 14, pp. 471 – 486.

Berkowitz, J. and Giogianni, L. (1997), 'Long–horizon exchange rate predictability?', IMF Working Paper No. 6.

Bollerslev, T. (1986), 'Generalised Autoregressive Conditional Heteroscedasticity', *Journal of Econometrics,* vol. 51, pp. 307 – 327.

Boothe, P. and Glassman, D. (1987), 'Comparing exchange rate forecasting models', *International Journal of Forecasting,* vol. 3, pp. 65 – 79.

Brooks, C. (1996), 'Testing for non-linearity in daily sterling exchange rates', *Applied Financial Economics,* vol. 6, pp. 307 – 317.

Brooks, C. (1997), 'Linear and non-linear non-forcastability of high-frequency exchange rates', *Journal of Forecasting,* vol. 16, pp. 125 – 145.

Cheung, Y. W. (1993),' Long memory in foreign-exchange rates', *Journal of Business and Economics Studies,* vol. 11, pp. 93 – 101.

Chinn, M. and Meese, R. (1995), 'Banking on currency forecasts: how predictable is change in money', *Journal of International Economics,* vol. 38, pp. 161 – 178.

Clark, P. B. and MacDonald, R. (1998), 'Exchange rates and economics fundamentals: A methodological comparison of BEERs and FEERs', *IMF Working Paper No. 67.*

Coakley, J. and A. Fuertes, A. (1997), 'New panel unit root tests of PPP', *Economics Letters,* vol. 57, pp. 17 – 22.

Coakley, J. and A. Fuertes, A. (2001), 'Nonparametric cointegration analysis of real exchange rates', *Applied Financial Economics,* vol. 11, pp. 1 – 8.

Cornell, B. (1977), 'Spot rates, forward rates and exchange market efficiency', *Journal of financial Economics,* vol. 5, pp. 55 – 65.

Dornbusch, R. (1976), 'Expectations and exchange rate dynamics', *Journal of Political Economy,* vol. 84, pp. 116 – 1176.

Engle, R. F. (1982), 'Autoregressive Conditional Heteroscedasticity, with estimation of the variance of United Kingdom inflation', *Econometrica,* vol. 50, pp. 987 – 1007.

Fama, E. F. (1965), 'The behaviour of stock market prices', *Journal of Business,* vol. 38, pp. 34 – 105.

Frankel, J. (1979), 'On the Mark: a theory of floating exchange rates based on real interest differentials', *American Economic Review,* vol. 69, pp. 610 – 622.

Frankel, J. and Rose, A. K. (1994), 'A survey of empirical research on nominal exchange rates', *NBER Working Paper No. 4685.*

Franses, P. H. and Homelen, P. V. (1998), 'On forecasting exchange rates using Neural Networks', *Applied Financial Economics,* vol. 8, pp. 589 – 596.

García-Ferrer, A., Del Hoyo, J. and Martín-Arroyo, A. S. (1997), 'Univariate forecasting comparisons: the case of the Spanish automobile industry', *Journal of Forecasting,* vol. 16, pp. 1 – 17.

Giddy, I. H. and Duffey, G. (1975), 'The random behaviour of flexible exchange rates: implication for forecasting', *Journal of International Business Studies,* vol. 6, pp. 1 – 33.

Goldfajn, I. and Valdes, R. (1999), 'The aftermath of appreciation', *Quarterly Journal of Economics,* vol. 114, pp. 229 – 262.

Gujarati, D. N. (1995), *Basic Econometrics*, US: McGraw-Hill Inc.

Hakkio, C. S. and Rush, M. (1986), 'Market efficiency and cointegration: an application to the Sterling and Deutschemark exchange markets', *Journal of International Money and Finance,* vol. 5, pp. 221 – 230.

Hallwood, C. and Macdonald, R. (1994), *International Money and Finance,* Oxford: Blackwell.

Johansen, S. and Juselius, K. (1990), 'Maximum likelihood estimation and inference on cointegration – with application to the demand for money', *Oxford Bulletin of Economics and Statistics,* vol. 52, pp. 169 – 210.

Kaminsky, S. and Reinhart, C.. (1999), 'Currency and banking crises: the early warnings of distress', *American Economic Review,* vol. 89, pp. 473 – 500.

Keller, A. (1989), 'Advanced time-series analysis', in C. Dunis and M. Feeny (eds), *Exchange Rate Forecasting*, England: Woodhead-Faulkner, pp. 206 – 299.

Kräger, H. and Kugler, P. (1993), 'Non-linearities in foreign exchange markets, a different perspective', *Journal of International Money and Finance,* vol. 12, pp. 195 – 208.

Lin, W. T. and Chen, Y. H. (1998), 'Forecasting foreign exchange rates with an intrinsically nonlinear dynamic speed of adjustment model', *Applied Economics,* vol. 30, pp. 295 – 312.

Litterman, R. B. (1986), 'Forecasting with Bayesian vector autoregressive – five years of experience', *Journal of Business and Economic Statistics,* vol. 4, pp. 25 – 38.

Lupoletti, W. M. and Webb, R. H. (1986), 'Defining and improving the accuracy of the macroeconomics forecasts: contribution of a VAR model', *Journal of Business,* vol. 59, pp. 263 – 284.

M-Azali, Habibullah, M. S. and Baharumshah, A.Z. (2001), 'Does PPP hold between Asian and Japanese economies? Evidence using panel unit root and panel cointegration', *Japan and the World Economy,* vol. 13, pp. 35 – 50.

Ma, Y. and Kanas, A. (2000), 'Testing for a nonlinear relationship among fundamentals and exchange rates in ERM', *Journal of International Money and Finance,* vol. 19, pp. 135 – 152.

Mackinnon, J. G. (1991), 'Critical Values for Cointegration Tests', in R.F. Engle and C.W.J. Granger (eds), *Long-Run Economic Relationship: Reading in Cointegration,* Oxford: Oxford University Press, pp. 267 – 276.

Mark, N. (1995), 'Exchange rates and fundamentals: evidence on long-run horizon predictability', *America Economic Review,* vol. 85, pp. 201 – 218.

Mckenzie, M. D. (1999), 'Power transformation and forecasting the magnitude of exchange rate changes', *International Journal of Forecasting,* vol. 15, pp. 49 – 55.

Meese, R. A. (1990), 'Currency fluctuations in the post-Bretton Woods era', *The Journal of Economic Perspectives,* vol. 4, pp. 117-134.

Meese, R. A. and Rogoff, K. (1983), 'Empirical exchange rate models of the seventies: do they fit out of sample', *Journal of International Economics*, vol. 14, pp. 3 – 24.

Meese, R. and Rogoff, K. (1988), 'Was it real? the exchange rate-interest differential relation over the modern floating rate period', *Journal of Finance,* vol. 43, pp. 933 – 948.

Meese, R. A. and Rose, A. K. (1991), 'An empirical assessment of non-linearities in models of exchange rate determination', *Review of Economics Studies,* vol. 58, pp. 603 – 619.

Montogomery, D. C., Johnson, L. A. and Gardiner, J. S. (1990), *Forecasting and Time Series Analysis*, US: McGraw-Hill Inc.

Mussa, M. (1996), 'Nominal exchange rate regimes and behaviour of real exchange rates: evidence and implications', *Carnegie-Rochester Series on Public Policy*, vol. 25, pp. 117 – 214.

Nelson, D. B. (1991), 'Conditional heteroskedasticity in asset returns: a new approach', *Econometrica,*, vol. 59, pp. 347–370.

Palma, W. and Chan, N. H. (1997), 'Estimation and forecasting of long-memory processes with missing values', *Journal of Forecasting,*, vol. 16, pp. 395 – 410.

Parikh, A. and Williams, G. (1998), 'Modelling real exchange rate behaviour: a cross-country study', *Applied Financial Economics,* vol. 8, pp. 577 – 587.

Plasmans, J., Verkooijen, W. and Daniels, H. (1998), 'Estimating structural exchange rate models by Artificial Neural Networks', *Applied Financial Economics*, vol. 8, pp. 541 – 551.

Taylor, M. P. and Peel, D. A. (2000), 'Nonlinear adjustment, long-run equilibrium and exchange rate fundamentals', *Journal of International Money and Finance,* vol. 19, pp. 33 – 53.

Wu, J. L. and Chen, S. L. (2001), 'Nonlinear exchange-rate prediction: evidence from a nonlinear approach', *Journal of International Money and Finance,* vol. 20, pp. 521 – 532.

PART III
TOWARDS A REGIONAL INTEGRATION

Chapter 7

Internal and External Deficits in the ASEAN-5 Economies

Evan Lau

Introduction

Analysts and politician have shown concern over the state of the external imbalances in the past two decades or so. Most observers consider large external deficit to have been the cause of macroeconomic imbalances. In attempt to study the external imbalances numerous researchers had explored the possible link between internal deficit and external deficit. The so-called twin deficits hypothesis erupted during the 'Reagan fiscal experiment' in the 1980s which marked a period of strong appreciation of the dollar with unusual shift hike in external deficit not in favor of the United States is an example in history.[1] This close connection between external and internal deficits, however, is not unique for the United States. In Europe, Germany and Sweden faced similar problems emerged in the early part of the 1990s where the rise in the internal deficit was accompanied by a real appreciation of their national currencies which adversely affect the current accounts (see Ibrahim and Kumah, 1996). Developing countries are no exception, most have also experienced problem with external debts in early 1980s. Several authors have documented that the unsustainable internal deficit during these periods has widens the external deficit. Indeed, authors like Laney (1984) found that the relationship between these two variables is much stronger for the developing countries. The emergence of internal-external deficits phenomena in many countries has drawn increasing attention to the problem of 'twin deficits'.

The aim of this chapter is to investigate the twin deficits hypothesis (internal-external deficits) for five Asian developing economies (ADE) namely Indonesia, Malaysia, Singapore, Thailand and the Philippines (ASEAN-5), that persistent internal deficit have been the prime 'cause' of the escalating external deficit observed in the late 1980s and for the most part of the 1990s.[2] More precisely, the purpose is to identify the causal relationship between these two variables. This in our view is important, as it will determine the source of the problem and provide the right policy mix for policymakers in addressing the issue of external imbalances in the ASEAN-5 countries. For instance, if large internal deficits cause the current account to move into deficit then the policy recommendation is clear – maintaining large internal deficits will not correct the external deficits. Therefore, policies that do not address the capital movements will not alter the external deficit.

The article differs from the earlier studies in the following ways. First, we choose ASEAN-5 because the issue seems to be currently relevant to these economies during the pre-crisis period. Four out of five of the countries under investigation were hardly hit by the recent Asian financial crisis and they are still undergoing structural and economics adjustments in the aftermath of the crisis.[3] Further, we observed that most of the crisis-affected countries (including those in this chapter) recorded large external and internal deficits for most part of the 1990s. Indeed, many analysts have questioned the sustainability of the external deficit in the pre-crisis period. For example, Lau *et al.* (2002) found that most of the crisis-affected economies (Indonesia, the Philippines and Thailand) are indeed on the unsustainable path in governing the external imbalances prior to the 1997 crisis.[4] Thus, the experience of ASEAN-5 will contribute to the debate on the 'twin deficits' issue particularly for developing countries, which are scarce in the literature.

Second, to our best knowledge, no previous work has attempted to address the 'twin deficits hypothesis' for the ASEAN-5 countries, with the exception of Anoruo and Ramchander (1998) and Khalid and Teo (1999).[5] In addition, this chapter extended the basic version model by including two additional mediating (transmitting) variables. The mediating variables namely the short-term interest rates, exchange rates are known to influence the twin deficits nexus.[6] These mediating variables allow us to map out the transmission mechanism between the four variables. Moreover, it is now well-known that the causality and cointegration inferences are strongly affected by omission of important causing variables. Finally, the modeling strategy adopted here differs from most of the earlier studies; in that, we deal with the issue of potential breakpoint(s) in cointegration relationship using Gregory and Hansen (1996) methodology. The breakpoints are imposed *a priori* and are estimated endogenously. In addition, we addressed the internal-external nexus using the powerful Toda and Yamamoto (1995) *Granger non-causality*.

Theoretical Framework and Previous Literature

The Theoretical Model

The model starts with the national income identity for an open economy that can be represented as:

$$Y = C + I + G + X - M \tag{1}$$

where Y= gross domestic product *(GDP)*, C = consumption, I = investment, G = government spending, X = export and M = import. Defining current account *(CA)* as the difference between export *(X)* and import *(M)*, equation 1 becomes:

$$CA = Y - (C + I + G) \tag{2}$$

where $(C + I + G)$ are the spending of domestic residents (domestic absorption). In a closed economy saving *(S)* equals investment *(I)* and given that $Y - C = S$, we have:

$$S = I + CA \tag{3}$$

Equation 3 states that unlike a closed economy, an open economy can seek domestically and internationally for the necessary funds for investments to enhance its income. In other words, external borrowing allows investment at levels beyond those that could be financed through domestic savings. The national savings can further be decomposed into private (S_p) and government savings (S_g) :

$$S_p = Y - T - C \qquad (4)$$

and

$$S_g = T - G \qquad (5)$$

where T is the government revenue. Using equations 4 and 5 and substituting into equation 3 yields:

$$S_p = I + CA + (G\text{-}T) \qquad (6)$$

or

$$CA = S_P - I - (G - T) \qquad (7)$$

Equation 7 states that a rise in the government (budget) deficit will increase the current account deficit if and only if, the rise in government deficit decreases total national saving. Assuming that current tax revenues are held constant and $(S_p - I)$ remains the same, an increase in temporary government spending (G) will cause government deficit to rise $(G - T)$ which will affect the current account positively. In this manner, the government deficit reduces the nation's current account surplus and hence suggesting the worsening of current account balance that supports the Keynesian (conventional) view. In the other end of the spectrum, lies the Ricardian Equivalence Hypothesis. This group of economists believed that the consumers foreseen the future increase in taxes. Knowing that their future disposable income will be reduced because of the impending increase in taxes, households reduce their consumption spending and raise savings to smooth out the expected reduction in income. Thus, no subsequent effect on the current account deficit as budget deficit increased.

Relevant Literature

Past literature on the twin deficits issue has mainly centered on two major theoretical paradigms: Keynesian and the Ricardian Equivalence Hypothesis. However, the 'twin deficits hypothesis' can be categories under four testable hypotheses. The first is based on the Keynesian (conventional) proposition. By using the well-known Mundell-Fleming framework, economist demonstrates that under flexible exchange rate regime, an increase in internal deficit could induce upward pressure on interest rates, causing capital inflows and the appreciation of domestic currency. The appreciated exchange rate in the host country will make exports less attractive and increase the attractiveness of imports and subsequently worsen of the current account balances. Under fixed exchange rate regime, the internal deficit generates higher real income or prices and this will also worsen the current account balance. In other words, the internal deficit ultimately widens the external deficit under both fixed or flexible exchange rate regimes although we have indicated earlier that the transmission mechanisms differ. Hence, two important conclusions emerged from the Keynesian proposition. First, a positive relationship exists between internal deficit and external deficit. Second, there exists a unidirectional Granger causality that runs from internal to external deficits. Researchers like Vamvoukas (1999), Piersanti (2000) and Akbostanci and Tunç (2001) among others found strong evidence to support the Keynesian view.[7]

Second, Buchanan (1976) rediscovered the Ricardo's proposition that is known as Ricardian Equivalence Hypothesis (hereafter REH) in the seminal work of Barro (1974).[8] According to this view, an intertemporal shift between taxes and internal deficit does not matter for the real interest rate, the quantity of investment or the current account balance. In fact, neither a crowding-out effect of domestic investment nor an external deficit necessarily emerges from an internal deficit. In other words, the absence of any Granger causality relationship between the two deficits would be in accordance with the REH. The statistical evidence provided by Miller and Russek (1989), Enders and Lee (1990), Evans and Hasan (1994) are all supportive to REH.

Third, a unidirectional causality also may exist from external to internal deficits. This possibility may occur when the deterioration in current account leads to slower pace of economic growth and hence increases the internal deficit. Several authors have pointed out that for a small open developing economy that depend highly on foreign capital inflows to finance their economic developments followed this pattern of causal relation. In other words, the fiscal position of a country will be affected by large capital inflows or through debt accumulations and with that a country will eventually run into internal deficit. The experiences of Latin American and to some extent East Asian countries illustrate this point (see Reisen, 1998). For instance, most of the Latin American recorded investment rate that was higher than national saving in the 1980s. These later led to the worsening of the current account. The budget (fiscal) position exacerbated the private sector imbalances. This reverse causality is termed as 'current account targeting' by Summers (1988), where he argued that external adjustment maybe sought via budget (fiscal) policy. Recently, Fountas and Tsoukis (2000) found the reverse causation for Canada while Alkswani (2000) documented the experience of Saudi Arabia.[9] According to them, this outcome is possible if government of a country utilized their fiscal stance to target the current account balance.

Lastly, feedback (bidirectional) causality between the two deficits is also possible. In other words, internal deficit Granger causes external deficit and vice-versa.[10] The above discussion suggests that the link between internal and external deficits is indeed an empirical issue.[11] While most of the research considered in the literature are devoted on the developed economies had provides remarkable insights into the issue, there has been very little attention focuses for the developing nations. Henceforth, the issue has become very important in developing nations and we are motivated to examine the relationship between the two if any, for ASEAN-5 economies.

Methodology and Data

Unit Root Tests

In carrying out the cointegration analysis, the first step is to implement the unit root tests. In this chapter, we deployed Said and Dickey (1984) Augmented Dickey-Fuller (ADF) and Kwiatkowski *et al.* (1992) (hereafter KPSS) testing principle. Unlike the ADF test, the KPSS semi-parametric procedure tests for level (η_μ) or trend stationary (η_τ) against the alternative of a unit root. Hence, by combining the ADF test with KPSS procedure, it is likely to provide more clear-cut conclusion with regard to the order of integration for all the series.

Multivariate Cointegration Test

The Johansen procedure poses several advantages over the residual-based Engle-Granger two-step approach in testing for cointegration. It does not suffer from problems associated with normalization and it is robust to departures from normality (Cheung and Lai, 1993). The test utilizes two likelihood ratio (LR) test statistics for the number of cointegrating vectors: the maximum eigenvalue [$-T \log(1-\lambda_I)$] and trace [$-T\Sigma(1-\lambda_I)$] statistics. The maximum eigenvalue test (λ-max) is based of the comparison on H_I (r-1) against the alternative H_I (r). In general, the null hypothesis (H_0: r=0) is tested against an alternative (H_1: r=1) against (H_1: r=2), and so on. In the trace test, the null hypothesis (H_0) is that there is at most r cointegrating relationship, for example, r= 0, 1, 2, 3 is tested against a general alternative. Readers may refer to Johansen and Juselius (1990) for a complete discussion on the procedure. Critical values for both the maximum eigenvalue and trace tests are tabulated in Osterwald-Lenum (1992).

Gregory and Hansen Cointegration Method

Results of the Johansen procedure are known to be sensitive to structural break(s) in the long run cointegrating relationship. Given that such break(s) is likely to exist in estimating a cointegrating relationship, we applied the Gregory and Hansen (1996) cointegration test that accounts for the break endogenously. A dummy variable is included to account for a shift in the cointegrating vector. The procedure offers four different models corresponding to the four different assumptions concerning the nature of the shift in the cointegrating vector.[12] As such, the Gregory and Hansen (1996) procedure allows us to determine the break point endogenously from the data set instead of selecting the break point based on *a priori* information. Hence, the problem of data mining can be avoided.

Toda-Yamamoto Test

Standard procedure in testing the non-causality such as error correction model (ECM) and vector error correction model (VECM) when the variables are cointegrated are cumbersome and sensitive to the values of nuisance parameters in finite samples and therefore 'the virtues of simplicity and ease of application have been largely lost' (Rambaldi and Doran, 1996 p.3). Alternatively, Toda and Yamamoto (1995)[13] have proposed a procedure for testing *Granger non-causality* which allows causal inference to be conducted in the level vector autoregression (VARs) that may contain integrated processes and require the determination of the true lag length in the model. This procedure imposes (non-) linear restrictions using the modified WALD (MWALD) test on the parameters of VARs models without pretest for unit root and cointegrating rank. Furthermore, Rambaldi and Doran (1996) had shown that the MWALD could be easily computed by Seemingly Unrelated Regression (SUR). Thus, causal ordering among the variables can be established without *prior* restrictions of exogeneity.

Data

Quarterly data from post Bretton Woods (1976:1 to 2000:4) is utilized in the analysis. For Malaysia, the data ended in 1998:2 before the pegging of the exchange rate to US dollar on September 1998. The data are gathered from several *International Financial Statistics* issues, published by the International Monetary Fund (IMF). The variables employed in the chapter are the current account (CAD), fiscal position (BD), short-term nominal interest rate[14] (IR) and nominal exchange rate (EX) denominated in US dollar. Both the CAD and BD are expressed as ratio of the nominal Gross Domestic Product (GDP). The IFS provided CAD denominated in US dollar while the BD and the nominal GDP is measured in domestic currency. For consistency, we express all the variables in domestic currency. Data for GDP are available on annual basis and hence, the quarterly GDP data for this chapter were extrapolated from the annual series employing the approach suggested by Gandolfo (1981). The data utilized in the analysis are seasonally unadjusted and expressed in nominal terms.

Empirical Results and Discussion

Univariate Integration

Both the testing principles support the hypothesis of ΔCAD, ΔBD, ΔIR and ΔEX being stationary or *I(1)*. Specifically, the ADF statistics strongly reject the unit root null in favor of stationary while the KPSS statistics strengthen this conclusion by failing to reject null at the usual confidence levels. The finding that all the variables have the same order of integration allows us to proceed with the Johansen-Juselius cointegration analysis.

Johansen Cointegration Analysis

To implement Johansen procedure, the appropriate lag length *k* in the VAR system must be determined. The standard Akaike's information criterion (AIC) is used to determine the optimal lag length.[15] This criteria yields VAR(5) for Philippines, Singapore and Thailand while VAR(3) is most appropriate for Malaysia and VAR(4) for Indonesia. Despite different lag structure employed in the analysis for each country, the residuals of each equation in the system do not exhibit any form of serial correlation or ARCH effects thus satisfying the normal specification criteria for residuals.

The importance of applying a correction factor for the Johansen procedure in small samples is now well known. The correction factor is necessary to reduce the excessive tendency of the test to falsely reject the null hypothesis of no cointegration often associated with data of relatively short span. A number of papers including Reimers (1992) and Cheung and Lai (1993) have documented the importance of this correction factor for the small sample. Cheung and Lai (1993) had provided the correction factor of Johansen likelihood ratio test while Reinsel and Ahn (1992) suggested an adjustment to the estimated maximum eigenvalue and trace statistics. In this chapter, we relied on the later suggestion to confirm the cointegration results from the Johansen statistics.[16]

Table 7.1 presents the results of the Johansen cointegration tests. The null hypothesis of no cointegrating vector (r=0) in favor of at least one cointegrating vector is rejected at 5 percent significance level for Indonesia, Malaysia and Thailand but not for Singapore and the Philippines. Rejecting the null hypothesis of no cointegrating between the *I(1)* variables as in the case of Indonesia, Malaysia and Thailand implies that the four variables do not drift apart and share at least a common stochastic trend in the long-run. Therefore, the Johansen test identifies a single unique cointegrating relationship in three out of five countries. Meanwhile, both maximal eigenvalue and trace statistics for the case of the Philippines Singapore are insignificant even at the 10 percent level and the results hold with or without applying the Reinsel and Ahn (1992) correction factor.

To determine if all the four variables in the system of twin deficits hypothesis (for three countries that are found to be cointegrated) belong to the cointegrating space, we apply the log-likelihood ratio (LR) test for the exclusion of each variable as discussed in Johansen and Juselius (1990: p. 195). Table 7.2 presents the tests of the exclusion restriction on CAD, BD, IR and EX. The null of restricting the coefficients of CAD, BD, IR and EX to zero can be easily rejected at the 5 percent significant level for all the three countries where the cointegrating relationship holds. Clearly, all the variables belong to the cointegrating space and cannot be excluded from the analysis. The empirical results show that both interest rate and exchange rate are key components in the twin deficits debate. Given the well-known problem of omitted relevant variables in the causality and cointegration inferences, the results from previous studies are highly questionable and potentially misleading. Again, the results tend to suggest that all the four series (CAD, BD IR and EX) are bound together by a single, unique long run equilibrium relationship for Indonesia, Malaysia and Thailand. Next, we turn to test the parameter instability for the long run cointegrated relationship in order to establish the robustness of our results due to structural break(s).

Structural Break

To allow for possible changes in the cointegrating vector over the estimation period, we relied on the Gregory and Hansen (1996) procedure. The results of the Gregory-Hansen cointegration tests are summarized in Table 7.3. The first model (level shift model) reveals that cointegration is present with a break for Indonesia (1981:4), Malaysia (1980:4) and Philippines (1986:4) implying that the data supports cointegration with change in intercept. The second model (level shift and trend model) shows that long run relationship is present with a break for Indonesia (1981:4) and Singapore (1987:1). Finally, the third model that takes into consideration the simultaneous presence of both a mean break and a slope break (regime shift) exhibits empirical support for the case of Malaysia (1987:2), Singapore (1986:4) and Thailand (1985:4). Taken together, the Gregory-Hansen test suggests that the four variables are cointegrated. Therefore, failure to reject the null hypothesis in the Johansen-Juselius procedure reported earlier for the case of Singapore and the Philippines is due to structural shift in the underlying parameters of the model. Therefore, our finding of a least one cointegrating vector in the system of four I(1) variables satisfy the sufficient condition for causality in at least one direction is fulfilled.

The break points detected by the Gregory and Hansen test coincide with three major events in the ASEAN-5 countries. First, aftermath of the second oil price shocks that occur in 1979; second, the collapse of commodity prices due to the world recession (Plaza Accord and its aftermath) in the mid-1980s. Third, and most importantly, Asian (particularly ASEAN-5) countries undertook significant macroeconomic stabilization and structural reforms in the 1980s and early 1990s due to the involvement of a sizeable deterioration in external imbalances. In addition, some of the countries also took steps to correct exchange rate overvaluation in mid to late 1980s that may contribute to the deterioration in the current account position. Notice that the result indicates that the four variables are in fact cointegrated with break in the case of Philippines and Singapore, a relationship that the Johansen framework failed to detect. This evidence shows that the cointegrating relationship is sensitive to the presence of structural break(s) and had to be considered before any conclusion can be drawn on the internal-external deficits hypothesis.

The MWALD Test

The long run *Granger non-causality* based on Toda and Yamamoto (1995) procedure are reported in Table 7.4. The null hypothesis that internal deficit do not cause external deficit is easily rejected at 5 percent significant level for all the countries but Indonesia. This is in line with results presented in Anoruo and Ramchander (1998) and Khalid and Teo (1999) where they found a significant reverse causation in Indonesia. Moreover, as noted in Table 7.4, there exists feedback causation in Malaysia and the Philippines. This suggests that in Malaysia and Philippines, internal deficit is not the prime cause of the external deficit and one could see that the reverse causation running from external to internal deficit is much more strong in terms of the significance. This finding is consistent with the results in a number studies conducted for the developing economies e.g. (Anoruo and Ramchander, 1998 and Khalid and Teo, 1999) and even in developed countries (Darrat, 1988). Moreover, Khalid and Teo (1999) pointed that two-way causality between the two deficits is more likely to occur in the developing rather than the developed economies. We view the mixed evidence found in this chapter may be due to structural and economic differences that exist between developed economies and those economies included in this chapter.[17]

As a summary, we found two countries (Singapore and Thailand) support the notion of Keynesian (conventional) views of twin deficits, one (Indonesia) country of Summer's external account targeting and the remaining two (Malaysia and the Philippines) of the feedback causation. In addition, exchange rate and interest rate are the important propeller in the internal-external deficits nexus.

Further, the results from Toda-Yamamoto Granger non-causality reported in Table 7.4 also useful for the examining the causal influence of the mediating variables (exchange rate and interest rate) on the twin deficits issues. As shown in Panel A, exchange rate is found to be statistically significant in all the countries, suggesting that devaluation policy option is feasible in managing the external deficit. As pointed out by Ostry (1997) and Baharumshah (2001) among others, that the currency appreciation (worsening term of trade) is one plausible explanation, why the ASEAN (particularly ASEAN-5) current account is in deficits several years prior to the crisis. Additionally, Panel B shows both interest rate and exchange rate Granger cause internal deficit in Indonesia and Singapore but not in Thailand and the Philippines. For Malaysia, the causal relationship that runs from exchange rate to internal deficit is detected. As such, any action taken to combat the external imbalances will lies on the importance of the influences in exchange rate, interest rate with simultaneous effect of reduction package in internal deficit.

Concluding Remarks and Policy Stance

Spurred by the dramatic surge in both United States external and internal deficits in the 1980s, a particular causal story (twin deficits) exits in the literature. Since then, research in this area has mushroomed. Motivated by this development, this chapter focuses on ASEAN-5 due to similar pattern in the comovements between current account (external) deficit and budget (internal) deficit. The objective of this chapter is to establish the causal relationship between the external and the internal deficits if any. We research the task by using the theory of integration and cointegration with (without) break in examining the issue. In testing for the causal relationship between the twin deficits, two important mediating variables (exchange rate and interest rate) known to influence the relationship are also included in the estimation procedures.

The empirical analysis leads to the following conclusions: First, the evidence of cointegration (without break) is found in only three countries (Indonesia, Malaysia and Thailand) suggesting a long run relationship between the four variables: current account, budget deficit, interest rate and exchange rate. This result suggests that most of the developing countries indeed rely more on external source of fund in building up infrastructure and economy which leads to the external imbalances. Moreover, future services of debts will impose an excessive burden on future generations, and thus lower the standard of livings, which will have to pay back high amounts of accumulated external debts and leads to economic imbalances.

Second, the more powerful cointegration analysis that accounts for parameter instability found the existence of long-run relationship in all the countries (at least in one scenario of the principle). This may have been due to the aftermath of second oil price shocks that occur in 1979, collapse of commodity prices due to the world recession in 1985 (Plaza Accord and its aftermath) and structural transformation taken by ASEAN-5 country authorities. Indeed, models that used long data span and failed to account for break(s) are likely to lead to unreliable conclusions. Further, the results obtained from Gregory-Hansen cointegration are more promising than the Johansen's approach.

Third, since both deficits are found to be simultaneously caused by the other mediating variables, a manipulation of these policy variables could be potentially employed to bring the internal-external deficits under control. In this sense, export promotion maybe one option that policy makers may pursue due to the dynamic positive spillover effect from the export sector growth. Recent empirical evidence tends to support this notion that export promotion policy is successful for developing countries, particularly ASEAN-5 (Islam, 1998b and Baharumshah and Rashid, 1999)

Fourth, the existence of unidirectional from external to internal deficits and a bi-directional relationship highlighted the exogeneity change in foreign variables. For instance, it is possible that a deteriorating in external account might contribute the contractionary effect of an internal deficit reduction package. This is because the results suggest internal deficit is not an exogenous variable in the policy equation. The real solution to the practical problem of twin deficits lies in a simultaneous attacks focusing on exchange rate and interest targeting (external policy) which acts as the transmission mechanism of external shocks, budget cut (internal policy), productivity improvement and some extent of monetary policy.

Finally, the problem of twin deficits is truly an empirical issue and the selection of the countries cannot lead one to generalization of results. Thus, we realize more emphasis on the empirical validity has to be taken in this field of academic interest.

Acknowledgments

A major part of this chapter was conducted whilst the author was pursuing his Ph.D in Universiti Putra Malaysia. The author is grateful to Professor Ahmad Zubaidi Baharumshah and his Ph.D committee members for their guidance, comments and suggestions throughout the period. Comments and suggestions from the seminar participants at the first Asia Pacific Economic and Business Conference (APEB), Kuching (2002) are gratefully acknowledged.

Notes

1. In the period 1980-1985, budget deficit in US rose from $74 billion to a total of $212 billion in 1985. In the same period, US real as well as nominal exchange rate depreciated. The depreciation leads to deterioration in current account balance from a surplus of $6.0 billion in 1980 to a deficit of $124 billion by the year 1985. It is widely believed that the US current account deficit rose mainly because of the skyrocketing in budget deficit.
2. Milesi-Ferretti and Razin (1996) and Monetary Authority of Singapore (1997) pointed out that the presence of budget deficit is also an explanation for the current account deficits in most of the ASEAN countries. Moreover, in the 1980s and early 1990s, ASEAN countries experienced budget deficits, except for Singapore, thus, their fiscal position had more or less generated to the current account deficit. Therefore, the choice of the countries in this chapter is not without merit.
3. Singapore is the only country in the sample that appears to be unaffected by the crisis. It is now facing problems with the electronic exports as an outcome of the economic slowdown in the United States.
4. The papers by Lau *et al.* (2002) and Corsetti *et al.* (1999) among others, provided evidence that the current account acts as a propagation in the financial crisis but did not discuss on the source of the problem.
5. Anoruo and Ramchander look at the case of Indonesia and the Philippines while Khalid and Teo examine the case for Indonesia.
6. The importance of the mediating variables in the internal-external deficits nexus are discussed in Abell (1990) and Anoruo and Ramchander (1998).
7. Some earlier work that attempted to resolve the issue includes Hutchison and Pigott (1984) and Bachman (1992). These studies also identify a causal relationship running from budget to current account deficits.
8. For a comprehensive understanding on the Ricardian Equivalence Hypothesis (REH), interested reader could refer to Barro (1989) and Seater (1993).
9. The work by Islam (1998a) for Brazil, Anoruo and Ramchander (1998) for Philippines, India, Indonesia and Korea while Khalid and Teo (1999) for Indonesia and Pakistan also supports this hypothesis.
10. For the bidirectional causal relationship between the two variables, one may refer to Darrat (1988) and Normandin (1999). The work by Darrat found a feedback relationship between government deficit and trade balance. Other variables (money stock, inflation and interest rates) were shown not to have causal link with trade balance.

11. Haug (1996) and Cardia (1997) found a contrast perspectives of the REH in which he nested Ricardian equivalence within a non-Ricardian equivalence. There is low correlation between the two series for the both nested and non-nested hypothesis. Moreover, they did not supports any testable hypothesis presented above.
12. Model 1 = standard cointegration, Model 2 = level shift (C), Model 3 = level shift with trend (C/T) and Model 4 = regime shift (C/S). We followed Gregory and Hansen (1996) to compute the ADF statistics for each breakpoint in the interval, 0.15T to 0.85T (where T is the number of observations). We chose the breakpoint associated with the smallest value as that point at which the structural break occurred.
13. They proven that in the integrated and cointegrated system, the WALD test for restrictions on the parameters of a VAR(k) has an asymptotic χ^2 distribution when a VAR ($k + d_{max}$) is estimated, where d_{max} is the maximum order of integration suspected to occur in the system.
14. The short-term nominal interest rate used are as follow: Malaysia, the Philippines and Singapore–3 month treasury bill rates, Indonesia-interbank call loan rates while discount rates for Thailand.
15. The multivariate generalization of AIC remains the best performing criterion as the system dimension increases (see Gonzalo and Pitarakis, 2002).
16. The correction factor suggested is to multiply the test statistic by *(T-pk)/T*, where T is the sample size, p is the number of variables, and k is the lag length for the VAR model.
17. We caution the reader that this finding do not contradict with the REH (of no clear relationship between the internal and external deficits) because the model adopted in our analysis does not allow for the direct test of Ricardian hypothesis.

Table 7.1 Johansen Multivariate Cointegration Results

A: Indonesia

Null	Alternative	k=4 r=1					
		λmax			Trace		
		Unadjusted	Adjusted	95 percent C.V.	Unadjusted	Adjusted	95 percent C.V.
r = 0	r = 1	42.103*	35.36*	31.000	69.668*	59.521*	58.930
r<= 1	r = 2	15.314	12.838	24.350	27.564	23.154	39.330
r<=2	r = 3	10.472	8.796	18.330	12.250	10.290	23.830
r<=3	r = 4	1.778	1.493	11.540	1.778	1.493	11.540

B: Malaysia

Null	Alternative	k=3 r=1					
		λmax			Trace		
		Unadjusted	Adjusted	95 percent C.V.	Unadjusted	Adjusted	95 percent C.V.
r = 0	r = 1	49.159*	42.604*	23.920	66.576*	56.832*	39.810
r<= 1	r = 2	8.638	7.486	17.680	17.417	15.095	24.050
r<=2	r = 3	7.229	6.266	11.030	8.7788	7.608	12.360
r<=3	r = 4	1.549	1.342	4.160	1.549	1.342	4.160

C: Philippines

Null	Alternative	k=5 r=0					
		λmax			Trace		
		Unadjusted	Adjusted	95 percent C.V.	Unadjusted	Adjusted	95 percent C.V.
r = 0	r = 1	20.970	16.550	27.100	39.080	30.860	47.200
r<= 1	r = 2	15.280	12.060	21.000	18.120	14.300	29.700
r<=2	r = 3	2.828	2.233	14.100	2.839	2.242	15.400
r<=3	r = 4	0.011	0.009	3.800	0.011	0.009	3.800

Table 7.1 (continued)

D: Singapore							
Null	Alternative	k=5 r=0					
		λmax			Trace		
		Unadjusted	Adjusted	95 percent C.V.	Unadjusted	Adjusted	95 percent C.V.
r = 0	r = 1	19.8400	15.660	27.100	44.460	35.100	47.200
r<= 1	r = 2	16.830	13.290	21.000	24.630	19.440	29.700
r<=2	r = 3	7.553	5.963	14.100	7.797	6.156	15.400
r<=3	r = 4	0.244	0.193	3.800	0.244	0.193	3.800
E: Thailand							
Null	Alternative	k=5 r=1					
		λmax			Trace		
		Unadjusted	Adjusted	95 percent C.V.	Unadjusted	Adjusted	95 percent C.V.
r = 0	r = 1	42.993*	34.395*	23.920	59.035*	47.228*	39.810
r<= 1	r = 2	13.089	10.471	17.680	16.042	12.8336	24.050
r<=2	r = 3	2.434	1.947	11.030	2.9532	2.363	12.360
r<=3	r = 4	0.519	0.415	4.160	0.519	0.415	4.160

Notes: Asterisk (*) denotes statistically significant at 5 percent level. The k is the lag length and r is the cointegrating vector(s).

Table 7.2 Test of Exclusion Restrictions

	Indonesia	Malaysia	Philippines	Singapore	Thailand
	χ^2-statistics (p-value)				
CAD	4.971(0.026)*	17.912(0.000)*	-	-	25.331(0.000)*
BD	7.279(0.007)*	38.541(0.000)*	-	-	18.618(0.000)*
IR	9.908(0.002)*	23.759(0.000)*	-	-	12.914(0.000)*
EX	10.837(0.001)*	28.035(0.000)*	-	-	8.127(0.004)*

Notes: Asterisk (*) denotes statistically significant at 5 percent level.

Table 7.3 Gregory-Hansen Cointegration Tests

Country	C	C/T	C/S
Indonesia	-9.980*	-8.837*	-5.546
	(1981:4)	(1981:4)	(1987:1)
Malaysia	-5.293*	-5.083	-7.829*
	(1980:4)	(1986:4)	(1987:2)
Philippines	-5.631*	-5.470	-3.024
	(1986:4)	(1986:4)	(1986:4)
Singapore	-2.099	-6.487*	-12.419*
	(1986:4)	(1987:1)	(1986:4)
Thailand	-4.456	-3.003	-6.199*
	(1979:3)	(1981:1)	(1985:4)

Notes: Asterisk (*) denote statistically significant at 5 percent level.

Table 7.4 Toda-Yamamoto Test Results

	Indonesia (n=100) k=4 d=1	Malaysia (n=90) k=3 d=1	Philippines (n=100) k=5 d=1	Singapore (n=100) k=5 d=1	Thailand (n=100) k=5 d=1
			χ^2-statistics (p-value)		
A: CAD/GDP equation:					
Null Hypothesis					
BD does not cause CAD	1.992 (0.574)	8.263 (0.041)*	12.358 (0.030)*	12.991 (0.023)*	12.140 (0.032)*
IR does not cause CAD	6.097 (0.107)	2.694 (0.441)	3.843 (0.572)	10.244 (0.068)	13.615 (0.018)*
EX does not cause CAD	11.359 (0.010)*	16.294 (0.001)*	13.693 (0.017)*	19.518 (0.001)*	28.779 (0.000)*
B: BD/GDP equation:					
Null Hypothesis					
CAD does not cause BD	8.816 (0.032)*	10.714 (0.013)*	14.838 (0.011)*	8.729 (0.120)	7.823 (0.166)
IR does not cause BD	23.583 (0.000)*	0.647 (0.885)	8.502 (0.131)	41.890 (0.000)*	3.776 (0.582)
EX does not cause BD	8.293 (0.040)*	27.973 (0.000)*	6.749 (0.239)	12.557 (0.027)*	4.033 (0.545)

Notes: Figures in the parentheses are the p-value. Asterisk (*) denotes statistically significant at 5 percent level. k = optimum lag and d = maximal order of integration.

References

Abell, J. (1990), 'Twin Deficits during the 1980s: An Empirical Investigation', *Journal of Macroeconomics*, vol.12, pp. 81-96.

Akbostanci, E. and Tunc, G. İ. (2001), 'Turkish Twin Deficits: An Error Correction Model of Trade Balance', Economic Research Center (ERC) Working Papers in Economics No. 6.

Alkswani, M.A. (2000), 'The Twin Deficits Phenomenon in Petroleum Economy: Evidence from Saudi Arabia', Presented in Seventh Annual Conference, Economic Research Forum (ERF), 26-29 October, Amman, Jordan.

Anoruo, E. and Ramchander, S. (1998), 'Current Account and Fiscal Deficits: Evidence from Five Developing Economies of Asia', *Journal of Asian Economics*, vol. 9, 487-501.

Bachman, D. D. (1992), 'Why is the US Current Account Deficit so Large? Evidence from Vector Autoregressions', *Southern Economic Journal*, vol. 59, pp. 232-240.

Baharumshah, A. Z. and Rashid, S. (1999), 'Exports, Imports and Economic Growth in Malaysia: Empirical Evidence Based on Multivariate Time Series', *Asian Economic Journal*, vol. 13, pp. 389-406.

Baharumshah, A. Z. (2001), 'The Effect of Exchange Rate on Trade Balance: The Experience Based on Two Neighboring ASEAN Countries', *Asian Economic Journal*, vol. 15, pp. 291-312.

Barro, R. J. (1974), 'Are Government Bonds Net Wealth?', *Journal of Political Economy*, vol. 82, pp. 1095-1117.

Barro, R. J. (1989), 'The Ricardian Approach to Budget Deficits', *Journal of Economic Perspectives*, vol. 3, pp. 37-54.

Buchanan, J. M. (1976), 'Barro on the Ricardian Equivalence Theorem', *Journal of Political Economy*, vol. 84, pp. 337-342.

Campbell, J. Y. and Perron, P. (1991), 'Pitfalls and Opportunities: What Macroeconomists Should Know About Unit Roots', in O. J. Blanchard and S. Fischer (eds), *National Bureau of Economic Research Macroeconomics Annual*, MIT Press, Cambridge, pp. 144-201.

Cardia, E. (1997), 'Replicating Ricardian Equivalence Tests with Simulated Series', *American Economic Review*, vol. 87, pp. 65-79.

Cheung, Y. W. and Lai K. S. (1993), 'Finite-sample Sizes of Johansen's Likelihood Ratio Tests for Cointegration', *Oxford Bulletin of Economics and Statistics*, vol. 55, pp. 313-328.

Corsetti, G., Pesenti, P. and Roubini, N. (1999), 'What Caused the Asian Currency and Financial Crisis?', *Japan and World Economy*, vol. 11, pp. 305-373.

Darrat, A. F. (1988), 'Have Large Budget Deficits Caused Rising Trade Deficits?', *Southern Economic Journal*, vol. 54, pp. 879-886.

Dickey, D. A. and Fuller, W. A. (1981), 'Likelihood Ratio Statistics for Autoregressive Time Series With a Unit Root', *Econometrica*, vol. 49, pp. 1057-1072.

Enders, W. and Lee, B. S. (1990), 'Current Account and Budget Deficits: Twins or Distant Cousins?', *The Review of Economics and Statistics*, vol. 72, 373-381.

Evans P. and Hasan, I. (1994), 'Are Consumers Ricardian? Evidence for Canada', *Quarterly Review of Economics and Finance*, vol. 34, pp. 25-40.

Fountas, S. and Tsoukis, C. (2000), 'Twin Deficits, Real Interest Rates and International Capital Mobility', Department of Economics, National University of Ireland, Working Paper No. 49.

Gandolfo, G. (1981), *Quantitative Analysis and Econometric Estimation of Continuous Time Dynamic*, North-Holland Publishing Company Amsterdam.

Gregory, A. W. and Hansen, B. E. (1996), 'Residual-Based Tests for Cointegration in Models with Regime Shifts', *Journal of Econometrics*, vol. 70, pp. 99-126.

Gonzalo, J. and Pitarakis, J. I. (2002), 'Lag Length Estimation in Large Dimensional Systems', *Journal of Time Series Analysis*, vol. 23, pp. 401-423.

Haug, A. A. (1996), 'Blanchard's Model of Consumption: An Empirical Study', *Journal of Business and Economic Statistics*, vol. 14, pp. 169-177.

Hutchison, M. M. and Pigott, C. (1984), 'Budget Deficits, Exchange Rates and Current Account: Theory and U.S. Evidence', *Federal Reserve Bank of San Francisco Economic Review*, vol. 4, pp. 5-25.

Ibrahim, S. B. and Kumah, F. Y. (1996), 'Comovements in Budget Deficits, Money, Interest Rate, Exchange Rate and the Current Account Balance: Some Empirical Evidence', *Applied Economics*, vol. 28, pp. 117-130.

Islam M. F. (1998a), 'Brazil's Twin Deficits: An Empirical Examination', *Atlantic Economic Journal*, vol. 26, pp. 121-128.

Islam, M. N. (1998b), 'Export Expansion and Economic Growth: Testing for Cointegration and Causality', *Applied Economics*, vol. 30, pp. 415-425.

Johansen, S. and Juselius, K. (1990), 'Maximum Likelihood Estimated and Inference on Cointegration with Application to the Demand for Money', *Oxford Bulletin of Economics and Statistics*, vol. 52, pp. 169-210.

Khalid, A. M. and Teo W. G. (1999), 'Causality Tests of Budget and Current Account Deficits: Cross-Country Comparisons', *Empirical Economics*, vol. 24, pp. 389-402.

Kwiatkowski, D., Phillips, P. C. B. Schmidt, P. and Shin, Y. (1992), 'Testing the Null Hypothesis of Stationarity Against the Alternative of a Unit Root. How Sure Are We that Economic Time Series Have a Unit Root?', *Journal of Econometrics,* vol. 54, pp. 159-178.

Laney, L. (1984), 'The Strong Dollar, the Current Account and Federal Deficits: Cause and Effect', *Federal Reserve Bank of Dallas Economic Review*, January, pp. 1-14.

Lau, E., Baharumshah, A. Z. and Fountas, S. (2002), 'On the Sustainability of Current Account Deficits in ASEAN-4 Countries', Department of Economics, National University of Ireland, Working Paper No. 62.

Mackinnon, J. G. (1991), 'Critical Values for Cointegration Tests', in R. F. Engle and C. W. J. Granger (eds), *Long-Run Economic Relationship: Reading in Cointegration,* Oxford: Oxford University Press, pp. 267-276.

Milesi-Ferretti, G. M. and Razin, A. (1996), 'Current Account Sustainability: Selected East Asian and Latin American Experiences', National Bureau of Economic Research (NBER) Working Paper No. 5791.

Miller, S. M. and Russek, F. S. (1989), 'Are the Twin Deficits Really Related?', *Contemporary Policy Issues*, vol. 7, pp. 91-115.

Monetary Authority of Singapore (1997), 'Current Account Deficits in the ASEAN-3. Is there Cause for Concern?', Occasional paper, No. 1.

Normandin, M. (1999), 'Budget Deficit Persistence and the Twin Deficits Hypothesis', *Journal of International Economics*, vol. 49, pp. 171-193.

Osterwald-Lenum, M. (1992), 'A Note with Quantiles of the Asymptotic Distribution of Maximum Likelihood Cointegration Rank Test Statistic', *Oxford Bulletin of Economics and Statistics,* vol. 54, pp. 461-472.

Ostry, J. D. (1997), 'Current Account Imbalances in ASEAN Countries: Are They a Problem?', IMF Working Paper No. 51.

Piersanti, G. (2000), 'Current Account Dynamics and Expected Future Budget Deficits: Some International Evidence', *Journal of International Money and Finance*, vol. 19, pp. 255-271.

Rambaldi, A. N. and Doran, H. (1996), 'Testing for Granger Non-Causality in Cointegrated Systems Made Easy', Department of Econometrics, University of New England, Working Paper in Econometrics and Applied Statistics No.88.

Reimers, H. E. (1992), 'Comparison of Tests for Multivariate Cointegration', *Statistical Papers*, vol. 33, pp. 335-359.

Reinsel, G. C. and Ahn S. K. (1992), 'Vector AR Models with Unit Roots and Reduced Rank Structure: Estimation, Likelihood Ratio Test and Forecasting', *Journal of Time Series Analysis,* vol. 13, pp. 353-375.

Reisen, H. (1998), 'Sustainable and Excessive Current Account Deficits', OECD Development Centre, Technical Paper No. 132.

Said, E. S. and D. A. Dickey (1984), 'Testing for Unit Roots in Autoregressive-Moving Average Models of Unknown Order', vol. *Biometrika,* vol. 71, pp. 599-607.

Seater, J. J. (1993), 'Ricardian Equivalence', *Journal of Economic Literature*, vol. 31, 142-190.

Summers, L. H. (1988), 'Tax Policy and International Competitiveness', in J. Frenkel (eds), *International Aspects of Fiscal Policies*, Chicago: Chicago UP, pp. 349-375.

Toda, H. Y. and T. Yamamoto (1995), 'Statistical Inference in Vector Autoregressive with Possibly Integrated Processes', *Journal of Econometric*, vol. 66, pp. 225-250.

Vamvoukas, G. A. (1999), 'The Twin Deficits Phenomenon: Evidence from Greece', *Applied Economics*, vol. 31, pp. 1093-1100.

Chapter 8

Financial Integration of East Asia: Is There a Yen Block?

Ahmad Zubaidi Baharumshah and Goh Wee Keat

Introduction

The East Asian economies namely, Japan, Hong Kong, Malaysia, Singapore, South Korea, Taiwan, Thailand, Indonesia and the Philippines have taken major steps to deregulate and liberalise their financial markets. Hong Kong and Singapore were the first to begin liberalising by removing or relaxing interest rate regulation and abolishing exchange controls in the mid-1970s. Japan and Malaysia followed soon by taking major steps toward deregulating their financial markets in the late 1970s and the Philippines and Indonesia in the early 1980s.[1] The two newly industrialised economies (NIEs) of Taiwan and Korea took much longer time to allow market forces to play a greater role in financial market. The financial reforms were intended to promote greater economic efficiency and increase the pace of economic progress in these countries. A well-integrated financial market allows a country to smoothen its consumption and attract productivity-enhancing investment from abroad, and hence propelling economic growth. Financial integration adds depth and liquidity to domestic capital market and permits it to intermediation and risk diversification roles more efficiently. Financial liberalisation covered areas in exchange rate, interest rate, capital control, and current account convertibility (Moosa and Bhatti, 1997; Mussa *et al.*, 2000). Together with this move towards liberalisation, most of these Asian countries undertook measures to relax international capital controls.[2]

The Asian countries have achieved different levels of economic development. The dynamic economies of Taiwan, South Korea, Singapore, Malaysia and Thailand grew at a much faster pace than Indonesia and the Philippines.[3] A distinguishing characteristic of these economies is that they all have strong administrative controls of domestic financial markets, heavily managed exchange rate, high saving and investment rates, rapid growth of international trade and until 1997, an admirable degree of financial stability. Current Asian currency arrangements span the range from fixed to floating rates. Hong Kong dollar is peg to the US dollar under a currency board. The remaining currencies (Taiwan dollar, Korean won, Singapore dollar, Malaysian ringgit, Thailand baht, Indonesian rupiah and Philippine peso) are managed, but the intensity of the management has declined over time. The frequency of management ranges from Indonesia, where the authorities intervene continuously, to Malaysia where intervention is episodic although when it occurs it is often quite substantial. The movement of the Singapore dollar and the Korean won was more flexible, compared to the other currencies, responding some to the Japanese yen movement. Generally speaking, the intensity of the managements has declined over time towards greater exchange rate flexibility (Moosa and Bhatti, 1997).

In the 1990s a number of studies have examine the role of the Japanese yen and US dollar in the East Asian countries (see Aggarwal and Mougoue, 1993, 1996; Chinn and Dooley, 1997; Frankel, 1993; Frankel and Wei, 1994; Moosa and Bhatti, 1997; Tse and Ng, 1997). The weight of the empirical evidence suggests that the East Asian countries are well integrated with the global financial markets. The present chapter focusses on the influence of yen in the East Asian countries and deals with two important issues. The first is to examine the relationship between the yen and other currencies of the East Asian by focusing on the dynamic linkages among the exchange rates. Specifically, the linkage between Japan and seven East Asian countries (Indonesia, Malaysia, Philippines, Singapore, South Korea, Taiwan and Thailand) is tested in an attempt to complement the empirical findings of earlier studies.[4] Unlike past studies that focus on the day-to day linkages among the currencies, this chapter extends the analysis to quarterly data in order to show the longer-term relationship among them.

The second aim of the chapter is to investigate the stability of the long-run relationship following several events that took place in the 1990s. We suspect that a number of events in the mid 1990s such as the Tequila crisis in Latin America initiated by the crash of Mexican peso in 1994, the appreciation of the U.S. dollar and the devaluation of the Chinese yuan during 1994-1996 period may have had some effect on the structure of these economies, and hence affect the interdependencies of these financial markets.[5] In addition, all the Asian economies were affected by the recent financial crisis. They suffered noticeable depreciation following the outbreak of the crisis in July 1997 but the extent of the slide differed from one country to another.[6] Hence, three sub-periods have been used in the analysis in order to better dissect the influence of the yen on these Asian currencies. Period 1 spans from 1978:1 to 1994:1; Period 2 covers from 1978:1 to 1996:2: Period 3 starts from 1978:1 and ends in 1998:3. The first sub-period excludes the turbulence during the 1994-96 period. The second sub-period includes the observation of 1994-96 but not he financial crisis. The third sub-sample includes observation covering the period after the crisis had subsided.

The present chapter is of interest for several reasons. First, we offer up-to date evidence on the existence of yen block in the Asian region that is based on the recent development in time-series econometrics. The time-series techniques include, multivariate cointegration, vector error correction modelling (VECM) and forecast variance decomposition (FEVD). Second, we examine the role of yen in the exchange rate policies of the selected countries to shed additional light on the issue of monetary cooperation and the usefulness of monetary policy in East Asia.

It has long been established that the extent of pursuing an independent domestic monetary policy by a country is limited when financial market is interrelated with the rest of world markets (see Moosa and Bhatti, 1997). Third, Malaysia and Singapore were the first to take major steps in deregulating their financial market while Taiwan and Korea took a little longer time to deregulate their financial markets. Government control can retard the development and financial intermediation and led to market inefficiencies. Hence, it is interesting to find out if the deregulation of the financial market was instrumental in making these markets more integrated, and by using variance decomposition we intend to show how foreign innovations may affect the movements of Asian currencies. Finally, evidence in favour of yen block may provide useful information to portfolio managers and businesses on how they can manage exchange rate risk. As pointed by Gray (1991) and Aggarwal and Mougoue (1996), evidence of cointegration of the minor currencies with a major currency may suggest a means of cross hedging with more liquid currencies.

Review of the Relevant Literature

Several authors have used the convergence of exchange rates to investigate financial integration in Asian countries. For instance, Aggarwal and Mougoue (1993) in an attempt to seek for the existence of a 'yen bloc' used the time-series stochastic behaviour and cointegration of five Asian currencies (Japanese yen, Hong Kong dollar, Malaysian ringgit, Philippines peso, and Singapore dollar). Based on daily frequency exchange rates data from 27 September 1982 to 22 December 1989, they found strong evidence of a yen block. This finding is in sharp contrast with the earlier results found in Frankel (1993).

Aggarwal and Mougoue (1996) re-examined the long-run relationship of the Asian currencies. In this chapter the stochastic properties as well as the cointegrating relationship of exchange rates between Japanese yen with two sets of Asian currencies were documented. The two sets of currencies consisted of (1) currencies of the Asian Tigers Hong Kong, South Korea, Singapore, and Taiwan, and (2) currencies of ASEAN, Malaysia, Philippines, Thailand, and Singapore. The sample period for the daily exchange rates covered from October 1983 to February 1992. In contrast to their earlier work, the possibility of structural break is taken into account using the procedure advocated by Park and Sung (1994). A structural break that coincided with the October 1987 stock market crash was detected and based on this result further analysis we concludes on two sub-periods. They showed that influence Japanese yen in the two-five dimensional systems of exchange rates has increased importance relative to the US dollar. They concluded that intra-Asia trade and investment flows have increased significantly in recent years. The strong currency linkages between Japan and Asian coupled with increasing intra-Asia trade and investments may be indicative of the quest of trading and currency block in Asia lead by Japan which is quietly forming.

Tse and Ng (1997) pointed out that the inclusion of Hong Kong dollar in the set of exchange rates may be inappropriate as the currency has been pegged to U.S. dollar and countries like South Korea and Taiwan that have close trade relationship with Japan should be included in the analysis. In this chapter, seven Asian currencies were considered: Japanese yen, Malaysian ringgit, Philippines peso, Singapore dollar, Thailand baht, South Korean won, and Taiwan dollar. To compare the results with the earlier article by Aggarwal and Mougoue (1993), they disaggregate the sample period into two sub-periods. The first sub-period corresponded with Aggarwal and Mougoue (1993), September 1982 to December 1989 and the second period ended in 30 June 1994. Contrary to the work by Aggarwal and Mougoue (1996), they found that if South Korean won and Taiwan dollar are excluded from the set of currencies, the evidence is not in favour of yen-dominated Asian exchange rate system. This finding illustrates the importance of these two economies in the Asian financial system. They also indicated that the number of cointegrating vectors increased when sample period includes the 1990s. Based on this observation, Tse and Ng concluded that the interdependence of Asian economies has increased with Japan as one moves to the present.

The relationship between real exchange rates in the Asian region has been investigated by Baharumshah and Ariff (1997), Aggarwal *et al.* (2000) and Azali *et al.* (2001), among others. Aggarwal *et al.* (2000) by taking into account of the possibility of structural breaks in the time series of real exchange rates find strong evidence of long-run quasi purchasing power parity (PPP) for most of ASEAN currencies in term of the Japanese yen. However, the evidence of PPP is much weaker when the US dollar, German mark and Australian dollar are used as numeraire.[7] These results allow them to conclude that there is evidence of yen block in the Asian region. Further tests conducted by Azali *et al.* (2001) using panel unit root tests and panel cointegration techniques find support for PPP when Japan is used as the base country. They provide evidence that real exchange rate was mean reverting for a panel of seven Asian developing countries. Again these papers were in favor of the yen block in the NICs and ASEAN countries. It is note worthy to point out here that earlier studies that used US as the reference country to test for PPP hypothesis found that PPP relationship does not hold for most of these countries (see for example, Baharumshah and Ariff, 1997). The results of all these studies tend to suggest economic integration is a consequence of regional integration policies.

Methodology

This chapter employed tests of unit root and cointegration tests to uncover the long-run and short-run dynamics relationship of the Asian currencies markets.

Tests for unit root are performed to identify the stationarity and order of integration of the series. For this purpose, we relied on standard augmented Dickey-Fuller (ADF) and Phillips-Perron (PP) tests. For the ADF tests, special attention was given to the selection of lag length, as different lag length often yield conflicting outcome. In this chapter, the procedure proposed by Campbell and Perron (1991) was adopted to identify the appropriate lag length, k. Following Campbell and Perron, we start with an upper bound of $k = 8$. If the maximum lag length eight is significant (at 10 percent level of significance), than this particular lag length is chosen. Otherwise, the lag length is reduced until the last lag becomes significant. In cases where none of the coefficients on the lagged variables are significant, no lags are used in the tests (DF). This procedure has better size and power properties than the alternative methods such as Akaike Information Criteria (AIC) or Bayesian Information Criteria (BIC) (Campbell and Perron, 1991). The PP test statistics reported in this chapter are based on the truncation lag indicated by Newey-West correction (see Newey and West, 1987).

The Johansen (1988) and Johansen and Juselius (1990) maximum likelihood method is employed to determine whether nominal exchange rates are cointegrated or not, by identifying the number of cointegrating vectors in the exchange rate system. If a set of variables (e.g., exchange rates of Asian countries) is cointegrated then, although each series may be individually nonstationary, there must exist at least one linear combination that is stationary. This linear combination can be thought of as a long-run relationship towards which there is a continual mutual tendency of the variables to adjust- in other words the series tend to move together over time (see Engle and Granger, 1987).

The vector error correction model (VECM) is utilized to seek the long-run and short-run relationship embedded in the system of exchange rates. The VECM is also more superior than standard Granger-causality for two reasons. First, it is possible to find no causal relationship between two variables that are cointegrated if the standard Granger causality is used. In contrast, the VECM approach allows for detection of a Granger causal relation from explanatory variables to dependent variable, even when the coefficients on the lagged difference terms of the dependent variables in right hand side of the equation are not jointly significance. Second, the VECM approach reintroduces any information lost in the differencing process, which allowed for long-run equilibrium and short-run dynamics (Miller, 1981). If the F-test shows that the difference explanatory variable is significant, this would imply the presence of short-term causal effect. Whilst when the lagged error-correction term(s) is found to be significant under the t-test, this would indicates the existence of long-term Granger causality between dependent variable with explanatory variables (Cheng, 1999).[8]

The inferences made from VECM however maybe interpret as within-sample causality tests. In other words, it indicates the Granger-exogeneity or endogeneity of the eight Asian exchange rates within the sample period. However, the Granger causality fails to provide information regarding the relative strength of the Granger-causal chain amongst the variables beyond the sample period (Masih and Masih, 1996). To provide the dynamic properties of the VECM, the Forecast Error Variance Decomposition (FEVD) is normally conducted. FEVD indicates the properties of the movements in a sequence due to its "own" shock versus shocks to others variables. If the shocks brought by others variables explain none of the forecast error of that particular sequence at all forecast horizons, it could be interpret as the investigated sequence is exogenous and it would evolve independently of the other variables' shocks (Enders, 1995).

For testing financial integration, we defined X=[YEN, SD, RM, PP, RP, TB, KW, NT]. The data set consists of quarterly frequency data for eight currencies: Yen, Singapore dollar (SD), ringgit Malaysia (RM), Philippines peso (PP), Indonesia rupiah (RP), Thailand bath (TB), Korean won (KW) and Taiwan dollar (NT). The sampling period starts from 1978:1 and ends in 1998:1, to capture the 1997 Asian financial crisis. The nominal exchange rate is expressed as a unit pf local currency per US dollar4. All the series are expressed in logarithm form. The data is collected from *International Financial Statistics* (Monthly Editions) published by International Monetary Fund (IMF).

Empirical Results

Unit root tests were performed first on model without time trend and then with trend for the three sub-periods. All series are transformed into logarithm form before conducting the unit root tests. For the first sub-period (1978:1 to 1994:1), the results of ADF provide no evidence against unit root hypothesis in all except for the Malaysian ringgit (RM) and Korean won (KW) (at 5 percent level of significance). For Taiwan, the unit root hypothesis could not be rejected even after first differencing, suggesting that the currency could be integrated of higher order (e.g. *I(2)*). The unit root test results for second sub-period too produced similar outcome, except for Malaysian Ringgit where the null hypothesis of integrated of order one could not be rejected. The results of PP unit root test suggest that null hypothesis of unit root could not be rejected for all exchange rate series but one (KW). The null hypothesis that the first difference of these series is non-stationary is, however, strongly rejected by the PP unit root test and to a large extent by ADF test. Similar results (not reported) were found for the full sample period.[9]

It is a widely acknowledged fact that the standard ADF and PP tests are not very informative to distinguish between a unit root and near unit root case. To address this issue, we adopt the approach advocated by Kwaitkowski *et al.* (1992) (KPSS). The KPSS tests assume the null is stationary and the alternative is that the variable does have a unit root. Table 8.1 presents the results of the KPSS tests for the full sample period. In all cases, the null is rejected in favour of the unit root hypothesis since the KPSS statistic is larger than the asymptotic critical values provided by KPSS. The results of KPSS tests confirm that all the series can be treated as *I(1)* process in their level: there is no variable which is *I(2)*. As the standard unit root tests are known to have low power against the alternative of trend stationarity, we relied on the KPSS statistics to arrive at the conclusion that each of the series is an *I(1)* process. Overall, these results are consistent with the earlier findings found in Aggarwal and Mougoue (1993,1996), Azali *et al.* (2001), and Tse and Ng (1997), among others. These results provide the requisite for the forthcoming multiple cointegration analysis.[10]

Next, the cointegration test is performed using the multivariate cointegration test developed by Johansen (1988) and its extension in Johansen and Juselius (1990). The lag structure of the exchange rate system is set up through a search process using AIC with a potential lag length of one through seven (as the sample size permits only up to lag length of seven). The criteria yield a vector autoregressive (VAR) model of order 3. The system is constructed with three lags (k=3) and the initial results (not reported) of the cointegration tests indicate that hypothesis of no cointegration can be easily rejected in full sample period at conventional significance levels.[11] Hence our preliminary results suggested there are seven common stochastic trends driving the currency markets of these Asian countries.

We are aware that although the cointegration may exist among the eight Asian currencies not all of these currencies will enter the cointegration vector. To this purpose, we perform test of restriction on the β coefficient using the log-likelihood ratio (LR) test as described in Johansen (1988). The LR statistic is asymptotically distributed as χ^2 distribution with one degree of freedom in the present case. The null hypothesis is that the currency does not share common trend with the other currencies. The exclusion tests conducted on cointegrating parameter in three sample periods suggest that all except the Philippine peso and Korean won reject the hypothesis null of cointegrating parameter equal to zero. This finding implies that these two currencies could be excluded from the system of exchange rate series, as they do not belong to the system. The six-vector VAR model (YEN, SD, RM, RP, TB, NT) is re-estimated in order to perform the cointegration tests on the six remaining series. Results of the cointegration tests for the three sample periods (excluding the Philippines peso and Korean won) are shown in Table 8.2.

Both the maximum eigenvalue test and trace test rejected the null hypothesis of no cointegrating vector at 5 percent level of significance or better.[12] In addition, the exclusion test result failed to reject the null hypothesis of cointegrating parameter equal to zero for all six currencies. Both cointegration and exclusion tests suggest that the six exchange rates (YEN, SD, RM, RP, TB, NT) are cointegrated with a unique cointegrating vector. From statistical point of view when exchange rates form cointegrating relationship, it implies that one currency in the exchange rate system may be use to predict the other. In other words, movements in one of the currencies will reflect the other, perhaps suggesting that in the Asian countries currencies are driven by the same fundamental variables. The evidence suggests that the six bilateral rates are tied to the yen, at least in the long run. This finding is robust since it holds for all three sample periods and is consistent with the result reported by Aggarwal and Mougoue (1996), and Tse and Ng (1997).

To sum, three important conclusions can be draw from the results of the Johansen multivariate cointegration test. First, not all of the East Asia currencies form a cointegrating relationship has shown by the exclusion test. The empirical results suggest that while there is strong co-movement among the eight currencies but not all belong to the cointegrating relationship. Second, the Asian region remains largely unaffected by the events in 1994-95 that include "tequila" crisis, rise of US dollar and the devaluation of the Chinese yuan. Indeed, that financial integration among the six East Asian countries with Japan maybe traced back as early as late 1970s. We view this result as supporting the evidence that these currencies are driven by the same fundamental factors, which is primarily driven by the trade-investment nexus. Third, the long run relationship of these six Asian currencies remains stable even in the volatile currency crisis period.

As the presence of cointegrating vector had been ascertain, the next step would be identifying the direction of causality among the Asian currencies. Table 8.3 reports the results of the Granger-causality test, along with the respective t-test and F-test result for sample periods 1978:1-1994:1, 1978:1-1996:2 and 1978:1-1998:3. The adequacy of the model was determined through a battery of diagnostic tests. The diagnostic test shows no autocorrelation, no ARCH effect, no functional misspecification, and homoskedastic and normality residuals. The hypothesis that coefficient of error-correction term (α) is equal to zero is easily rejected for the Taiwan and Singapore equations in all sub-periods, and Malaysia for sub-period 3 (see Table 8.3), implying that the currency of these three countries endogenously react to past deviations from the cointegrating relationship and adjusts to restore the long-run equilibrium.

The small magnitude of the coefficient of the error-correction term indicates that the adjustment towards equilibrium is rather slow. Notice that speed of adjustment is much faster for case of Taiwan (9-10 percent) as compared to Singapore (4-7 percent). It is interesting to find that the speed of adjustment has increased somewhat when sample is extended to the post-crisis period.[13] The error-correction terms for the remaining countries (Indonesia and Thailand) are not statistically significant, suggesting that these exchange rates are weakly exogenous in both time period.[14] An important conclusion that can be drawn here is that the movement of the yen is not affected by most of the Asian currencies, except the more developed financial markets of Singapore (both in the short-run and long-run) and Taiwan (only in the long-run).

Short-run causal relationship is detected running from yen to the Indonesian rupiah and no other short-run channel is active except in the equation for Taiwan dollar (NT) for all the sub-periods. In addition, Singapore dollar is found to be granger cause by Malaysian Ringgit, Indonesian Rupiah, and Thailand bath in the whole sample period. We view this finding in itself as interesting since it supports the view that some of the Asian countries compete among themselves in the global market in order to be competitive. Notice also that the movements of the currencies of Malaysia, Indonesia and Thailand Granger cause the Taiwan dollar to move while yen and Singapore dollar causes the Taiwan dollar to move only in the long run. In other words, all the six currencies may be used to predict the Taiwan dollar. Taiwan dollar emerged as the most sensitive currency in the region. Similarly the same thing can be said about the Singapore dollar but the causal relationship holds only in the longer term through error-correction term. The results also show that there are close links between the yen and the Singapore dollar and between Singapore dollar and Taiwanese dollar as indicated by the feedback causal links. There is no evidence to suggest that changes in the Malaysian ringgit and Indonesian rupiah are caused by the Thai bath. Hence, ruling out the bath as the contagion factor in the ASEAN region. However, the empirical results support the view that the weaker ASEAN currencies as a contagion factor in the Asian region and that currency crisis spread to Japan via the Singapore dollar.

The methodology pursued thus far tells nothing about the way in which Asian currencies have affected the individual currencies. The FEVD analysis is conducted for all sample periods, and to conserve space only the results of the pre-crisis period (1978:1-1996:2) and the sample period that include the post-crisis period (1978:1-1998:3) are reported and discussed here.[15] It is well established that the results of FEVD based on Choleski decomposition are generally sensitive to the ordering of the variables (see, for example, Lutkepohl, 1991). To overcome this shortcoming we apply the generalized variance decomposition provided and applied by Lee *et al.* (1992), Lee and Pesaran (1993), Pesaran *et al.* (1993) and Pesaran and Shin (1998).

Results of the generalized FEVD from one-standard deviation shocks to each series over selected horizons from 1 to 24 quarters for the pre-crash period are given in Table 8.4. Table 8.4 may have several points bear noting: First, it appears that most of the variability in the ringgit (40-59 percent) and Singapore dollar (54-59 percent) is attributable to external shocks, perhaps indicating that these two countries have limited ability to control its exchange rates both in short and long run. Notice that after a 24-quarter horizon, variability due to its own shock account for only about 41 percent of the variation. This result coincides with our expectation since these two ASEAN were among the earliest to reform their financial markets. In Indonesia and Taiwan, the influence of foreign shocks is relative small, less than 30 percent at a horizon of 8-quarters. Indonesia appears to be the most exogenous in the system as most of its shock is explained by its own innovation. Notice that the influence of foreign shocks (mainly Japan) tends to increase with time horizon.

Second, all the Asian currencies are influenced by the shocks originating form Japan. Indeed, the yen is the most important source of foreign shocks in all the sample countries except for one (Malaysia). The strong influence of the yen on the Taiwan dollar (Singapore dollar) and vice versa suggests that the two high performing countries place more emphasis on export expansion. In other words, the yen is perceived as the currency of a competitor country in the exports market by the two NIEs. The currencies of the two NIEs were built on large foreign exchange surplus and they have appreciated against the yen gradually until the crisis hit the region. However, the impact of the other Asian countries on the yen is generally more modest or insignificant even in the long run (e.g. in the case of the rupiah it is less than 1 percent).

Third, among the six currencies, the Indonesia rupiah seems to be least affected by foreign. As indicates in Table 8.4, only about 18 percent of the variation in the rupiah is attributed to foreign shocks even after 24-quarter horizon. In the short-run the rupiah appears not to be affected by the foreign rates, reflecting the attempt by the monetary authority to limit changes in exchange rate. This accords with the fact that monetary authority in Indonesia tends to emphasise price stability in the short-run. Fourth, the interconnectness between the ringgit, Singapore's dollar, and the bath is fairly strong. The results also suggest that Taiwan dollar (perhaps Korean won) are important to the ASEAN countries. Thus, it is consistent with the notion that intra-regional integration among the Asian countries (Japan excluded) has increased.

Finally, the FEVD for period 1978:1-1998:3 are computed and the results are presented in Table 8.5. Overall, the results indicate that the proportion of exchange rate movements that can be explained by its own shocks (or the degree of exogeneity) has been significantly reduced. The degree of exogeneity in Indonesia, Taiwan and Malaysia increases that most (51, 44 and 25 percent respectively). This suggests that these economies actively responded to the other East Asian country's innovation following the period of the currency turmoil. In other word, no country in the sample is exogenous to the currency crisis. Even in the short horizon, very little of the forecast variance in exchange rate is caused by its own innovations. It is particularly interesting to note that Japanese influence is greatest on Taiwan and Singapore while Taiwan has a bigger influence in Malaysia, Thailand and Indonesia. The Japanese yen will response more to innovations in Singapore dollar rather than those of the other Asian currencies.

Summary and Policy Conclusions

In this chapter, we utilized the theory of cointegration to investigate the influence of yen and interdependence among the Asian currencies. The basis is that convergence between two currencies means that they cannot drift apart in the long run and hence have to be cointegrated. The empirical results provide some further evidence that the currencies of Indonesia, Malaysia, Singapore, Taiwan, Thailand, and Japan are cointegrated over the 1978-1998 period, implying that these currencies are closely related in the long run. Hence, there exists an underlying equilibrium relationship binding these six currencies, perhaps suggesting that the set of nominal currencies is driven by the same fundamental. In this regard, our results mirror the existing literature (Aggarwal and Mougoue, 1993, 1996; Tse and Ng, 1997; Chinn and Dooley, 1997, 1999; Moosa and Bhatti, 1997). Indeed, they all have interpreted this finding as plausible sign of yen block formation in the region. In this chapter, we showed that the result holds regardless of the sampling period. This is because of the massive and growing trade integration with Japan and their trading relationship with each other. Indeed, Kwan (2000) finds that for the last two decades intra-trade (including Japan) has raised mush faster than trade with the US. Now, about 50 percent of gross East Asian exports end up in the Japanese market. Tavlas and Ozeki (1992) examined the role of yen in the region concluded that Asian central banks increased their holdings of yen and the yen is also being used more widely to invoice trader and finance in Asia. Together, we find these explanations fit well with the notion of the formation of a yen block.

The following conclusions that may be drawn about the East Asian currencies: First, contrary to the findings found in earlier papers, we showed that the Philippines peso and Korean won do not belong to the cointegrating relationship. The exclusion of the peso and won contradicted the findings by Aggarwal and Mougoue (1993, 1996), Tse and Ng (1997), Chinn and Dooley (1997, 1999), but not for Moosa and Bhatti (1997) where they showed that the peso is not financially cointegrated with the other Asian countries. The exclusion of peso from the system may rest on its unstable political climate. Specifically, Zhou (1996) has identified several economic and political events that have made Philippines economy more turbulent as compared to its counterparts in East Asia. In addition, the currency market of the Philippines had also experienced shuffle and disturbances, including adjustments and change of fixed to floating system (Houben, 1997). Similarly, South Korea also experienced political and civil unrest after the assassination of President Park in 1979. Park's successor pursued a restrictive policy on foreign holdings of many types of financial instrument to maintain domestic control over monetary policy (Moreno, 1993). Another reason for the Korean won not sharing a common trend with the other Asian countries is the closed nature of the financial markets in Korea and may partly explained why its financial market is segmented with the other East Asia counterparts, including Japan. It is note worthy to point out that several author that focus on the integration of Asian equity markets have also found that the Korean market is far from conclusive (see e.g. Faruqee, 1992; Dooley and Mathieson, 1994; Reisen and Yeches, 1993). Most have pointed out that the probable cause is due to the closedness of the Korean economy. The regulations and imperfections are often sited as the cause of information to disseminated less efficiently than with those with less stringent markets. We find this explanation to be plausible.

Second, the evidence suggests that macroeconomic shocks experienced in 1994-1996 (the Mexico tequila crisis, rise of U.S. dollar, devaluation of yuan) have not distorted the yen's influence in the region. We showed that the relationship remained unaffected by including and excluding periods during these episodes.

One plausible reason for this convergent movement in exchange rates is that using the quarterly frequency data in the analysis could have averaged out shocks from these events. Besides the temporal aggregation, we also cannot over rule the fact that these events are not important to the region. For instance, the actual nominal exchange rate devaluation of the yuan was much smaller than implied by the official exchange rate devaluation, primarily because it merely unified the prevailing dual exchange rates in that period. China's devaluation was not important economic event as the strong export performance following the devaluation was matched by the other Asian economies (Fernald *et al.*, 1999).

Third, some high performance countries (Taiwan and Singapore) perceived the yen as a competitor currency in the international markets and therefore follow the yen up and down. For instance, the empirical result suggest that the yen is likely to follow the Taiwan (or Singapore) dollar and vice versa. The two currencies are highly correlated with the yen. This observation is consistent with the emphasis placed on export expansion by the two NIC. On the other hand, the empirical results suggest that high inflation countries like Indonesia paid little attention to the movement of yen in the short run, in the pre-crisis period. This accords with the view that the monetary authority in Indonesia emphasised more on domestic price stability rather than on competitiveness of their exports during the pre-crisis period.

The results from this chapter have several important policy conclusions. The East Asian countries financial markets are highly integrated with their trading partners, implying that they no longer can isolate the domestic economy from external shocks. Hence, the scope to pursue an independent monetary policy appears to be quite limited for most of the East Asian countries in the long run. Cointegrating relationship of minor currencies with major currency may suggest a means of cross hedging with more liquid currencies. Hence the yen (or Singapore dollar) could be use by business to hedge against exchange rate risk. This is important as it is well known that most of the forward markets in the Asian countries have not gained sufficient experience to function efficiently in the price discovery role due to liquidity problems.

Notes

1. For example, with the implementation of the 1980 Foreign Exchange and Foreign Trade Control Law, most of the capital control in Japan was eliminated.
2. This point is illustrated by the recent events in the region. For instance, the five East Asian countries of Indonesian, Malaysia, the Philippines, South Korea and Thailand received a substantial inflow of private capital until 1996 (US$97.1 billion). This suddenly reversed into an outflow of US$11.9 billion by July 1997.
3. The Philippines has had the consistently the slowest GNP growth rates among the East Asian countries.
4. We have excluded China and Hong Kong from the analysis for these reasons. China's currency remains inconvertible and its currency appears to hold within a wide fluctuation band and is significantly realigned from time to time. Hong Kong is excluded from the analysis because it adopted a strong form of currency board and the Hong Kong dollar has been effectively fixed to the U.S. dollar since October 1983.
5. Most of the East Asian economies experienced investment boom due to the high domestic saving rates and large capital inflows. China devalued its currency by 35 percent in early 1994 and the dollar appreciated globally after mid-1995 as the yen weakened. Together these forces adversely affect the competitiveness position of these countries.
6. Following the crisis, the value of the Indonesian rupiah depreciated to a level one-sixth of the pre-crisis level, and other ASEAN countries and the Korean won depreciated to the level half of the pre-crisis level.
7. Aggarwal *et al.* (2000) pointed out that earlier studies failed to support the PPP relationship due to lack of power in the classical unit root tests. To enhance the power of these statistical tests, they have made allowance for some structural breaks in the series. Their results showed evidence of mean reversion with mean exhibiting some shifts and termed this phenomenon as quasi PPP.
8. The non-significance of the error-correction term is equivalent to say that the variable is weakly exogenous with respect to long run parameters. The absence of short run causality (Granger causality in the strict sense) is established from the non-significance of the sums of lags of each explanatory variables. Finally, the non-significance of all the explanatory variables including the error-correction term indicates the econometric strong exogeneity of the dependent variable.
9. The computed ADF and PP statistics for the all periods are not reported here to conserve space but they are available upon request from the authors.
10. It is worth mentioning here that the Johansen procedure requires that the variables not to be $I(2)$, but can admit only both $I(1)$ and a mixture of $I(1)$ and $I(0)$ processes, in system used for testing for order of cointegrating rank.
11. The choice of maximum lag length is in the specification of the VAR model can affect the determination of the number of cointegrating vectors. Insufficient lag length would lead to rejection of the null hypothesis of no cointegration too often where over parameterization of the dynamic model would lead to loss of power.
12. We carried out both the maximum eigenvalue (max) and trace tests. Of the two, the later is more powerful when the eigenvalues are evenly distributed; the appropriate is true in the presence of either large or small eigenvalues (see Johansen and Juselius, 1990).

13. The error correction term for the Malaysian ringgit is also significant, implying that the rinngit is more responsive to the currencies in the system in the full sample period.
14. They may be considered as weakly exogenous when (1) their α's is insignificant, and (2) not granger-caused by the other variables in the system in the long run (Ericsson, 1992).
15. All computations are carried out using Microfit 4.0. The FEVD analysis for the 1978:1 to 1994:1 can be found in Goh (2001). Overall, the results are similar to those presented for the 1978:1 to 1996:2.

Table 8.1 KPSS Unit Root Tests (Sample Period 1978:1-1998:3)

Series	Level		First Difference		Conclusion
	μ	τ	μ	τ	
YEN	1.795**	0.173**	0.140	0.119	I(1)
	(3)	(3)	(3)	(3)	
SD	0.989**	0.169**	0.093	0.083	I(1)
	(4)	(4)	(4)	(4)	
RM	1.961**	0.165**	0.081	0.074	I(1)
	(3)	(3)	(3)	(3)	
PP	1.391**	0.246**	0.116	0.092	I(1)
	(5)	(5)	(5)	(5)	
RP	3.969**	0.188**	0.114	0.079	I(1)
	(1)	(1)	(1)	(1)	
TB	2.657**	0.169**	0.050	0.049	I(1)
	(2)	(2)	(2)	(2)	
KW	2.648**	0.129*	0.034	0.033	I(1)
	(2)	(2)	(2)	(2)	
NT	2.974**	0.139*	0.044	0.040	I(1)
	(1)	(1)	(4)	(4)	
5 percent critical values					
	0.463	0.146	0.463	0.146	
10 percent critical values					
	0.347	0.119	0.347	0.119	

Notes: The μ and τ statistics for the KPSS unit root test. μ and τ are the model with constant and a time trend respectively. Asterisks (***), (**) and (*) shows significant at 1 percent, 5 percent and 10 percent level. The following notations applies in all the tables followed: YEN = Japanese yen, SD = Singapore dollar, RM = Malaysia ringgit, Philippines peso, RP = Indonesia rupiah, TB =Thailand baht, KW = South Korean won, NT = Taiwan dollar. The null hypothesis in the KPSS is that the series is stationary against the alternative hypothesis of a unit root (see Kwiatkowski *et al.*, 1992).

Table 8.2 Cointegration Test Result

		Sub-period 1 (k=3, r=1)		Sub-period 2 (k=3, r=1)		Sub-period 3 (k=3, r=1)		95percent C.V.	
		Max	Trace	Max	Trace	Max	Trace	Max	Trace
r = 0	R = 1	71.58*	136.78*	79.72*	147.72*	80.37*	146.54*	39.83	95.87
r<= 1	R = 2	33.29	65.2	31.61	68	32.77	66.17	33.64	70.49
r<= 2	R = 3	12.37	31.91	14.71	36.39	15.25	33.4	27.42	48.88
r<= 3	R = 4	11.52	19.53	13.18	21.68	12.3	18.16	21.12	31.54
r<= 4	R = 5	7.08	8.01	7.36	8.5	5.08	5.58	14.88	17.86
r<= 5	R = 6	0.93	0.93	1.14	1.14	0.78	0.78	8.07	8.07

Notes: Asterisk (*) denotes statistically significant at 5 percent. Sub-period 1 refers to 1978Q1-1994Q1, sub-period 2 refers to 1978Q1-1996Q2, and sub-period 3 refers to 1978Q1-1998Q3.

Table 8.3 Granger Causality Results

Dependent Variable	Independent Variable							
	YEN	SD	RM	IR	TB	NT	ECT_{t-1}	t-stats
	Sub-period 1: 1978:1-1994:1							
	F-statistics							
YEN	2.97	6.06*	0.01	0.13	0.63	2.42	-0.01	-0.01
SD	1.90	3.44	2.76	2.18	0.01	0.32	-0.05	-2.78*
RM	1.34	1.16	1.16	0.02	0.10	0.01	-0.04	-2.04
IR	6.27	2.68	0.29	1.50	0.26	0.41	0.03	0.57
TB	0.95	0.00	0.06	0.11	0.10	0.00	0.01	0.39
NT	0.63	0.46	10.97*	5.42*	6.12*	24.05*	-0.09	-6.42*
	Sub-period 2: 1978:1-1996:1							
	F-statistics							
YEN	1.95	4.56*	0.00	0.26	0.31	1.97	0.02	0.45
SD	2.75	3.03	3.09	3.13	0.00	0.72	-0.04	-2.34*
RM	2.34	0.41	0.97	0.01	0.01	0.08	-0.04	-1.83
IR	6.13*	2.38	0.02	1.28	0.20	0.32	0.04	0.59
TB	0.56	0.03	0.06	0.12	0.12	0.01	0.01	0.46
NT	0.03	0.51	11.69*	5.08*	6.36*	22.16*	-0.09	-6.19*
	Sub-period 3: 1978:1-1998:3							
	F-statistics							
YEN	2.15	4.63*	0.00	0.37	0.96	2.48	-0.00	-0.02
SD	1.78	1.77	5.07*	10.21*	5.17*	1.17	-0.07	-3.95*
RM	2.11	0.05	2.09	1.81	2.49	0.63	-0.10	-3.17*
IR	11.32*	1.74	2.58	0.51	2.00	0.03	-0.07	-1.12
TB	0.11	0.70	0.47	0.04	2.62	0.28	-0.07	-1.69
NT	0.13	1.34	16.98*	17.86*	13.94*	19.26*	-0.10	-6.62*

Notes: Asterisk (*) denotes statistically significant at 5 percent. F-statistics tests the joint-significance of the lagged values of the independent variables, and t-statistic tests the significance of the error correction term (ECT).

Table 8.4 Variance Decomposition for Sub-period 1978:1-1996:2

Percentage of variations in	Horizon	Due to innovation in: YEN	SD	RM	RP	TB	NT	FOREIGN
YEN	1	53.05	21.03	7.57	0.25	8.10	10.00	46.95
	8	51.74	14.27	7.23	0.25	6.01	20.52	48.28
	16	51.58	13.29	6.85	0.25	5.94	22.09	48.42
	24	51.49	12.95	6.75	0.25	5.88	22.67	48.50
SD	1	26.07	46.30	17.59	0.38	9.64	0.01	53.69
	8	24.52	42.21	10.07	0.23	22.92	0.06	57.80
	16	25.38	41.07	8.56	0.14	24.76	0.08	58.92
	24	25.68	40.67	7.97	0.11	25.49	0.08	59.33
RM	1	10.88	20.33	60.20	1.03	7.53	0.03	39.80
	8	12.98	18.42	45.70	4.56	18.10	0.24	54.30
	16	14.71	18.14	42.40	4.80	19.56	0.38	57.59
	24	15.40	18.06	40.94	4.91	20.27	0.42	59.06
RP	1	0.10	0.06	2.06	95.85	0.32	1.61	4.15
	8	11.59	0.12	0.99	82.83	0.55	3.92	17.17
	16	12.14	0.14	0.83	82.19	0.32	4.38	17.81
	24	12.54	0.13	0.75	81.73	0.22	4.63	18.27
TB	1	13.34	11.36	6.90	0.08	61.83	6.49	38.17
	8	15.12	12.07	8.28	0.18	55.48	8.87	44.52
	16	15.75	11.88	7.81	0.17	54.83	9.55	45.16
	24	15.95	11.82	7.67	0.17	54.61	9.79	45.40
NT	1	13.12	0.00	0.44	2.83	10.11	73.49	16.39
	8	22.06	0.19	6.20	1.16	20.32	50.07	29.61
	16	23.67	0.23	5.62	1.06	19.68	49.75	30.58
	24	24.11	0.24	5.52	1.02	19.59	49.53	30.89

Notes: The last column provides the percentage of forecast error variances of each country explained collectively by the foreign countries.

Table 8.5 Variance Decomposition for Sub-period 1978:1-1998:3

Percentage of variations in	Horizon	Due to innovation in: YEN	SD	NT	RM	TB	RP	FOREIGN
YEN	1	24.78	22.42	21.72	12.94	9.91	8.20	75.21
	8	30.72	27.16	22.68	7.43	7.38	4.60	69.28
	16	29.96	28.64	19.94	6.99	9.60	4.85	70.03
	24	29.89	29.45	18.92	6.73	10.38	4.61	70.10
SD	1	20.53	22.62	16.98	15.87	14.23	9.74	77.37
	8	28.09	29.31	16.88	8.67	11.41	5.61	70.68
	16	26.60	30.77	13.84	8.12	15.25	5.41	69.22
	24	26.24	31.33	12.92	8.05	16.40	5.03	68.66
NT	1	21.59	20.13	22.89	14.39	12.78	8.19	77.11
	8	28.68	23.25	25.40	8.28	8.99	5.35	74.59
	16	27.84	23.17	24.72	8.67	10.46	5.11	75.27
	24	26.89	22.48	24.58	9.33	11.52	5.17	75.41
RM	1	12.65	15.86	11.37	24.30	22.61	13.19	75.69
	8	21.58	23.49	13.09	15.26	18.62	7.93	84.73
	16	18.41	23.01	9.54	15.43	24.65	8.93	84.56
	24	16.63	22.15	7.95	16.11	27.96	9.17	83.88
TB	1	9.43	13.89	8.98	24.24	31.55	11.88	68.44
	8	18.14	21.62	11.24	16.71	25.01	7.24	74.98
	16	16.51	21.74	8.91	16.32	29.49	7.01	70.50
	24	15.68	21.55	8.09	16.50	31.65	6.50	68.34
RP	1	10.86	11.98	9.55	18.78	16.42	32.39	67.60
	8	6.13	9.16	3.25	21.64	28.44	31.35	68.64
	16	4.36	6.89	2.79	22.25	32.42	31.27	68.72
	24	3.53	5.73	2.27	24.34	33.49	30.63	69.37

Notes: As per Table 8.4.

References

Aggarwal, R, Montanes A. and Ponz, M. (2000), 'Evidence of Long-Run Purchasing Power Parity: Analysis of Real Asian Exchange Rates in Term of Japanese Yen,' *Japan and the World Economy,* vol. 12, pp. 351-361.

Aggarwal, R. and Mougoue, M. (1993), 'Cointegration Among Southeast Asian and Japanese Currencies,' *Economics Letters,* vol. 41, pp. 161-166.

Aggarwal, R. and Mougoue, M. (1996), 'Cointegration Among Asian Currencies: Evidence of the Increasing Influence of the Japanese Yen,' *Japan and the World Economy,* vol.8, pp. 291-308.

Azali, M., Habibullah, M.S. and Baharumshah, A.Z., (2001), 'Does PPP Hold Between Asian and Japanese Economies? Evidence Using Panel Unit Root and Panel Cointegration,' *Japan and the World Economy*, vol. 13, pp. 35-50.

Baharumshah, A.Z. and Ariff, M. (1997), 'Purchasing Power Parity in Southeast Asian Countries Economies,' *Asian Economic Journal*, vol. 11, pp. 141-153.

Campbell, J.Y. and Perron, P. (1991), 'Pitfalls and Opportunities: What Macroeconomists Should Know About Unit Roots,' in O.J. Blanchard and S. Fischer (eds), *National Bureau of Economic Research Macroeconomics Annual*, MIT Press, Cambridge, pp. 144-201.

Cheng, B.S. (1999), 'Beyond Purchasing Power Parity: Testing for Cointegration and Causality Between Exchange Rates, Prices, and Interest Rates,' *Journal of International Money and Finance,* vol. 18, pp. 911-924.

Chinn, M.D. and Dooley, M.P. (1997), 'Asia-Pacific Capital Markets: Measurement of Integration and the Implications for Economic Activity,' in T. Ito and A.O. Krueger (eds), *Regionalism versus Multilateral Trading Arrangement*, Chicago: Chicago University Press for NBER, pp. 169-196.

Chinn, M.D. and Dooley, M.P. (1999), 'International Monetary Arrangements in the Asia Pacific Before and After,' *Journal of Asian Economics,* vol. 10, pp. 361-384.

Dooley, M.P. and Mathieson, D.J. (1994), 'Exchange Rate Policy, International Capital Mobility, and Monetary Instruments,' in Glick, R. and M.M. Hutchison (eds), *Exchange Rate Policy and Interdependence: Perspective from the Pacific-Basin,* Cambridge, New York, pp. 68-95.

Enders, W. (1995), *Applied Econometric Time Series,* New York: John Wiley & Sons, Inc.

Engel, R.F. and Granger, C.W.J. (1987), 'Cointegration and Error-Correction: Representation, Estimation, and Testing,' *Econometrica,* vol. 55, pp. 251-276.

Ericsson, N.R. (1992), 'Cointegration, Exogeneity, and Policy Analysis: An Overview,' *Journal of Policy Modeling,* vol. 14, pp. 251-280.

Faruqee, H. (1992), 'Dynamic Capital Mobility in Pacific-Basin Developing Countries,' IMF *Staff Paper,* vol. 39, pp. 706-717.

Fernald, J., Edison, H. and Loungani, P. (1999), 'Was China the first domino? Assessing Links Between China and other Asian Economies,' *Journal of International Money and Finance,* vol. 18, pp. 515-535.

Frankel, J. A. (1993) 'Is Japan Creating A Yen Bloc in East Asia and the Pacific?,' in J. A. Frankel and M. Kahler (eds), *Regionalism and Rivalry: Japan and the United States in Pacific Asia*, Chicago: University of Chicago Press, pp. 53-85.

Frankel, J.A. and Wei, S.J. (1994), 'Yen Bloc or Dollar Bloc? East Asian Exchange Rate Policies,' in T. Ito and A. Krueger (eds), *Macroeconomic Linkage*, Chicago: University of Chicago Press.

Goh, W.K. (2001), 'Financial Integration In East Asia,' *Unpublished Master of Science Thesis,* Universiti Putra Malaysia, Serdang, Malaysia.

Gray, G. (1991), 'Dealing with Exotic Currencies,' *Corporate Finance*, vol. 38, pp. 9-11.

Houben, A.C.F.J. (1997), 'Exchange Rate Policy and Monetary Strategy Options in the Philippines- the Search for Stability and Sustainability,' *IMF Paper on Policy Analysis and Assessment PPAA/97/4*.

Johansen, S. (1988), 'Statistical Analysis of Cointegration Vectors,' *Journal of Economic Dynamics and Control,* vol.12, pp. 231-254.

Johansen, S. and Juselius, K. (1990), 'Maximum Likelihood Estimation and Inference on Cointegration with Applications to the Demand for Money,' *Oxford Bulletin of Economics and Statistics,* vol. 52, pp. 169-210.

Kwiatkowski, D., Phillips, P.C.B. Schmidt, P. and Shin, Y. (1992), 'Testing the Null Hypothesis of Stationarity Against the Alternative of a Unit Root. How Sure Are We that Economic Time Series Have a Unit Root?', *Journal of Econometrics,* vol. 54, pp. 159-178.

Kwan, C.H. (2000), *The Economics of A Yen Block*, The Brooking Institute and Nomura Research Institute.

Lee, K.C., Pesaran, M.H. and Pierse, R.G. (1992), 'Persistence of Shocks and its Sources in Multisectoral Model of UK Output Growth,' *Economic Journal*, vol. 102, pp. 342-356.

Lee, K.C. and M.H. Pesaran, M.H. (1993), 'Persistence Profiles and Business Cycle Fluctuations via Dissaggregate Model of UK Output Growth,' *Rierche Economiche*, vol. 47, pp. 293-322.

Lutkepohl, H. (1991), *Introduction to Multiple Time Series Analysis*, Springer-Verlag, Berlin.

Masih, R. and Masih, A.M. (1996), 'Macroeconomic Activity Dynamics and Granger Causality: New Evidence from a Small Developing Economy Based on a Vector-Error Correction modelling analysis,' *Economic Modelling,* vol. 13, pp. 407-426.

Miller, S. (1981), 'Monetary Dynamics: An Application of Cointegration and Error-Correction Modelling,' *Journal of Money, Credit, and Banking,* vol. 23, pp. 139-154.

Moosa, I.A. and Bhatti., R.H. (1997) 'Are Asian Markets Integrated? Evidence for Six Countries vis-à-vis Japan.,' *International Economic Journal,* vol. 11, pp. 51-67.

Moreno, R. (1993), 'Exchange rate policy and insulation from external shocks: the experience of Taiwan and Korea: 1970-1990,' Center for Pacific Basin Monetary and Economic Studies, Federal Reserve of San Francisco, Working Paper 93-05.

Mussa, M., Masson, P., Swoboda, A., Jadresic, E., Mauro, P. and Berg, A. (2000), 'Exchange Rate Regimes in An Increasingly Integrated World Economy,' IMF Occasional Paper 193.

Newey, W. and West, K. (1987), 'A Simple Positive Semi-Definite, Heteroskedasticity and Autocorrelation Consistent Covariance Matrix,' *Econometrica*, vol. 51, pp. 703-708.

Park, J.Y. and Sung, J. (1994), 'Testing for Unit Roots in Models with Structural Change,' *Econometric Theory,* vol. 44, pp. 917-936.

Pesaran, M.H., Pierse, R.G. and Lee, K.C. (1993), 'Persistence, Cointegration, and Aggregation: a Dissaggregate Analysis of Output Fluctuations in the US economy,' *Journal of Econometrics*, vol. 56, pp. 57-88.

Pesaran, M.H and Shin, Y. (1998), 'Generalized Impulse Response Analysis in Linear Multivariate Models,' *Economic Letters*, vol. 58, pp. 17-29.

Reisen, H. and Yeches, H. (1993), 'Time-Varying Estimates on the Openness of the Capital Account in Korea and Taiwan,' *Journal of Development Economy,* vol. 41, pp. 285-305.

Talvas, W. and Ozeki, Y. (1992), 'The Internationalisation of Currencies: An Appraisal of the Japanese Yen, IMF Occasional Paper No. 90.

Tse, T.K. and Ng., L.K. (1997), 'The Cointegration of Asian Currencies Revisited,' *Japan and the World Economy,* vol. 9, pp. 109-114.

Zhou, S. (1996), 'Trade Connections and Interest Rate Linkages among ASEAN, Japan, and the USA: An Empirical Analysis, *Applied Economics,* vol. 28, pp. 617-630.

Chapter 9

Measuring Capital Mobility in the Pacific Rim

Chan Tze Haw and Ahmad Zubaidi Baharumshah

Introduction

Two decades ago, Feldstein and Horioka (1980) proposed a study of the saving-investment nexus that initiated a major controversy on the extent and implications of international finance. They found high correlation between savings and investments in OECD countries (including the US and Japan), which apparently implied a low degree of global capital mobility. Surprisingly, the disputable findings were confirmed by many other subsequent studies.[1] Such event challenges the conventional wisdom which characterises the post-Bretton Woods floating-rate era as one that is experiencing a seeming increase in capital mobility (Obstfeld and Taylor, 2001), following the abandonment of fixed exchange rate regimes and the removal of capital controls since 1970s. In addition, the accelerated pace of globalisation and financial market deregulations as well as the revolutionary changes in information and communication technologies have further demonstrated an increasingly integrated world economy. Capital and trade flows expand remarkably and economic growth began its most rapid spurt in history worldwide. In other words, the Feldstein-Horioka criterion (FHC hereafter) contradicts the fact that capital movements across countries are getting mobile, as the global capital market has become more integrated and thus creating a puzzle[2] in modern economics.

This chapter revisits the issue in an effort to examine the extent of capital mobility, focusing on ten Asia Pacific nations of different level of economic development and financial openness, during the past three decades. Countries included in the analysis are the two economic giant: the US and Japan; the NIE-4:[3] Hong Kong, Singapore, South Korea and Taiwan; and the ASEAN-4:[4] Indonesia, Malaysia, Philippines and Thailand. To perform a robust analysis, advances in econometric such as the unit root test, cointegration procedure, unrestricted VAR causality, and dynamic OLS (DOLS) are deployed. These empirical tools are capable of demonstrating the dynamic channel of the saving-investment nexus and our estimations take account of the non-stationarity of the time series data to avoid the inferential biases due to non-stationary variables under investigation.

The investigation of capital mobility in the Asia Pacific rim is of interest for a number of reasons. For analysts, assumptions on the level of capital mobility have profound implications for their modelling strategy. For policy makers, the degree of capital mobility has an important bearing on the short-run effects of stabilisation policies. For academicians, evaluation of the Feldstein-Horioka puzzle by employing different empirical specification enhances the application of modern econometrics methods.

Our chapter differs from the previous works in at least three significant ways. First, this chapter offers an up-to date study of the saving-investment relationship based on the evidence from both developed and developing countries. Empirical research of capital mobility in developing countries has been meagre while previous studies mostly focused on the OECD and European community. Second, we counter the problem of country size by studying ten countries, which are different in the size of capital markets and production capacities. Our findings indicate that the heftiness of FHC in measuring capital mobility is more subjected to econometric specifications rather than country size alone. Third, the endogeneity problem of the saving-investment model is confronted by adopting the dynamic OLS (DOLS) estimation. As suggested in Inder (1995) and Hussein (1998), the inclusion of lags and leads of the first difference of savings in DOLS eliminates the effect of endogeneity, while the lags of the first difference of investment corrects for the impact of the remaining autocorrelation of the residual term in the model.

Review of the Saving-Investment Puzzle

The FHC has gained numerous attentions in both theoretical and empirical works. However, anomalous results were reported without convincing conclusion, leaving the 'Feldstein-Horioka Puzzle' even more controversial. In many settings, arguments were reflecting on the statistical method used rather than on any inherent deficiency in the saving-investment relationship. Obstfeld and Rogoff (2000) reveal their concern, arguing that most explanations (on the FH puzzle) tend to be clever but empirically inadequate, and more troublesome still, tend to fix one puzzle at the expense of creating others.

Conventionally, the FHC has been subjected to several theoretical criticisms including the country size and the endogeneity of saving and investment. A small country would take the world interest rate as given while changes in savings and investment of a large country will affect world interest rates (see Obstfeld, 1986; Summers, 1988; Frankel, 1992). An increase in savings of large economies would lower the world's interest rates and, increase the investments in that country. Consequently, saving-investment will be correlated but it would be erroneous to conclude that this implies low capital mobility. In addition, Dooley *et al.* (1987) documented that any economic variable in addition to the cost of capital that influences the investment rate will probably be correlated with the national saving rate. If factors that determine investment happen to be uncorrelated with national savings, then there will be no endogeneity problem. But since the difference between national savings and investment is identically equal to current account, the lack of correlation would imply that the factor in question has an identical effect on the current account as on investment. Moreover, the current account targeting policies would have resulted in association of savings and investment (e.g. Bayoumi, 1990; Bayoumi and MacDonald, 1995). If there is trade deficit induced by increase in investment, government may react by expenditure cuts or raising taxes, and if current account targeting is successful, it could provide a strong saving-investment correlation. The high saving-investment correlation, however, has nothing to do with capital mobility.

Empirically, the assessments of the saving-investment nexus have focused more on time series data than cross-sectional data. Several studies have argued that the use of time-averaged data in cross-sectional regression analysis tends to bias the results against capital mobility. Gundlach and Sinn (1992) claim that the average value obtained from a cross-section of countries might be the result of divergent individual observations. Countries may contribute to a high β (the saving retention coefficient) either because they have imposed capital controls or because they are simply large. Moreover, advances in time series estimation lead to the application of cointegration procedure and error correction modelling that allow for the investigation of long run equilibria and short run dynamics of saving-investment. If there is cointegration between the two aggregates, capital flows are immobile. Otherwise, capital is regarded as highly mobile across countries. Authors such as Gulley (1992), Bodman (1995), Lemmen and Eijffinger (1995) and Rubio (1998), among others applied the cointegration procedure on saving-investment nexus and support the hypothesis of capital mobility. By contrast, a few articles show that current account balances tend to be mean-reverting, implying that saving and investment are in fact cointegrated with a unit coefficient (e.g. Gundlach and Sinn, 1992, Jansen, 1996; Coakley, 1996). However, this could be also a reflection of the external solvency constraint requiring the current account to be stationary in order for the external debt to be bounded.

Recent studies have extended their analyses to the panel approach. Notably, panel data comprises information from both cross-sectional and time series dimension that provides great flexibility for researchers in modelling differences in behaviour across individuals. Specifically, Ho (2002) pointed out that the low power of univariate tests against persistent alternatives, which is typical for sample sizes that occur in practice, has motivated the use of panel data analysis. Applying a panel regression on 21 OECD countries, Krol (1996) easily rejected the FH puzzle. Jansen (2000) re-examined the same panel set and argued that Krol's conclusion is due to the presence of Luxembourg in the panel set. Coiteux and Oliver (2000) reconciled Krol with FHC by addressing the FH's finding as a long proportion while revealing a much higher degree of capital mobility in the short run. Alternatively, Athanasios and Romain (1998) measure the world capital mobility by subjecting their analyses to a panel of 103 countries, comprising the OECD countries, middle- and low-income countries. Taking into consideration the business cycle effects and country-specific fixed effects, they found that the saving retention coefficient of OECD panel alone is on average, higher than that of developing countries as a whole. Such occurrence is explained by the increased size sample of more diverse countries. Athanasios and Romain also argued that official capital transactions may cause a low correlation of saving-investment even if capital markets are not well integrated, as for LCDs. Indeed, the sources of capital flows in LCDs are often linked to the financial aid, debt repayments and financial outflows. Ho (2002) then applies fully modified and dynamic OLS estimators to a panel of 12 OECD countries and found no evidence of cointegration between savings-investment, suggesting that international capital mobility is at least high in the long run. Lately, in a comprehensive study, Banerjee and Zanghieri (2003) reconcile the FH puzzle by exploring both the current account dynamics and the saving-investment nexus. Nonetheless, their findings are neither impeccable, having the results of heterogeneous panel-based tests inconsistent with those of time series-based tests (e.g. unit root and cointegration). In brief, disagreements persist in the panel analyses, which are sensitive to the country grouping and the panel size. Hence, the FH puzzle remains.

Theoretical Framework

Following Frankel (1992) and Lemmen and Eijffinger (1995), the FHC can be algebraically linked to three interest parity conditions: the covered interest rate parity (CIP), the ex ante uncovered interest rate parity (UIP) and the ex ante real interest rate parity (RIP). These interest rate parities rely on the co-movement of domestic and foreign prices (*i.e.,* interest rates) and are characterised as the price approach. The FHC, however, relies on the co-movement of domestic quantities and is characterised as the quantity approach. Table 9.1 summarises the cumulative working assumptions to be fulfilled for each condition to hold.

The CIP states that for countries to be financially integrated in the absence of capital controls, default risks and transaction costs, covered interest arbitrage equates the forward premium or discount on foreign exchange to the nominal interest rate differential between comparable domestic and foreign currency assets. UIP, the hypothesis of perfect asset substitution, measure the financial integration in the sense of zero country premium (CIP holds) and zero exchange risk premium. The exchange risk premium captures the information of forward exchange rate as an unbiased predictor of the future spot rate and hence, an extent of 'efficient market hypothesis'. RIP, on the other hand, will hold if the domestic and foreign real interest rates are equalised. It requires the assumptions of CIP (zero country premium) and UIP (zero exchange risk premium) plus zero expected real exchange rate change.

CIP and UIP conditions coincide with two important theoretical aspects of financial integration, *i.e.* the ability and willingness to move financial assets across countries in response to expected difference in exchange-adjusted returns. Two assets are substitutable if investors are willing to change relative shares of their portfolio in response to a change in expected relative returns. Whether asset stocks actually change depends on the ability of investors to adjust their portfolios. The CIP examines the ability; whereas the UIP examines the ability and willingness of capital movements. Subsequently, the RIP examines the perfect financial and non-financial assets movements across countries including the goods and services or, production factors such as labour and physical capital. In other words, preceding studies that showed real interest rate inequality could be due to the failure of the UIP and the PPP or imperfect integration of goods markets but not imperfect integration of financial markets.

The FHC examines capital mobility through the saving-investment nexus. Under perfect capital mobility hypothesis, domestic savings and domestic investments should not share a common movement but vary independently across countries. There are two important assumptions underlying the saving-investment model. First, the investment rate depends linearly on the expected real interest rates and the stochastic error term (μ_i) that capture all other determinants of the investments is uncorrelated with the savings ratio; second, the savings ratio is not affected by the expected real foreign interest rate and uncorrelated with the deviation of RIP. Since the FHC requires two additional assumptions to the RIP condition, it is thereby the strongest criterion for measuring capital mobility.

Data and Methodology

Unit Root and Cointegration Procedure

It is essential for one to first examine the stationarity of the time series properties and determine their order of integration before any further investigation of relationships among variables. For this purpose, we rely on the standard Augmented Dickey Fuller (ADF), Philips-Perron (PP) and the KPSS unit root tests. If any series is identified to have a unit root, then the series are found to be non-stationary. If so, data transformation such as taking first differences of the series to detrend the regression will be necessary. If a series must be differenced d times before it becomes stationary, then it is said to be integrated of order d, denoted *I(d)* and it is unusual in practice for economic series to be integrated of an order greater than two. If two time series are stationary after first difference, they are said to be integrated of order 1 or *I(1)*.

Notably, the Johansen-Juselius (JJ hereafter) cointegration procedure requires that variables are *I(1)* but not *I*(2). It is, however, possible to have a mixture of different order series when there are three or more series under consideration (see Granger and Lee, 1990; Charemza and Deadman, 1992; Masih and Masih, 1999). More particular, the Johansen procedure requires variables not to be *I(2)* but can admit both *I(1)* only or a mixture of *I(1)* and *I(0)* processes in the system, providing that the dependent variable is *I(0)* while at least two explanatory variables are integrated of *I(1)*, if the necessary condition for stationarity of the error term is to be met.

Cointegration refers to the possibility that non-stationary variables may have a linear combination that is stationary, which implies a long run equilibrium relationship between variables. Cointegrated variables move together over time so that any short run deviation from the long-term trend will be corrected. In recent studies, the JJ cointegration procedure is preferred over the two-step Engle-Granger (1987) cointegration procedure. The arguments of deficiencies and lacking of robustness were pointing to the Engle-Granger approach, which relies on ordinary least squares (OLS) analysis[5] as noted in Banerjee, *et al.* (1988), MacDonald and Taylor (1993), Masih and Masih (1997), among others. The test for number of cointegrating vectors in the JJ procedure can be conducted using two likelihood ratio (LR) test statistics namely the trace statistic and maximum eigenvalue statistic as shown below:

$$L_{trace\,(r)} = -T \sum \ln (1 - \lambda_i) \quad (1)$$

$$L_{max\,(r,\, r+1)} = -T \ln (1 - \lambda_{r+1}) \quad (2)$$

where λ_i is the estimated eigenvalues and T is the number of valid observations. The null hypothesis of trace statistic tests that the number of distinct cointegrating vector is less than or equal to r against a general alternative in which it gives result of at most r cointegrating vectors. The latter λ-max statistic tests the null hypothesis that there is r cointegrating vector(s) against the alternative of r+1 cointegrating vectors. The saving-investment cointegration regression can be specified as follows:

$$(I/Y)_{t+k,i} = \alpha + \beta(S/Y)_{t+k,i} + \varepsilon_{t+k,i} \quad (3)$$

where I/Y is the domestic investment ratio, S/Y is the domestic savings ratio, β is the saving retention coefficient and $\varepsilon_{t+k,I}$ is the error term.

Causality Tests

If cointegration is detected, Granger-causality within Vector Error Correction Model (VECM) will be conducted to avoid the problem of mis-specification. Otherwise if there is no cointegration, the causality channel will then be carried out through the restriction Wald tests within the unrestricted VAR. VECM analyses the short run relationship, indicating the short run adjustment to long run equilibrium and the direction of causal effect from one variable to another. A valid error-correction representation of (3) may be specified in the following way:

$$\Delta(I/Y)_{t+k,i} = \alpha + \beta\Delta(S/Y)_{t+k,i} + \gamma[(I/Y)_{t+k-1,i} - \delta(S/Y)_{t+k-1,i}] + \eta_{t+k-1,i} \quad (4)$$

where β is the impact multiplier, γ is the error correction coefficient, δ is the long run multiplier and $[(I/Y)_{t+k-1,i} - \delta(S/Y)_{t+k-1,i}]$ is the error correction term.

Dynamic OLS

Stock and Watson (1993) have proposed a more robust parametric approach of extracting the long run coefficient, particularly for small sample size (like ours). While estimating the long-run equilibrium via dynamic OLS (DOLS), the Stock-Watson method corrects for possible simultaneity bias among the regressors. The potential of simultaneity bias and small sample bias among the regressors is dealt with the inclusion of lagged and led values of the change in the regressors. The Stock-Watson DOLS is similar to the methods proposed by Phillips and Hansen (1990) and Phillips and Loretan (1991), but is practically much more convenient to implement and estimate. A valid Stock-Watson DOLS representation may be specified in the following way:

$$I_t = B'X_t + \sum_{j=-k}^{j=k} \eta_j \Delta S_{t-j} + \sum_{j=-l}^{j=l} \lambda_j \Delta I_{t-j} + \xi_t \qquad (5)$$

where $B = [c, \alpha, \beta]'$, $X = [1, \; S_t, \; I_t]$ while I_t and S_t represent the domestic investment ratio and domestic savings ratio respectively. The DOLS procedure of estimating the saving-investment long run parameters basically involves regressing any *I(1)* variables on other *I(1)* variables, any *I(0)* variables and leads and lags of the first difference of any *I(1)* variables. These estimates will facilitate inferences made for the long run. In our case, the DOLS equations are estimated including up to $j = \pm 3$ leads and lags for first difference of savings to eliminate the effect of endogeneity. For first difference of investments, the estimation includes up to $j = -3$ lags to correct for the impact of remaining autocorrelation of the residual term.

Data Description

Our analyses occupy the annual ratio of gross domestic savings (GDS/GDP) and ratio of gross domestic investments (GDI/GDP) concerning the United States and Japan, NIE-4 and ASEAN-4, spanning from 1971 to 1999. Gross domestic savings comprises the private and government savings, which can be estimated by subtracting both the private and government consumption expenditure from gross domestic product. Gross domestic investment then takes account of the fixed capital formation and changes in the capital stock. All raw data are sourced from IFS, SEACEN Financial Statistics and the respective central banks. Annual frequency data are chosen for the analysis due to the fact that higher frequency data are not available for most of the developing countries. Indeed, annual data generally convey more information and avoid the contamination of seasonal elements (see Bayoumi and Macdonald, 1995). It is also well known that cointegration analyses are sensitive to seasonal elements in the data. Further data description can be referred to in Appendix A.

Results Discussion

Correlation Analysis

Figure 9.1 demonstrates the scatter and regression plots of saving-investment ratios over the past three decades. For most East Asian countries, the domestic investments tend to be drifting far apart from the domestic savings, implying a low correlation between the two variables. This pattern appears to suggest high capital mobility within the Pacific Rim. Nonetheless, Japan seems to have their saving-investment closely correlated while the US data yields a positive steep regression slope, which may suggest a highly dependent savings and investments. These figures seem to support the puzzling findings by earlier studies: capital flows in the highly developed and open countries such as the US and Japan are subsequently less mobile when compared to the developing East Asia countries.

Unit Root and Cointegration Analysis

The application of cointegration requires savings and investments ratios to be non-stationary. All series are first transformed into natural logarithm form before being subjected to the unit root tests of stationarity. The computed Augmented Dickey Fuller (ADF) and Philips-Perron (PP) statistics indicate that the null hypothesis of a unit root cannot be rejected for all the series in level (Table 9.2). For series in first difference, many cases in the ADF test still fail to reject the null hypothesis of unit root at standard significant levels. This finding implies that some series are not stationary even after first differencing, perhaps suggesting that the series are integrated at a higher order (e.g. *I(2)*). On the other hand, the non-parametric PP test has rejected the hypothesis of unit root for all series except the investment rates of Hong Kong, implying that most series are integrated of order one or *I(1)*.

It is widely acknowledged that the standard ADF and PP tests are not very informative on how to distinguish between a unit root and near unit root case and they are known to be of low power in small sample size such as ours. The ADF test, in particular experiences the loss of power when the autoregressive parameter is close to unity. The PP test, on the other hand, has poor size properties, i.e. it is biased towards the rejection of the null hypothesis when the series follows a MA process, as highlighted by Schwert (1989). The power of these two tests to distinguish between trend stationary and difference stationary processes has been further questioned by Schwert (1987) and De Jong *et al.* (1989). Therefore, the alternative KPSS test proposed by Kwaitkoski *et al.* (1992) can be used in a complementary way to confirm the *I(1)* specification. KPSS procedure assumes the univariate series can be decomposed into the sum of a deterministic trend, random walk and stationary *I(0)* disturbance and is based on a Lagrange Multiplier score testing principle. This test reverses the null and the alternative hypothesis. A finding favourable to a unit root in this case requires strong evidence against the null hypothesis of stationarity. As reported in Table 9.3, the null hypothesis is rejected in favour of the unit root hypothesis for all cases, wherein the computed statistics are larger than the asymptotic critical values. These KPSS results have further confirmed that all series are stationary after first difference and no variable is *I(2)*. We thus relied on the KPSS tests to arrive at the conclusion that both domestic savings and investments are of the *I(1)* process for all the sample countries. Hence, the series are expedient in a cointegration analysis.

Although the JJ procedure is a multivariate approach, it is also widely used in two-dimensional cases (such as ours) to test for the unique cointegrating vector in the system (Table 9.4), which may exist between the saving-investment ratios. Both the trace and maximum eigenvalue tests indicate no evidence of cointegrating vector(s) at 5percent significant level, suggesting the absence of long run common stochastic trend between domestic savings and domestic investments for all studied countries. The absence of long run comovements of domestic investments and domestic savings leads us to conclude that there is no reason to expect that higher domestic savings in any particular country will reflect a higher domestic investments in that country. In addition, the difference between saving-investment is identically equal to current account balance. The lack of cointegration would imply that savings in each country react to cross country differences in rates of return on capital while a country's level of investment is financed by the world capital market through a current account deficit. This can only happen if the financial markets are open and allow for free capital flows. The finding is further supported by the fact that financial inflows and FDI to the Asian region have accelerated since mid-1980s, attributed to the deregulated regional financial markets and the sustained decline of world interest rates as well as the less-exceptional performance of industrial economies.

Unrestricted VAR Analysis

Table 9.5 presents the results of restricted Wald tests within the unrestricted VAR. The findings have informed us about the causal channels between domestic savings and domestic investments. Most countries (except Indonesia and Japan) fail to reject the null hypothesis of perfect capital mobility ($\beta s=0$) at conventional significance levels. This indicates an inactive temporal causality chain of savings to investments, suggesting that domestic savings are not being utilised in a significant proportion to finance domestic investment even in the short run. By contrast, when the restriction of unique coefficient is imposed ($\beta s=1$), all countries strongly reject the null hypothesis of perfect capital immobility. To this end, the findings are in agreement with the cointegration results and further support the presence of a high regional capital mobility (although it is not perfectly mobile).

DOLS and Long Run Equilibria

Long run parameters for variables in levels, with approximate asymptotic standard errors appear in Table 9.6, with the endogeneity of savings and investments taken into account. For most countries, domestic savings fail to be the significant explanatory variables for domestic investments, even when allowing for simultaneity bias in the DOLS estimation. All saving retention coefficients (βs) are statistically significant at vary confidence levels, and seven out of ten have reported below 0.5, suggesting a considerable degree of capital mobility in the Asia Pacific Rim. Indeed, near perfect capital mobility is detected in the case of Singapore (0.05). Overall, the long run capital mobility is more apparent for the NIEs while capital flows in ASEAN economies seem to be more restricted (especially Indonesia and Thailand). Despite the fact that ASEAN members have aggressively taken parts in international trades, their financial controls and interest rates ceilings were only removed gradually since mid-1980s. By contrast, most NIEs (except South Korea) have experienced the interest rates and capital accounts liberalisation since late 1970s. Moreover, both Hong Kong and Singapore have been the Asia financial centres for the past two decades. As for the US and Japan, their long run saving retention coefficients are in the moderate range (0.56 and 0.45) but seems to be much lower than those of previous studies. Our empirical evidences have, to some extent, not supported the argument that country size (or production capacity) encounters for the proficiency of FHC.

Concluding Remarks and Policy Implication

The analyses based on cointegration tests, unrestricted VAR and DOLS have provided sufficient evidence that capital movements have been highly mobile in the Pacific Rim during our study period. This finding is in contrast to that of FH but is in line with recent studies that found massive influx of capital flows from developed countries into developing countries, especially to the East Asian countries (see Hussein, 1998 and Gabriele *et al.*, 2000). We attribute the result of our finding to the endogeneity of savings in the saving-investment relationship.

On one hand, high capital mobility allows small economies such as the ASEAN countries that have a relatively smaller domestic market and insufficient capital (savings), to rely on foreign investments and court funds from the capital-surplus countries to generate capital formation, productive capacity and national wealth. On the other hand, it enables investors from capital-surplus countries (US, Japan and NIEs) to diversify and minimise their portfolio investment risk and achieve higher risk-adjusted rates of return, leading to a much more efficient allocation of resources. In turn, higher return rates encourage more savings and investments that stimulate greater economic growth. In addition, countries with high capital mobility and trade integration across each other are more likely to harmonise currency arrangements and trade policies.

Nevertheless, growing capital mobility across countries is often associated with costly financial problems. The size and speed of international capital movements can very quickly overwhelm the domestic authorities and narrow their policy options, building up pressure on the domestic price and monetary instruments hence causing the macroeconomics imbalance and distortion of the financial system. It is hard to govern capital inflows and to maintain exchange rate stability when international currency and financial markets are dominated by speculative and herding behaviour. Problems become worse when asymmetric information takes place in the immature Asia Pacific financial markets. Asymmetric information implies information gap in financial transactions (e.g. between loan officer and borrower) that contribute to financial problems including moral hazard[6] and adverse selection. Such asymmetric behaviour, at minimum, can lead to inefficiencies; while in extremes will lead to costly financial crises such as the recent Asia crisis (Eichengreen *et al.*, 1999).

The non-cointegrated saving-investment nexus has as well implied that unit roots present in the government saving gaps, which support neither the current account targeting nor the Ricardian Equivalence. Current account balances are thus not mean-reverting to the equilibria level and government could remain insolvent even in the long run. This has indeed reflected the raison d'être of recent Asia crisis. Prior to 1997, a surge of capital inflows increases current account deficits to an unsustainable level. It then causes an appreciation of real exchange rate in the receiving country, which further leads the tradable sector of the economy to become less competitive in the global market. The unsustainability of the current account deficit as well as the appreciation of real exchange rate causes the receiving country to become more vulnerable to foreign shocks. Indeed, the financial crisis demonstrated that different countries in the region were affected differently according to the level of development in the capital market. The badly affected countries are Indonesia, Malaysia, Philippines, Thailand and South Korea. Singapore, Hong Kong, Taiwan and Japan who have relatively matured capital markets were less affected by the crisis.

In conclusion, despite the potential benefits gained form increased capital mobility, open economies with small shares of world output and trade (e.g. ASEAN) will have a narrow monetary and fiscal apparatus to contain exposure to external shocks. Countries can only take advantage of a greater mobility of capital once they have developed a somewhat advanced domestic financial market (Edwards, 2001). Despite building up strong economic fundamentals including the sustainability of current account balances and fiscal stance, it is essential for developing Asia countries to reinforce their domestic financial system. Laws, rules and regulations governing the operations of equity market should be strengthened, to provide a collective defence mechanism against systemic failures and monetary instability.

Notes

1. These include the studies in both cross-sectional and time series. Examples are Penati and Dooley (1984), Dooley, Frankel and Mathieson (1987), Summers (1988), Argimon and Roldan (1994), Taylor (1996), Jansen, (1996), Coakley (1996), Oh *et al.* (1999), among others.
2. Obstfeld and Rogoff, (2000) in their recent survey, remarked the 'Feldstein-Horioka Puzzle' as one of the six puzzles in international macroeconomics in conjunction with the McCallums' home bias in trade puzzle, the French-Poterba equity home bias puzzle, the Backus-Kehoe-Kydland consumption correlation puzzle, the PPP puzzle and the Exchange Rate Disconnect Puzzle.
3. NIE-4 corresponds to the four Newly Industrialised Economies in Asia.
4. ASEAN, which refers to the Association of Southeast Asian Nations, has five original members, Indonesia, Malaysia, Philippines, Singapore and Thailand. However in our context, we characterise Singapore as one of the NIE-4 according to the level of financial development and the size of the capital market.
5. More detail, Masih and Masih (1997) added that the Johansen-Juselius procedure assumes all variables to be endogenous while the Engle-Granger procedure is sensitive to the choice of dependent variables. The JJ procedure does not priori assume the existence of at most a single cointegrating vector; instead it explicitly tests for a number of cointegrating relationships. Also, the JJ procedure avoids the arbitrary choice of the dependent variables in the Engle-Granger approach and is insensitive to the variable being normalised when it comes to extracting the residual from the cointegrating vector. Furthermore, the JJ procedure is established on a unified framework for estimating and testing cointegrating relations within the vector error correction modelling (VECM) formulation. Finally, the JJ procedure provides the appropriate statistics and the point of distribution to test a hypothesis for the number of cointegrating vectors and also tests any restriction upon the coefficients of the vectors.
6. The role of moral hazard in the onset of the Asian crisis has been stressed by a number of authors, namely Krugman (1998) and Sarno and Taylor (1999). According to them, before the financial crisis, Asia's leading national banks were excessively borrowing from abroad and lending excessively at home. These capitals have flowed to lots of risky and dubious profitable projects, which later put the investors/ bankers into large debts and even bankruptcy when the currency crisis occurred.

Table 9.1 Cumulative Assumptions of Interest Parities and FHC

Table 9.1 Cumulative Assumptions of Interest Parities and FHC

Interest Parities and FHC	Assumptions	
CIP		
$i_t - i_t^* = f_t^{t+k} - s_t$	$i_t - i_t^* - (f_t^{t+k} - s_t) = 0$	Zero country premium
UIP		
$i_t - i_t^* = E_{t(}s_{t+k} - s_{t)}$	$i_t - i_t^* = f_t^{t+k} - s_t$	Zero country premium
	$E_t(s_{t+k} - s_t) = f_t^{t+k}$	Forward exchange rate is an unbiased predictor of expected future spot exchange rate
RIP		
$E_t(r_{t+k}) = E_t(r^*_{t+k})$	$i_t - i_t^* = f_t^{t+k} - s_t$	Zero country premium
	$E_t(s_{t+k} - s_t) = f_t^{t+k}$	Forward exchange rate is an unbiased predictor of expected future spot exchange rate
	$E_t(s_{t+k} - P_{t+k} + P^*_{t+k}) = s_t - P_t + P^*_t$	Zero expected real exchange rate change
FHC		
$(I/Y)_{i,\,t+k} = \alpha + \beta(S/Y)_{i,\,t+k} + \varepsilon_{i,\,t+k}$		
	$(I/Y)_{t+k,\,i} = -\varnothing E_t(r_{i,\,t+k}) + \mu_i$ and	
	$i_t - i_t^* = f_t^{t+k} - s_t$ $E_t(s_{t+k} - s_t) = f_t^{t+k}$ $E_t(s_{t+k} - P_{t+k} + P^*_{t+k}) = s_t - P_t + P^*_t$	$\mathrm{Cov}\,(E_t(r_{i,\,t+k}) - E_t(r^*_{i,\,t+k}), (S/Y)_{I,\,t+k}) = 0$
	$\mathrm{Cov}\,(\mu_i, (S/Y)_{i,\,t+k}) = 0$	
	$\mathrm{Cov}\,(E_t(r^*_{i,\,t+k}), (S/Y)_{i,\,t+k}) = 0$	

Table 9.1 (continued)

Symbols	
i_t	domestic nominal interest rate at time t on a k period bond held between time t and t+k
f_t^{t+k}	forward exchange rate agreed at time t for the delivery of foreign currency at time t+k
s_t	spot exchange rate at time t
$f_t^{t+k} - s_t$	forward premium (+ve) or discount (-ve) on foreign currency at time t
$E_t(s_{t+k})$	expected spot exchange rate at time t +k
$E_t(s_{t+k} - s_t)$	expected spot exchange rate change of the domestic currency vis-à-vis the foreign currency between time t+k
P_t	domestic price level at time t
$E_t(r_{t+k})$	expected domestic real interest rate at time t on a k-period bond held between time t and t+k
E_t	conditional expectations operator based upon the information available at time t, i.e., $E(. \mid I_t)$
μ_i	a stochastic error term that captures all other determinants (besides interest rates) of the investment ratio uncorrelated with $E_t(r_{i,\ t+k})$ and $S_{i,\ t+k} / Y_{i,\ t+k}$
I	gross domestic investment
S	gross domestic savings
Y	gross domestic product
k	holding period of the underlying debt period
*	foreign variable
i	domestic country i

Notes: All variables (except interest rates) are expressed in natural logarithms, represented by the lower case letters. Take for instance that the exact CIP is expressed as $F_t^{t+k}/ S_t = (1+ I_t)/ (1+ I^*_t)$. By taking natural logarithms of both sides, noting that $f_t^{t+k} = \ln (F_t^{t+k})$; $s_t = \ln (S_t)$; $\ln (1+ I_t) = i$, and $\ln (1+ I^*_t) = i^*$, the logarithm approximation of CIP will be: $i_t - i_t^* = f_t^{t+k} - s_t$

Table 9.2 ADF and PP Unit Root Tests

	ADF				PP			
	Level		1st Difference		Level		1st Difference	
	No Trend	Trend	No Trend	Trend	No Trend	Trend	No Trend	Trend
Savings								
IND	-2.10[1]	-1.73[1]	-2.96[1]*	-4.20[1]*	-2.16[1]	-1.36[1]	-5.63[1]*	-7.16[1]*
MAL	-2.37[1]	-2.16[1]	-3.70[2]*	-3.68[2]*	-2.27[1]	-3.15[1]	-6.81[1]*	-6.66[1]*
PHI	0.07[1]	-2.32[1]	-4.20[1]*	-4.51[1]*	0.03[1]	-2.30[1]	-4.65[1]*	-5.26[1]*
TH	-1.32[1]	-3.11[1]	-3.52[2]*	-3.45[2]*	-1.15[1]	-3.09[1]	-7.28[1]*	-7.14[1]*
HK	-2.19[1]	-2.14[1]	-4.19[1]*	-4.22[1]*	-2.39[1]	-2.33[1]	-4.21[1]*	-4.23[1]*
SIN	-2.27[1]	-2.77[1]	-3.89[2]*	-3.83[2]*	-2.61[1]	-2.75[1]	-7.74[1]*	-7.63[1]*
SK	-1.78[2]	-2.24[2]	-2.59[4]	-2.59[4]	-2.82[1]	-3.25[1]	-4.74[1]*	-4.69[1]*
TW	-1.61[1]	-2.15[1]	-2.39[4]	-2.41[4]	-1.74[1]	-2.24[1]	-4.81[1]*	-4.78[1]*
JAP	-2.40[1]	-2.47[1]	-3.06[3]*	-3.12[3]	-2.25[1]	-3.41[1]	-8.38[1]*	-8.31[1]*
US	-1.17[1]	-2.67[1]	-3.72[2]*	-3.68[2]*	-1.17[1]	-2.73[1]	-6.23[1]*	-6.18[1]*
Investments								
IND	-1.94[1]	-0.23[1]	-2.03[1]	-2.71[1]	-1.93[1]	0.14[1]	-5.33[1]*	-5.97[1]*
MAL	-1.81[1]	-0.79[1]	-2.20[1]	-2.36[1]	-2.01[1]	-1.28[1]	-3.35[1]*	-3.63[1]*
PHI	-1.49[2]	-2.26[2]	-2.49[2]	-2.39[2]	-1.79[1]	-2.19[1]	-3.52[1]*	-3.55[1]*
TH	-1.17[1]	-0.11[1]	-3.76[1]*	-4.30[1]*	-1.43[1]	-0.52[1]	-3.84[1]*	-4.33[1]*
HK	-2.28[1]	-2.85[1]	-2.67[1]	-2.67[1]	-1.87[1]	-1.81[1]	-2.87[1]*	-2.68[1]
SIN	-1.55[1]	-1.85[1]	-2.54[1]	-2.47[1]	-1.67[1]	-1.99[1]	-4.52[1]*	-4.43[1]*
SK	-1.85[2]	-1.54[2]	-1.32[3]	-1.52[3]	-2.19[1]	-2.11[1]	-4.41[1]*	-4.68[1]*
TW	-1.79[1]	-2.12[1]	-4.44[1]*	-4.36[1]*	-1.95[1]	-2.29[1]	-4.47[1]*	-4.39[1]*
JAP	-1.16[1]	-3.12[1]	-3.22[2]*	-3.18[2]	-1.16[1]	-3.25[1]	-7.34[1]*	-7.19[1]*
US	-1.20[4]	-2.08[4]	-2.28[6]	-2.13[6]	-2.82[1]	-3.34[1]	-6.40[1]*	-6.31[1]*

Notes: Asterisk (*) denotes significant at 5percent level. 5percent critical values for no trend and trend are –2.86 and –3.41 respectively. The optimal lag structure is determined using the Akaike Information Criteria (AIC) and are provided in the parentheses. All sample periods (except Malaysia) cover from 1971-1999, accounting for 29 observations. The following notations apply in all the forthcoming tables: IND = Indonesia, MAL = Malaysia, PHI = Philippines, SIN = Singapore, TH = Thailand, HK = Hong Kong, SK = South Korea, TW = Taiwan, JAP = Japan and US = United States.

Table 9.3 KPSS Unit Root Tests

	Level		First Difference		Conclusion
	μ	τ	μ	τ	
Savings					
IND	0.802[1]*	0.333[1]*	0.455[2]	0.060[2]	I(1)
MAL	0.720[1]*	0.147[1]*	0.122[5]	0.118[5]	I(1)
PHI	0.818[2]*	0.221[2]*	0.350[1]	0.059[1]	I(1)
TH	1.349[1]*	0.155[1]*	0.074[1]	0.074[1]	I(1)
HK	0.465[8]*	0.158[8]*	0.100[2]	0.041[2]	I(1)
SIN	1.064[1]*	0.153[1]*	0.098[1]	0.052[1]	I(1)
SK	0.493[5]*	0.181[15]*	0.073[1]	0.035[1]	I(1)
TW	0.481[1]*	0.256[1]*	0.137[1]	0.043[1]	I(1)
JAP	0.920[1]*	0.152[1]*	0.106[2]	0.078[2]	I(1)
US	0.792[2]*	0.159[2]*	0.056[1]	0.061[1]	I(1)
Investments					
IND	1.046[1]*	0.247[1]*	0.434[2]	0.105[2]	I(1)
MAL	0.639[1]*	0.152[1]*	0.226[3]	0.080[3]	I(1)
PHI	0.734[1]*	0.222[1]*	0.113[1]	0.081[1]	I(1)
TH	0.693[1]*	0.211[1]*	0.229[6]	0.127[6]	I(1)
HK	0.463[1]*	0.241[1]*	0.082[3]	0.070[3]	I(1)
SIN	0.531[1]*	0.221[1]*	0.064[2]	0.062[2]	I(1)
SK	0.766[1]*	0.150[1]*	0.219[4]	0.111[4]	I(1)
TW	0.560[1]*	0.146[1]*	0.060[1]	0.061[1]	I(1)
JAP	0.926[1]*	0.184[1]*	0.072[2]	0.071[2]	I(1)
US	0.729[1]*	0.152[1]*	0.072[2]	0.064[2]	I(1)

Notes: Asterisk (*) denotes significant at 5percent level obtain from Kwiatkowski *et al.* (1992). The null hypothesis of KPSS unit root tests is that the series contain no unit root (stationary) against the alternative hypothesis of a unit root (non-stationary). The μ and τ are the models with constants and a time trend respectively. Optimal lag lengths are provided in parentheses. All sample periods (except Malaysia) covers from 1971-1999, accounting for 29 observations.

Table 9.4 Multivariate Cointegration Tests of Saving-Investment

Model	Null Ho	Alternative H_1	λ-Max	Trace	Critical Value (95percent) λ-Max	Critical Value (95percent) Trace
IND (K=3)	r = 0	r = 1	14.30	21.75	19.22	25.77
	r ≤ 1	r = 2	7.44	7.44	12.39	12.39
MAL (K=3)	r = 0	r = 1	7.04	11.23	19.22	25.77
	r ≤ 1	r = 2	4.18	4.18	12.39	12.39
PHI (K=3)	r = 0	r = 1	11.94	18.59	19.22	25.77
	r ≤ 1	r = 2	6.65	6.65	12.39	12.39
TH (K=3)	r = 0	r = 1	9.22	12.59	19.22	25.77
	r ≤ 1	r = 2	3.37	3.37	12.39	12.39
HK (K=2)	r = 0	r = 1	11.14	15.95	19.22	25.77
	r ≤ 1	r = 2	4.80	4.80	12.39	12.39
SIN (K=1)	r = 0	r = 1	18.89	22.55	19.22	25.77
	r ≤ 1	r = 2	3.66	3.66	12.39	12.39
SK (K=3)	r = 0	r = 1	8.47	13.16	19.22	25.77
	r ≤ 1	r = 2	4.69	4.69	12.39	12.39
TW (K=2)	r = 0	r = 1	9.53	15.02	19.22	25.77
	r ≤ 1	r = 2	5.49	5.49	12.39	12.39
JAP (K=2)	r = 0	r = 1	15.75	23.53	19.22	25.77
	r ≤ 1	r = 2	7.79	7.79	12.39	12.39
US (K=1)	r = 0	r = 1	7.89	11.11	19.22	25.77
	r ≤ 1	r = 2	3.22	3.22	12.39	12.39

Notes: (K=n) represents the optimal lag lengths selected according to the AIC criteria. No cointegration is detected for saving-investment relationships of all 10 countries.

Table 9.5 Restriction Test of Saving-Investment

		Perfect Mobility Hypothesis (β=0)		Perfect Immobility Hypothesis (β=1)	
		Independent Variable		Independent Variable	
	Dependent	ΔI	ΔS	ΔI	ΔS
Model	Variable	χ^2		χ^2	
IND (k=3)	ΔI	-	5.48[0.02]*	-	4.44[0.04]*
	ΔS	0.38[0.54]	-	7.75[0.01]*	-
MAL (k=3)	ΔS	-	2.21[0.14]	-	23.65[0.00]*
	ΔI	2.74[0.10]	-	9.89[0.00]*	-
PHI (k=3)	ΔI	-	0.22[0.64]	-	59.61[0.00]*
	ΔS	0.08[0.78]	-	132.40[0.00]*	-
TH (k=3)	ΔI	-	0.40[0.53]	-	13.12[0.00]*
	ΔS	1.29[0.26]	-	12.13[0.00]*	-
HK (k=2)	ΔI	-	2.96[0.09]	-	48.31[0.00]*
	ΔS	0.00[0.98]	-	50.49[0.00]*	-
SIN (k=1)	ΔI	-	0.07[0.80]	-	379.03[0.00]*
	ΔS	2.82[0.09]	-	47.02[0.00]*	-
SK (k=3)	ΔI	-	1.02[0.31]	-	479.26[0.00]*
	ΔS	3.31[0.07]	-	17.23[0.00]*	-
TW (k=2)	ΔI	-	2.35[0.13]	-	74.90[0.00]*
	ΔS	1.33[0.25]	-	479.26[0.00]*	-
JAP (k=2)	ΔI	-	7.64[0.01]*	-	33.36[0.00]*
	ΔS	1.61[0.21]	-	6.39[0.01]*	-
US (k=1)	ΔI	-	1.19[0.28]	-	15.18[0.00]*
	ΔS	0.01[0.93]	-	38.19[0.00]*	-

Notes: Asterisk (*) denotes 5percent significant level while P-values are presented in parentheses [ ]. (K=n) represents the optimal lag lengths selected according to the AIC criteria. The joint-significance of the lagged values of the independent variables is tested using the Wald test and Chi-square (χ^2) statistics.

Table 9.6 DOLS Long Run Parameter Estimations

Country	β	SSR	Adj R^2
IND	0.76 (0.21) ***	0.09	0.81
MAL	0.50 (0.24) **	0.69	0.14
PHI	0.34 (0.11) ***	0.22	0.78
TH	0.69 (0.15) ***	0.40	0.45
HK	0.20 (0.35) *	0.05	0.60
SIN	0.05 (0.18) *	0.02	0.19
SK	0.32 (0.14) **	0.16	0.24
TW	0.14 (0.34) *	0.03	0.63
JAP	0.45 (0.25) *	0.02	0.50
US	0.56 (0.10) ***	0.03	0.74

Notes: Asterisks *, ** and *** denote 10percent, 5percent and 1percent significance level respectively. Standard errors are presented in parentheses ( ), while SSR represents the sum of squared residuals. The DOLS equations are estimated including up to $j = \pm 3$ leads and lags for first difference of savings and up to $j = -3$ lags for the first difference of investments. The results presented refer to a parsimonious version of the more general specification with only the insignificant lead/lag regressors omitted.

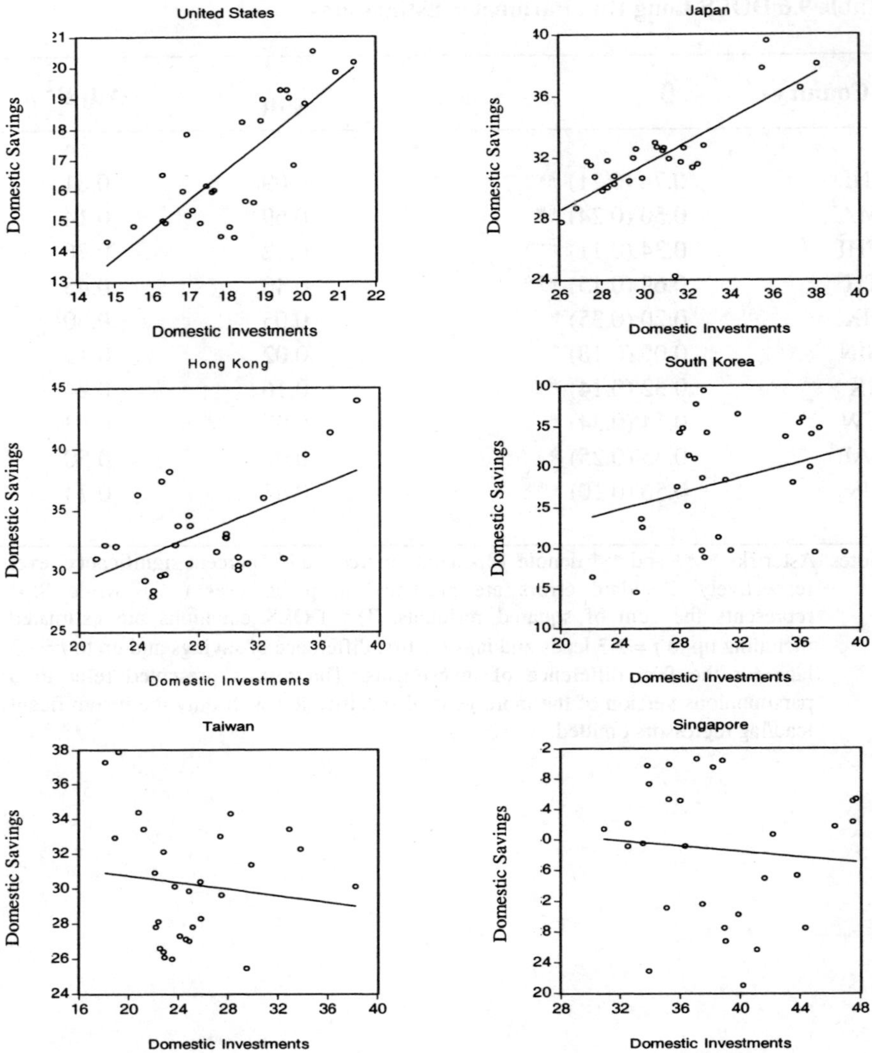

Figure 9.1 Plots of Saving-Investment Ratio

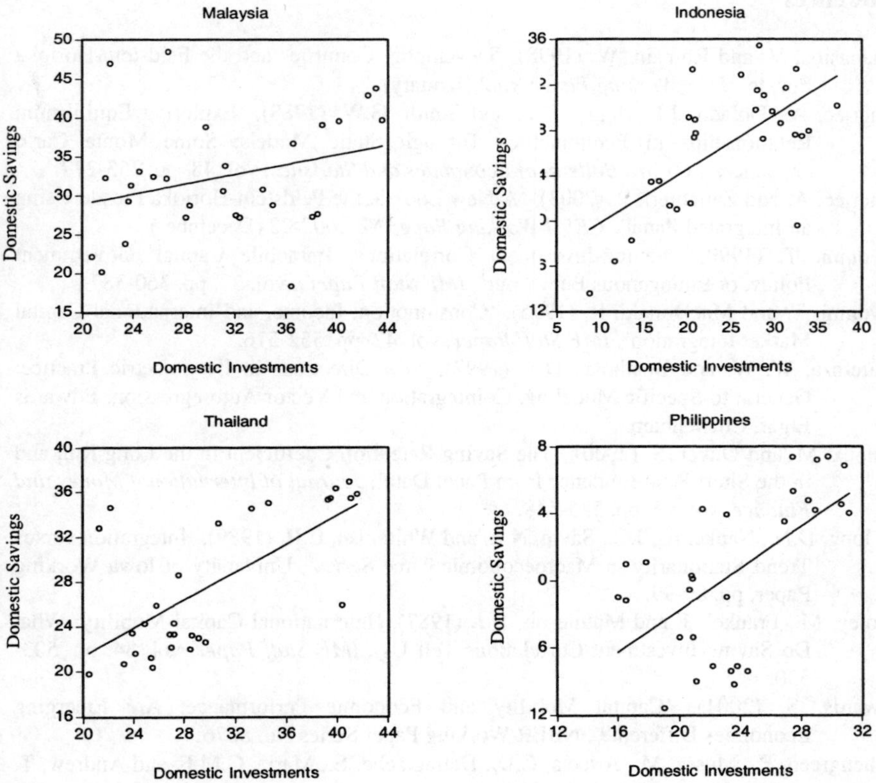

Figure 9.1 (continued)

References

Athanasioa, V. and Romain, W. (1998), 'Developing Countries and the Feldstein-Horioka Puzzle', *IMF Working Paper No.2* (January).

Banerjee, A., Dolado, J.J., Henry, D.F. and Smith, G.W. (1988), 'Exploring Equilibrium Relationships in Econometrics Through Static Models: Some Monte Carlo Evidences', *Oxford Bulletin of Economics and Statistics*, vol. 48, pp. 253-277.

Banerjee, A. and Zanghieri, P. (2003), 'A New Look at the Feldstein-Horioka Puzzle Using an Integrated Panel', *CEPII Working Paper No 2003-22* (December).

Bayoumi, T. (1990), 'Saving-Investment Correlations: Immobile Capital, Government Policy, or Endogenous Behaviour', *IMF Staff Papers*, vol. 37, pp. 360-387.

Bayoumi, T. and MacDonald, R. (1995), 'Consumption, Income, and International Capital Market Integration', *IMF Staff Paper*, vol. 42, pp. 552-576.

Charemza, W. W. and Deadman, D.F. (1992), New Directions in Econometric Practice: General to Specific Modeling, Cointegration and Vector Autoregression, Edwards Elgar, Cheltenham.

Coiteux, M. and Oliver, S. (2000), 'The Saving Retention Coefficient in the Long Run and in the Short Run: Evidence from Panel Data', *Journal of International Money and Finance*, vol. 19, pp. 535-548.

De Jong, D.N., Nankervis, J.C., Savin, N.E. and Whiteman, C.H. (1989), 'Integration versus Trend Stationarity in Macroeconomic Time Series', University of Iowa Working Paper, pp. 89-99.

Dooley, M., Frankel, J. and Mathieson, D.J. (1987), 'International Capital Mobility: What Do Saving-Investment Correlations Tell Us', *IMF Staff Paper*, vol. 34, pp. 503-530.

Edwards, S. (2001), 'Capital Mobility and Economic Performance: Are Emerging Economies Different?', NBER Working Paper Series No. 8076.

Eichengreen, B., Mussa, M., Ariccia, G.D., Detragiache, E., Maria, G.M.F. and Andrew, T. (1999), 'Liberalizing Capital Movements: Some Analytical Issues', *IMF Economic Issues 17*.

Engle, R.F. and Granger, C.W.J. (1987), 'Cointegration and Error Correction: Representation, Estimation, and Testing', *Econometrica*, vol. 55, pp. 251-276.

Feldstein, M. and Harioka, C. (1980), 'Domestic Saving and International Capital Flows', *Economic Journal*, vol. 90, pp. 314-329.

Frankel, J. A. (1992), 'Measuring International Capital Mobility: A Review', *American Economics Review*, vol. 82, pp. 197-202.

Gabriele, A., Boratav, K. and Parikh, A. (2000), 'Instability and Volatility of Capital Flows to Developing Countries', *The World Economy*, vol. 23, pp. 1031-1056.

Gundlach, E. and Sinn, S. (1992), 'Unit Root Tests of the Current Account Balance: Implications for International Capital Mobility', *Applied Economics*, vol. 24, pp. 617-623.

Ho, T.W. (1999), 'Export-orientation and Investment-Saving Correlation: A Case of Taiwan', *Applied Economics*, vol. 31, pp. 805-813.

Ho, T.W. (2002), 'A Panel Cointegration Approach to The Investment-Saving Correlation', *Empirical Economics*, vol. 27, pp. 91-100.

Hussein, K. A. (1998), 'International Capital Mobility in OECD Countries: The Feldstein-Horioka Puzzle revisited', *Economic Letters*, vol. 59, pp. 237-242.

Inder, B. (1995), 'Finite Sample Arguments for Appropriate Estimation of Cointegrating Vectors', Mimeo, Department of Economics, Monash University.

Jansen, W.J. (1996), 'Estimating Saving-Investment Correlations: Evidence For OECD Countries Based on an Error Correction Model', *Journal of International Money and Finance*, vol. 18, pp. 13-26.

Jansen, W.J. (2000), 'International Capital Mobility: Evidence form Panel Data', *Journal of International Money and Finance*, vol. 19, pp. 507-511.

Johansen, S. and Juselius, K. (1990), 'Maximum Likelihood Estimation and Inference on Cointegration with Applications to Money Demand', *Oxford Bulletin of Economics and Statistics*, vol. 52, pp. 169-210.

Kim, S.H. (1999), 'The Saving-Investment Correlation Puzzle is Still a Puzzle', Mimeo, Department of Economics, Brandeis University, United States.

Krol, R. (1996), 'International Capital Mobility: Evidence from Panel Data', *Journal of International Money and Finance*, vol. 15, pp. 467-474.

Krugman, P. (1998), 'What Happened to Asia', Mimeo, MIT, Cambridge, Massachusetts.

Lemmen, J.J.G. and Eijffinger, S.C.W. (1993), 'The Degree of Financial Integration in the European Community', *De Economist*, vol. 141, pp. 189-213.

Lemmen, J.J.G. and Eijffinger, S.C.W. (1995), 'The Quantity Approach to Financial Integration: The Feldstein-Horioka Criterion Revisited', *Open Economies Review*, vol. 6, pp. 145-165.

MacDonald, R. and Taylor, P.M. (1993), 'The Monetary Approach to the Exchange Rate: Rational Expectations, Long Run Equilibrium and Forecasting', *IMF Staff Papers*, vol. 40, pp. 89-107.

Masih, A.M.M. and Masih, R. (1997), 'A Comparative Analysis of The Propagation of Stock Market Fluctuations in Alternative Models of Dynamic Causal Linkages', *Applied Financial Economics*, vol. 7, pp. 59-74.

Masih, A.M.M. and Masih, R. (1999), 'Are Asian Stock Market Fluctuations due Mainly to Intra-Regional Contagion Effects? Evidence Based on Asian Emerging Stock Markets', *Pacific-Basin Finance Journal,* vol. 1 7, pp. 251-282.

Moosa, I. A. (1996), 'A Note on Capital Mobility', *Southern Economics Journal*, vol. 63, pp. 248-254.

Nelson, C.R. and Plosser, C. I. (1982), 'Trends and Random Walks in Macroeconomics Time Series: Some Evidence and Implications', *Journal of Monetary Economics*, vol. 10, pp. 139-162.

Obstfeld, M. and Rogoff, K. (2000), 'The Six Major Puzzles in International Macroeconomics: Is There A Common Cause?', NBER Working Paper Series, 7777.

Oh, K.Y., Kim, B.H., Kim, H.K. and Ahn, B.C. (1999), 'Saving-Investment Cointegration In Panel Data', *Applied Economics Letters*, vol. 6, pp. 477-480.

Phillips, P.C.B. and Perron, P. (1988), 'Testing For A Unit Root In Time Series Regression', *Biometrika*, 75, 335-346.

Phillips, P.C.B. and Hansen, B.E. (1990), 'Statistical Inference In Instrument Variables Regression With *I(1)* Processes', *Review of Economic Studies*, vol. 57, pp. 99-125.

Phillips, P.C.B. and Loretan, M. (1991), 'Estimating Long Run Equilibria', *Review of Economic Studies*, vol. 58, pp. 407-436.

Rubio, O.B. (1998), 'The Saving-Investment Correlation Revisited: the Case of Spain, 1964-1994', *Applied Economics Letters*, vol. 5, pp. 769-772.

Sachsida, A. and Caetano, M.A.R. (2000), 'The Feldstein-Horioka Puzzle Revisited', *Economics Letters*, vol. 68, pp. 85-88.

Sarno, L. and Taylor, M.P. (1999), 'Moral Hazard, Asset Price Bubbles, Capital Flows, and the East Asian Crisis: the First Tests', *Journal of International Money and Finance*, vol. 18, pp. 637-657.

Schwert, G.W. (1987), 'Effects of Model Specification on Tests for unit Roots in Macroeconomic Data', *Journal of Monetary Economics,* vol. 20, pp. 73-101.

Schwert, G.W. (1989), 'Tests for unit roots: A Monte Carlo investigation', *Journal of Business and Economic Statistics*, vol. 7, pp. 147-159.

Stock, J.H. and Watson, M. (1993), 'A Simple Estimator of Cointegrating Vectors in Higher Order Integrated Systems', *Econometrica*, vol. 61, pp. 783-820.

Summers, L.H. (1988), 'Tax Policy and International Competitiveness', in J. Frenkel (eds), *International Aspects of Fiscal Policies*, Chicago: Chicago UP, pp. 349-375.

Taylor, A.M. (1996), 'International Capital Mobility In History: The Saving-Investment Relationship', NBER Working Paper Series No. 5742.

Appendix A

Unit Root Tests

The ADF procedure extends the Dickey-Fuller test by allowing a higher order of autoregressive process whereas the PP test is a nonparametric method controlling for serial correlation when testing for a unit root. As these two tests are commonly used in the literature and to conserve space, we do not intend to discuss the details here. Unlike the ADF and PP, the KPSS test assumes the series to be (trend-) stationary under the null hypothesis. The KPSS statistic is based on the residuals from the OLS regression of Y_t on the exogenous variables x_t:

$$Y_t = x_t{}'\delta + \mu_t \tag{1}$$

with the LM statistics defined as:

$$LM = \sum_t S(t)^2 /(T^2 f_0) \tag{2}$$

where f_0 is an estimator of the residual spectrum at frequency zero and $S(t)$ is a cumulative residual function such that $S(t) = \sum_{r=1}^{t} \hat{\mu}_r$ based on the residuals of the $\hat{\mu}_t = Y_t - x_t{}'\hat{\delta}(0)$. However, the estimator of δ used in this calculation differs from the estimator for δ used by GLS detrending since it is based on a regression involving the original data, and not on the quasi-differenced data. The reported critical values for the LM test statistic are based upon the asymptotic results presented in Kwiatkowski *et al.* (1992, Table 1, p. 166).

Data Sources

Country	Raw Data	Derived data	Period	Sources
US	Government Consumption & Investment, Household Consumption Expenditure, Consumption of Fixed Capital, Private Gross Fixed Capital Formation, Changes in Inventories, GDP	GDS/GDP, GDI/GDP	1971-1999	IFS
JAP	Gross Saving, Household Consumption Expenditure, Gross Fixed Capital Formation, Changes in Inventories, GDP	GDS/GDP, GDI/GDP	1971-1999	IFS
NIE-4				
HK	Government consumption expenditure, Private consumption expenditure, Gross domestic fixed capital formation, Changes in inventories, GDP	GDS/GDP, GDI/GDP	1971-1999	IFS, Hong Kong Monetary Authority
SNG	Government Consumption Expenditure, Household Consumption Expenditure, Gross Fixed Capital Formation, Changes in Inventories, GDP	GDS/GDP, GDI/GDP	1971-1999	IFS, Monetary Authority of Singapore
SK	Government Consumption Expenditure, Consumption of Fixed Capital, Capital Formation, Changes in Inventories, GDP	GDS/GDP, GDI/GDP	1971-1999	IFS, SEACEN Financial Statistics
TW	Gross national savings, gross domestic investment, GDP	GDS/GDP, GDI/GDP	1971-1999	National Statistics of Taiwan

Data Sources (continued)

Country	Raw Data	Derived data	Period	Sources
ASEAN-4				
IND	Government consumption of fixed capital, private consumption, Gross Fixed Capital Formation, Changes in Inventories, GDP	GDS/GDP, GDI/GDP	1971-1999	IFS, SEACEN Financial Statistics
MAL	Government Consumption Expenditure, Household Consumption Expenditure, Gross Fixed Capital Formation, Changes in Inventories, GDP	GDS/GDP, GDI/GDP	1971-1997	IFS, SEACEN Financial Statistics
PHI	Government Consumption Expenditure, Household Consumption Expenditure, Gross Fixed Capital Formation, Changes in Inventories, GDP	GDS/GDP, GDI/GDP	1971-1999	IFS, SEACEN Financial Statistics
THAI	Government Consumption Expenditure, Household Consumption Expenditure, Consumption of Fixed Capital, Gross Fixed Capital Formation, Changes in Inventories, GDP	GDS/GDP, GDI/GDP	1971-1999	IFS, SEACEN Financial Statistics

Notes: IFS refers to the International Financial Statistics published by IMF. SEACEN represents the South East Asian Central Banks Research and Training Central. For details of Taiwanese data, please visit http://www.stat.gov.tw/main.htm. For Malaysia, the study period only covers 1971-1997 due to the imposed capital control and fixed bilateral exchange rate (against US) since 2 September 1998.

Chapter 10

Financial Integration and its Implication for Economic Union in Asia

Sarinder Kumari, Muzafar Shah Habibullah, M. Azali,
Mohammed B. Yusoff and Yoke-Kee Eng

Introduction

The general move towards international financial liberalisation by countries has been motivated by the fact that integration of financial markets allows for more efficient use and allocation of investment funds over time. Financial integration and capital mobility are closely related and often used interchangeably as the integration of financial markets involves the deregulation of national markets and the liberalisation of international capital flows. Therefore, financial market integration is conducive to capital mobility or increases the potential of capital flows and it can be implied that capital mobility is a sufficient condition for financial integration or that a high level of capital mobility indicates a high level of market integration (Moosa, 1996).

While the gains from financial integration and the associated capital mobility are quite clear, the measurement criteria for financial integration have proven to be more difficult. This chapter focuses on the savings-investment criterion highlighted by Feldstein and Horioka (1980) as a way of measuring international capital mobility. Feldstein and Horioka ran a cross-sectional regression on 16 industrial countries and found a high correlation between savings and investment. This was interpreted as indicating low capital mobility because if there was high capital mobility, there would be no *a priori* reason for savings and investment to be correlated across countries as savings in each country would respond to the worldwide opportunities for investment, while the worldwide pool of capital would finance investments in each country. However, if capital mobility were restricted, then there would be a wedge between the cost of domestic and foreign savings and the incremental savings would tend to be invested domestically. Therefore a positive close-to-one correlation between the savings rate and investment would be suggestive of imperfect capital mobility while in the extreme case of zero capital mobility; savings and investment would be perfectly correlated.

The finding of a high correlation between savings and investment by Feldstein and Horioka (1980) implying imperfect capital mobility has jolted the widespread analytical approach by researchers that international capital mobility is nearly perfect. If international capital mobility does not require a close correlation between savings and investment, it is difficult to rationalise the Feldstein-Horioka finding – corroborated in many similar studies – that savings and investment are in fact highly correlated. Referred to as the Feldstein-Horioka puzzle, this has raised considerable doubt on whether national markets for physical capital are highly integrated. Despite this, the savings-investment correlation proposed by Feldstein and Horioka (1980) has been widely accepted as a measure of financial integration and capital mobility.

However, the Feldstein-Horioka finding has been subjected to both econometrics and theoretical criticisms. The cross-sectional regression not only ignores the time-series and non-stationary properties of investment and savings in each country, which could lead to spurious regressions, but it could also be subjected to simultaneity bias (e.g. Dooley *et al.*, 1987; Miller, 1988; Sinn, 1992). There have also been difficulties in interpreting the results of tests based on the Feldstein and Horioka method, as the regression equations are not explicitly derived from theory. There is therefore, no information on the size of the regression coefficient under the null hypothesis of perfect capital mobility. Indeed, there are many cases in which savings and investment are correlated even under perfect capital markets (Obstfeld, 1993).

Due to these criticisms, alternative econometric approaches have been employed to study the savings-investment relationship. Cointegration techniques of analysis pioneered by Miller (1988) have been considered as they take into account the non-stationarity time-series properties of savings and investment in each country. The cointegration analysis essentially extends the Feldstein-Horioka interpretation by arguing that cointegration between savings and investment implies that capital is highly immobile internationally. Absence of cointegration between savings and investment means that capital mobility is high. Results from various unit root and cointegration tests (Miller, 1988; Barkoulas, 1996; Bajo-Rubio, 1998) among others show either no cointegration between savings and investment or reducing savings retention coefficients over time. However, recently it has been argued that savings and investment tend to be cointegrated variables (Coakley *et al.*, 1996; Coakley and Kulasi, 1997; Coiteux and Olivier, 2000). The cointegration between savings and investment has been taken to imply inter-temporal budget constraints rather than as an evidence against capital mobility.

Although cointegration analysis is able to address the issue of non-stationarity of investment and savings, the conventional unit root and cointegration tests have been found to have low testing power, which could therefore lead to erroneous conclusion (Coakley *et al.*, 1996; Coakley and Kulasi, 1997; Oh *et al.*, 1999).

To take into account the econometric issues of the Feldstein-Horioka approach, this study employs the panel data approach to analyse international capital mobility. Panel data analysis has been shown to improve the statistical power of the conventional unit root and cointegration tests by pooling data and increasing the number of observations (Coakley *et al.*, 1996; Coakley and Kulasi, 1997; Oh *et al.*, 1999).

Literature Review

The Feldstein-Horioka finding of a high correlation between investment rates and their national savings rates has been confirmed by many subsequent studies using a variety of techniques encompassing both cross-section and time-series regressions over different time periods for both industrialised and developing countries (e.g. Feldstein, 1983; Penati and Dooley, 1984; Dooley *et al.*, 1987; Vos, 1988; Tesar, 1991). In fact, Feldstein (1983) finds no evidence that this correlation has weakened over time.

Currently, however, there is little agreement on explanations of this apparent empirical regularity of a high correlation between savings and investment. Economists are unwilling to accept the statistical evidence that financial markets are not highly integrated and argue that the results do not necessarily imply low capital mobility in the international economy (e.g. Finn, 1990; Baxter and Crucini, 1993; Coakley *et al.*, 1996; Coakley and Kulasi, 1997).

A number of hypotheses have been used to rationalise the Feldstein-Horioka regression result without concluding that capital is immobile. For example, a number of studies suggest that the savings-investment correlation increases with country size due to its effects on the world interest rate (Murphy, 1984; Dooley *et al.*, 1987; Baxter and Crucini, 1993; Krol, 1996). Another alternative proposition is that savings and investment can be correlated even in the presence of capital mobility if exogenous variables like productivity shocks or non-traded consumption goods affect both savings and investment (Wong, 1990; Tesar, 1991).

The inter-temporal approach to the current account or the solvency constraint arguments have also been used to explain the relationship between savings and investment as both a short run and long run phenomenon (Sachs, 1982; Finn, 1990; Sinn, 1992; Baxter and Crucini, 1993; Coakley *et al.*, 1996; Coakley and Kulasi, 1997; Jansen, 2000). According to the inter-temporal approach to current account, domestic savings and investment should be perfectly correlated in the long run, since current account balances (i.e. differences between savings and investment) should add up to zero. Due to the inter-temporal budget constraints in an open economy, current account deficits/surpluses cannot be sustained indefinitely. In the long run therefore, investments cannot deviate too much from savings. This implies that savings and investment should keep a one-to-one relation in the steady state; in other words, savings and investment are cointegrated variables. On the other hand, in the short run, the size and sign of the correlation between savings and investment would depend on the structure of the economy, as well as on the nature of the shocks. So while small positive, zero or negative correlations would suggest a significant degree of capital mobility, high positive correlations would not necessarily imply imperfect capital mobility.

One main criticism of the Feldstein-Horioka finding is that national savings and investment are both endogenous variables that respond to a set of common factors. For example, one version of the endogeneity critique that results in investment and savings being correlated has been attributed to government policy whereby governments react systematically to current account imbalances so as to offset these imbalances (Tobin, 1983). Although endogeneity of savings arises especially in time-series analysis, it may also arise in cross-section analysis. One way to deal with the cyclical endogeneity (to remove the effects of the business cycle) is to use averaged rates of savings and investment over a period of time as in a cross-sectional regression (Feldstein and Horioka, 1980; Hussein, 1998).

There are essentially two ways that the relationship between savings and investment have been analysed. The first is to use time-averaged or cross-sectional data (Feldstein and Horioka, 1980; Feldstein, 1983; Wong, 1990) and the second is to use time-series data (Sinn, 1992). However, the use of cross-sectional data to primarily remove the business cycle effects has been a subject of contention. For example, Sinn (1992) and Krol (1996) argue that cross-sectional data analysis resulted in biases against capital mobility. Firstly, the averaging of data over five or ten years may not be sufficient to establish a long-run relationship between savings and investment. Secondly, averaging data can introduce an empirical problem of offsetting changes in investment and savings over time suggesting a relationship between investment and saving when none may exist. For instance, the inter-temporal budget constraints imply that there is a high correlation between savings and investment in the long run (Sachs, 1982; Sinn, 1992). Therefore, the savings and investment ratios averaged over sufficiently long periods must be close despite capital mobility. This implies that the correlation between savings and investment should be higher in the long run, compared to the short-run although this may not always be the case as indicated by Sarno and Taylor (1998).

To overcome the shortcomings of the cross-sectional method, time-series estimation approaches have been advocated. One important aspect of the time series estimation is that the same correlation coefficient is not imposed across different countries (Sinn, 1992). Therefore, the time series estimates have the advantage as the countries that are more open and integrated with the world capital markets are not merged together with economies that are more closed in a single regression. Modern theory of inter-temporal economics also shows that even with financial integration, a country may experience net capital inflows and outflows at different points in time (Genberg and Swoboda, 1992). This variability would not be captured by a cross-sectional analysis that is based on time-averaged data and would therefore result in a bias against capital mobility. A re-estimation of the Feldstein-Horioka model using annual data shows not only lower correlation coefficients but also considerable variability between savings and investment (Sinn, 1992).

Despite its apparent advantages, there have been concerns that the time series estimates may be subject to greater bias than cross-section regressions because of the problems of identification and estimation induced by simultaneity bias or the endogeneity of both savings and investment. For instance, the time-series estimates do not take into account business cycle effects on both savings and investment (Krol, 1996; Oh *et al.*, 1999).

As a result, there is now a growing interest in panel data methodology that utilises information from both the time-series and cross-sectional variation in the data. It does not require the averaging of data and there is no loss of information associated with it while at the same time allowing for specific country effects such as country size to be taken into account.

Krol (1996) employs the panel data approach to re-estimate the savings-investment regression as he atttributes the high savings-investment coefficient obtained in the Feldstein-Horioka (1980) to the problem of the estimation technique. It is argued that although the cross-sectional data employed by Feldstein-Horioka takes into account time-effects like the business cycle, it does not take into account unobserved or unmeasured country effects like country size. On the other hand, time-series data does not take into account the business cycle effects. A panel data approach would allow for both these effects to be taken into account as it controls for business cycle effects without averaging the data or suffering any loss of information associated with it and it also takes into account country effects. Using the panel approach, a considerably smaller correlation between savings and investment than previous estimates is found. Country effects are found to have more significant effects than international business cycle effects in the savings-investment analysis. The findings of Krol are corroborated by a number of studies adopting the panel data approach (Corbin, 2001; Oh *et al.*; 1999; Coakley *et al.*, 1996).

One common criticism raised in the literature is that of the low testing power of the conventional cointegration tests. Coakley and Kulasi (1997) employ a variety of cointegration tests to analyse the relationship between savings and investment. Besides the conventional ADF cointegration tests, a panel unit root test using the t-bar statistic based on the average ADF proposed by Im *et al.* (1995) is also employed as it has a higher power than the conventional time-series tests. The results of the panel cointegration show that there is cointegration between savings and investment in all the 11 countries studied as compared to only 8 countries by the conventional tests. Oh *et al.* (1999) used conventional and panel unit root and cointegration tests and confirm the low testing power of conventional cointegration tests as they fail to detect cointegration between savings and investment in contrast to the finding of the panel cointegration tests.

Methodology

The empirical model to test the capital mobility hypothesis applied here employs the panel data approach to the basic regression model used by Feldstein and Horioka (1980) to analyse the relationship between savings and investment. This approach utilises information from both time series and cross-sectional variation in the data and allows for the use of advances made in estimating models of individual behaviour over time without having to aggregate time-series data. It does not require the averaging of data and there is no loss of information associated with it.

The regression model that is employed in this study is as follows:

$$(I/Y)_{it} = \alpha_i + \beta(S/Y)_{it} + \varepsilon_{it} \qquad (1)$$

where I is the gross domestic investment, S is the gross national savings, Y is the gross domestic product, i is the country index, α is the constant term and β is the saving-investment coefficient, ε is the error term and t is the observation year.

In this regression, β is subjected to the equality restriction and is constrained to have the same value for all countries and does not vary across countries. However, to capture the country specific effects, the equality condition is not imposed on α and it is allowed to differ across countries. These constraints define the fixed-effects model (Krol, 1996; Coiteux and Olivier, 2000).

Under the assumption of high capital mobility, β should be closer to zero than to one. The null hypothesis that is tested is $\beta = 0$ against the alternative hypothesis of $\beta = 1$. If β is not found to be significantly different from zero, then the null hypothesis cannot be rejected and it can be inferred that capital is mobile internationally. However, if the null hypothesis is rejected, it can be inferred that capital is not perfectly mobile.

The conventional unit root and cointegration tests used in time-series data have been found to be limited due to their low testing power especially for panels of moderate size where the existing test procedures may not be computationally feasible or sufficiently powerful. This may therefore lead to erroneous results. The panel data approach employs the panel unit root tests and panel cointegration tests that have been found to improve the power of these tests. In this respect, the panel unit root tests developed by Im *et al.* (1997: IPS hereafter) and the cointegration tests by Pedroni (1995) and Kao and Chiang (1998) are used.

To determine the stationarity of the individual variables, the conventional unit root tests of Augmented Dickey-Fuller (ADF) (Dickey and Fuller, 1981) and Phillips-Peron (PP) (Phillips and Peron, 1988) are conducted. However, as these tests have low testing power, this study employs a panel unit root test proposed by IPS to test the null hypothesis of unit root (that is, non stationarity). This test is substantially more powerful than the individual time-series ADF or PP tests.

The IPS test is based on the average of the statistics obtained from individual tests. In other words, in the IPS procedure an ADF equation is estimated separately for each individual country and this allows for differing parameter values, variance and even different lag lengths. The null hypothesis for the presence of unit root is $H_o : \beta_i = 0$ for all i against the alternative H_1: $\beta_i < 0$ for $i = 1, 2, \ldots, N_1$; $\beta_i = 0$ for $i = N_1 + 1, N_1 + 2, \ldots N$. The alternative hypothesis allows for β_i to differ across groups.

The IPS procedure looks at the stochastic process generated by the first-order autoregressive process:

$$Y_{it} = (1 - \phi_i)\mu_i + \phi_i Y_{i,t-1} + \varepsilon_{it} \tag{2}$$

where $i = 1, 2, \ldots, N$; $t = 1, 2, \ldots, T$ and the initial values $Y_{t,0}$ are given. The following equation is estimated:

$$\Delta Y_{it} = \alpha_i + \beta_i Y_{i,t-1} + \varepsilon_{it} \tag{3}$$

where $\alpha_i = (1 - \phi_i)\mu_i$, $\beta_i = (1 - \phi_i)$ and $\Delta Y_{it} = Y_{i,t} - Y_{i,t-1}$. The errors ε_{it} are assumed to be serially uncorrelated.

IPS proposed two test statistics to test the null hypothesis of the unit root test. These are the Lagrange multiplier or the LM-bar statistic and the t-bar statistic. In this study only the t-bar test statistic is used as in the absence of autocorrelation, the t-bar test tends to perform better than the LM-bar test with finite samples. The t-bar test statistic can be calculated as follows:

$$\Gamma_i = \frac{\sqrt{N}\{\bar{t}_{NT} - E(t_T \mid \beta_I = 0)\}}{\sqrt{Var(t_T \mid \beta_i = 0)}} \Gamma_i \tag{4}$$

where $\bar{t}_{NT}$ is the cross-sectional average of the standard individual ADF unit root t-statistics, such that $\bar{t}_{NT} = \frac{1}{N}\sum_{i=1}^{N} t_{iT}$. The terms $E\ (t_T \mid \beta = 0)$ and $Var(t_T \mid \beta = 0)$ are the respective finite common mean and variance of t_{iT} for $i = 1, 2, \ldots, N$, obtained under the null hypothesis of $\beta_i = 0$. The test statistic t_{iT} is the individual t-statistic for testing the null hypothesis of the unit root ($\beta_i = 0$) in the standard individual ADF and its critical values are reported by Im *et al.* (1997).

Cointegration on the individual time-series data is conducted using the Engle-Granger (1987) cointegration test. However, the conventional cointegration tests tend to suffer from unacceptably low power especially when applied to series of moderate length. Hence, the panel cointegration tests will be employed. Panel cointegration tests generally allow for selective pooling of information regarding common long-run relationships from across the panel while allowing the associated short run dynamics and fixed effects to be heterogenous across different members of the panel.

Two cointegration tests proposed by Kao (1999) and Pedroni (1995) are employed to test whether a cointegration relationship exists between savings and investment. For this study, these tests apply to homogenous panels whereby β is assumed to be the same across all individuals. In these tests the null hypothesis of no cointegration in the variables in each member of the panel is tested.

Kao (1999) proposes two types of panel cointegration tests, namely the Dickey-Fuller (DF) and augmented Dickey-Fuller (ADF). The DF-type tests are calculated from the estimated residuals as follows:

$$\hat{e}_{i,t} = \gamma \hat{e}_{i,t-1} + v \tag{5}$$

where $\hat{e}_{i,t}$ is the estimated residual from the estimated equation. To test the null of no cointegration, (H_o: $\gamma = 1$), four DF-type tests are constructed as follows:

$$1.\ DF_\gamma = \frac{\sqrt{NT}(\hat{\lambda} - 1) + 3\sqrt{N}}{\sqrt{10.2}} \tag{6}$$

$$2.\ DF_t = \sqrt{1.25}\, t_\gamma + \sqrt{1.875N} \tag{7}$$

$$3.\ DF_\gamma^* = \frac{\sqrt{NT}(\hat{\gamma}-1)+(3\sqrt{N}\hat{\sigma}_v^2/\hat{\sigma}_v^2}{\sqrt{3+(7.2\hat{\sigma}_v^4/\hat{\sigma}_{0v}^4)}} \quad (8)$$

$$4.\ DF_t^* = \frac{t_\gamma+(\sqrt{6N}\hat{\sigma}_v/2\hat{\sigma}_{0v}}{\sqrt{(\hat{\sigma}_{0v}^2/2\hat{\sigma}_v^2+(3\hat{\sigma}_v^2/10\hat{\sigma}_{0v}^2)}} \quad (9)$$

where $\hat{\sigma}_v^2 = \Sigma_p - \Sigma_{\mu\varepsilon}\Sigma_\varepsilon^{-1}$ and $\hat{\sigma}_{0v}^2 = \Omega_\mu - \Omega_{\mu\varepsilon}\Omega_\varepsilon^{-1}$. DF_γ and DF_t are based on strict exogeneity of the regressors with respect to the errors in the equation while DF_γ^* and DF_t^* are based on endogenous regressors. The ADF test is calculated from the following regression:

$$\hat{e}_{i,t} = \gamma\hat{e}_{i,t-1} + \sum_{j=1}^{P}\vartheta_i\Delta\hat{e}_{i,t-j} + v_{i,t} \quad (10)$$

The ADF test statistic is constructed as follows:

$$\text{ADF} = \frac{t_{ADF}+\left(\sqrt{6N}\,\hat{\sigma}_v/2\,\hat{\sigma}_{0v}\right)}{\sqrt{\left(\hat{\sigma}_{0v}^2/2\,\hat{\sigma}_v^2\right)+\left(3\,\hat{\sigma}_v^2/10\,\hat{\sigma}_{0v}^2\right)}} \quad (11)$$

where t_{ADF} is the t-statistic of γ in equation (6). The distributions of all these statistics are normal *N(0, 1)*.

Pedroni (1995) constructs a panel autoregressive coefficient estimator $\hat{\gamma}_{N,T}$ based on a pooled Phillips and Perron-type test as follows:

$$\hat{\gamma}_{N,T} - 1 = \frac{\sum_{i=1}^{N}\sum_{t=2}^{T}\left(\hat{e}_{i,t-1}\Delta\hat{e}_{i,t} - \hat{\lambda}_i\right)}{\left(\sum_{i=1}^{N}\sum_{t=2}^{T}\hat{e}_{i,t-1}^2\right)} \quad (12)$$

where $\hat{\lambda}_i$ is the scalar equivalent to the correlation matrix and corrects for any correlation effect. The two test statistics proposed by Pedroni (1995) are:

$$1.\ PC_1 = \frac{T\sqrt{N}\left(\hat{\gamma}_{N,T}-1\right)}{\sqrt{2}} \Rightarrow N(0,1) \quad (13)$$

$$2.\ PC_2 = \frac{\sqrt{NT(T-1)}\left(\hat{\gamma}_{N,T}-1\right)}{\sqrt{2}} \Rightarrow N(0,1) \quad (14)$$

The cointegration relationship in the panel data is estimated using Kao and Chiang's (2001) dynamic OLS (DOLS) and fully modified (FMOLS) estimators. The FMOLS estimator does not in general improve on the OLS estimator while the DOLS estimator is better than both the bias-corrected OLS and FMOLS estimators. The OLS estimator of β is

$$\hat{\beta}_{OLS} = \left[\sum_{i=1}^{N} \sum_{i=1}^{N} (X_{i,t} - \overline{X}_i)(X_{i,t} - \overline{X})' \right]^{-1} \left[\sum_{i=1}^{N} \left(\sum_{t=1}^{T} (X_{i,t} - \overline{X}_i) \hat{y}_{i,t}^{+} - T\hat{\Delta}_{\varepsilon u}^{+} \right) \right] \quad (15)$$

where $\overline{X}_i = (1/T) \sum_{t=1}^{T} X_{i,t}$ and $\overline{Y}_i = \left(\sum_{t=1}^{T} Y_{i,t} \right)$. The FM estimator is obtained by correcting for endogeneity and serial correlation to the OLS estimator in (15) above and is given as follows:

$$\hat{\beta}_{FM} = \left[\sum_{i=1}^{N} \sum_{t=1}^{T} \left(X_{i,t} - \overline{X} \right) \left(X_{i,t} - \overline{X}_i \right)' \right]^{-1} \left[\sum_{i=1}^{N} \left(\sum_{t=1}^{T} \left(X_{i,t} - \overline{X}_{i,t} \right) \hat{Y}_{i,t}^{+} - T \hat{\Delta}_{\varepsilon\mu}^{+} \right) \right] \quad (16)$$

where $\hat{\Delta}_{\varepsilon\mu}$ is the kernel estimates of $\Delta_{\varepsilon\mu}$. The DOLS estimator can be obtained from the following regression:

$$Y_{i,t} = \alpha_i + X_{i,t}' \beta + \sum_{j=-q1}^{q2} c_{ij} \Delta X_{i,t+j} + v_{i,t} \quad (17)$$

The DOLS (p,q) where p and q denote the number of leads and lags respectively are estimated. To test for panel cointegration, the residual based ADF statistic proposed by Kao (1999) to test the null of no cointegration is employed. If there is a unit root then there is no cointegration in the model. As a comparison with the conventional cointegration test, the Engle Granger cointegration test is also carried out.

Empirical Results

This study uses the savings and investment data of 11 countries having different stages of financial and economic development. The sample period extends from 1963 to 1997.

The stationarity of individual data is analysed using two standard unit root tests, namely the ADF and PP tests. The ADF and PP statistics are calculated for regressions with a constant and a constant plus a time trend. Table 10.1 and Table 10.2 present the unit root test results for both levels and first-differenced. The null hypothesis of unit roots in the savings rate and investment rate data could not be rejected for almost all the data indicating that the majority of investment and savings rates are non-stationary or I(1) processes. Panel unit tests based on the IPS procedure are used to confirm whether these results from the individual unit root tests arise due to low testing power. Table 10.3 reports results of the panel unit root tests using the same data. The results confirm that even the panel tests cannot reject the null hypothesis of the non-stationarity of the data.

The cointegration analysis is carried out for both individual and panel data and the results are presented in Table 10.4 and Table 10.5 respectively. Both the individual cointegration test (except for India and Indonesia) based on Engle and Granger (1987) and the panel cointegration tests of Kao (1997) and Pedroni

(1995) reject the null hypothesis of no cointegration advocating that savings and investment are cointegrated.

The results for the panel cointegration regression are shown in Table 10.6. Although the t-statistic of the OLS estimate is significantly large, the OLS estimate is generally biased due to the endogeneity in the variables. The estimates of savings retention coefficient (β) derived from the bias-corrected OLS, FMOLS and DOLS are quite different. The OLS with bias correction (0.622) and the FMOLS (0.596) imply that investment and savings are related. However the DOLS estimate (0.093) suggests otherwise; that the impact of savings on investment is insignificant. This is corroborated by the results of the R^2 which indicates that while the FMOLS model is able to explain about 50percent of the variation in investment rates, the DOLS model explains the same variation rather poorly. Since the DOLS is a better estimator than FMOLS (Kao and Chiang, 2001), it can be concluded that the savings retention coefficient tends to be low and there is very low correlation between savings and investment for the set of Asian countries under investigation.

Conclusion

The findings of this study corroborates other studies that savings and investment are cointegrated and this can be interpreted as a manifestation of the inter-temporal budget constraint rather than evidence of low capital mobility (see for example: Coakley et al., 1996; Coakley and Kulasi, 1997; Coiteux and Oliver, 2000). The long-run equilibrium between savings and investment is in line with the inter-temporal budget constraints of an open economy as current account deficits cannot be sustained indefinitely. In this line of research, Baharumshah *et al.* (2003) have also provided evidence that most of the major Asian economies do not violate the inter-temporal budget constraints.

The low savings retention coefficient further implies that there need not be a close relationship between savings and investment as domestic investments can be financed from the worldwide pool of savings. The low correlation between savings and investment may be explained by higher investment opportunities in the Asian region. One explanation for the high degree of capital mobility (especially East Asian economies) is gradual elimination of restrictions on capital inflow (FDI) so as to take advantage of the substantial benefits from higher investments, faster growth and higher living standards in these Asian countries. One important conclusion of this study is that low savings investment retention suggests that Asian countries have already satisfied one of the criterion of the optimum Currency Area (OCA) put forward by Mundell (1961).

Table 10.1 Results of ADF Unit Root Test

	Savings Rate		Investment Rate	
	Constant	Constant & Trend	Constant	Constant & Trend
Level				
India	-1.175	-1.844	1.591	2.708
Indonesia	-1.254	-1.494	-0.996	-1.923
Japan	-1.701	-1.954	-1.659	-2.691
Korea	-1.634	-2.807	-2.878	-4.200**
Malaysia	-0.966	-3.176	-0.990	-2.720
Myanmar	-1.874	-1.877	-1.743	-1.785
Pakistan	-2.295	-1.608	-1.943	-3.336**
Philippines	-1.951	-1.923	-2.452	-2.411
Singapore	-1.435	-2.728	-2.324	-1.853
Sri Lanka	-2.098	-2.509	1.752	2.087
Thailand	-1.074	-2.024	1.745	-2.506
First Differences				
India	-4.170*	-4.074**	-7.144*	-7.091*
Indonesia	-3.976*	-4.054**	-4.268*	-4.379*
Japan	-3.790*	-3.724**	-4.848*	-4.862*
Korea	-5.164*	-5.416*	-5.475*	-5.646*
Malaysia	-6.824*	-6.716*	-3.496*	-3.432**
Myanmar	-4.236*	-4.225**	-4.426*	-4.455*
Pakistan	-5.859*	-6.564*	-4.296*	-4.118**
Philippines	-4.550*	-4.719**	-4.865*	-4.791*
Singapore	-4.565*	-4.602*	-2.991**	-3.084
Sri Lanka	-3.730*	-3.768**	-3.384**	-3.387**
Thailand	-4.237*	-4.190**	-3.644**	-3.487

Notes: The ADF test is implemented to test the null hypothesis of I(1) for the test labeled 'Level' and that of I(2) for the test indicated with 'First-Differenced.' The critical values are obtained from MacKinnon (1991). A full sample is used for the calculation. Asterisks (*) indicate statistics are significant at 1percent level while (**) indicate statistics are significant at 5 percent level.

Table 10.2 Results of PP Unit Root Test

	Savings Rate		Investment Rate	
	Constant	Constant & Trend	Constant	Constant & Trend
		Levels		
India	-0.850	-2.014	-1.714	-4.061**
Indonesia	-1.337	-1.820	-1.117	-2.302
Japan	-1.695	-2.079	-1.391	-2.330
Korea	-1.493	-2.099	-1.810	-2.622
Malaysia	-0.783	-3.704**	-0.809	-2.451
Myanmar	-4.578*	-5.083*	-8.937*	-8.779*
Pakistan	-1.698	-1.828	-2.035	-2.698
Philippines	-1.717	-1.641	-2.082	-2.046
Singapore	-1.292	-2.290	-2.424	-1.921
Sri Lanka	-2.057	-2.343	-1.678	-2.236
Thailand	-1.172	-1.999	-1.466	-2.397
		First Differences		
India	-5.166*	-5.099*	-10.859*	-10.947*
Indonesia	-6.044*	-6.007*	-6.588*	-6.542
Japan	-4.961*	-4.875*	-4.598*	-4.516*
Korea	-4.974*	-5.077*	-5.089*	-5.219*
Malaysia	-8.488*	-8.322*	-4.638*	-4.567*
Myanmar	-11.289*	-11.099*	-3.053**	-2.999
Pakistan	-7.452*	-8.868*	-6.232*	-6.173*
Philippines	-5.692*	-5.788*	-4.311*	-4.221*
Singapore	-5.543*	-5.617*	-5.655*	-5.874*
Sri Lanka	-5.207*	5.209*	3.384**	-3.387**
Thailand	-5.331*	-5.235*	-4.176*	-4.057**

Notes: The PP test is implemented to test the null hypothesis of I(1) for the test labeled 'Level' and that of I(2) for the test indicated with 'First-Differenced.' The critical values are obtained from MacKinnon (1991). A full sample is used for the calculation. Asterisks (*) indicate statistics are significant at 1 percent level while (**) indicate statistics are significant at 5 percent level.

Table 10.3 Results of Engle-Granger Test

	ADF
India	-1.521
Indonesia	-0.545
Japan	-1.998**
Korea	-2.562**
Malaysia	-3.686*
Myanmar	-2.159**
Pakistan	-2.228**
Philippines	-2.678*
Singapore	-1.929**
Sri Lanka	-2.074**
Thailand	-3.684*

Notes: Asterisks (*) indicate statistics are significant at 1 percent level and (**) indicates statistics are significant at 5 percent level.

Table 10.4 Results of Panel Unit Root Test

	Savings Rate		Investment Rate	
	Time trend	**No time trend**	**Time trend**	**No time trend**
IPS	-0.026	-0.244	-1.572	-1.124
(1995)	(0.489)	(0.404)	(0.058)	(0.131)
IPS	0.001	-0.248	-1.554	-10128
(1997)	(0.499)	(0.402)	(0.060)	(0.130)

Notes: Figures in parenthesis indicate the *p-values*.

Table 10.5 Panel Cointegration Test Results

	Kao (1999)
DF_ρ	-5.3374 (0.000)
DF_t	-3.3204 (0.004)
DF^*_ρ	-13.0659 (0.000)
DF^*_t	-3.5085 (0.0002)
ADF	-2.5951 (0.0047)
	Pedroni (1995)
PC_1	-18.5960 (0.0000)
PC_2	-18.3284 (0.0000)

Notes: The critical probabilities are reported in parentheses. Cointegration test statistics are calculated through the residuals from the OLS estimates.

Table 10.6 Results of Panel Cointegration Regression Procedure

	OLS	Bias Corrected OLS	FMOLS	DOLS
β	0.604	0.622	0.596	0.093
t-ratio	19.352	9.304	8.658	1.230
Prob. (N)	0.000	0.000	0.000	0.110
R^2	0.494	0.494	0.494	0.123
Adj. R^2	0.492	0.492	0.492	-1.231
Bias of β	Nil	-0.606	Nil	Nil

References

Baharumshah, A.Z., Lau, E. and Fountas, S. (2003), 'On the Sustainability of Current Account Deficits: Evidence from Four ASEAN Countries, *Journal of Asian Economics*, vol. 14, pp. 465-487.

Bajo-Rubio, O. (1998), 'The Saving-Investment Correlation Revisited: The Case of Spain, 1964-1994', *Applied Economics Letters,* vol. 5, pp. 769-772.

Barkoulas, J., Filizetkin, A. and Murphy, R. (1996), 'Time Series Evidence on the Saving-Investment Relationship', *Applied Economics Letters,* vol. 3, pp. 77-80.

Baxter, M. and Crucini, M.J. (1993), 'Explaining Saving-Investment Correlations', *American Economic Review,* vol. 83, pp. 416-436.

Coakley, J. and Kulasi, F. (1997), 'Cointegration of Long Span Saving and Investment', *Economics Letters,* vol. 54, pp. 1-6.

Coakley, J., Kulasi, F. and Smith, R. (1996), 'Current Account Solvency and the Feldstein-Horioka Puzzle', *The Economic Journal,* vol. 106, pp. 620-627.

Coitex, M. and Oliver, S. (2000), 'The Saving Retention Coefficient in the Long Run and in the Short Run: Evidence from Panel Data', *Journal of International Money and Finance* vol. 19, pp. 535-548.

Corbin, A. (2001), 'Country Specific Effect in the Feldstein-Horioka Paradox: Panel Data Analysis', *Economic Letters,* vol. 72, pp. 297-302.

Dickey, D.A. and Wayne A.F. (1981), 'Likelihood Ratio Statistics for Autoregressive Time Series with a Unit Root', *Econometrica,* vol. 49, pp. 1057-1072.

Dooley, M., Frankel J. and Mathieson, D.J. (1987), 'International Capital Mobility: What do Saving-Investment Correlations tell us?', *IMF Staff Papers,* vol. 34, pp. 503-530.

Engle, R.F. and Granger, C.W.J. (1987), 'Cointegration and Error Correction. Representation, Estimation and Testing', *Econometrica,* vol. 55, pp. 251-276.

Feldstein, M. (1983), 'Domestic Savings and International Capital Movements in the Long Run and the Short Run', *European Economic Review,* vol. 21, pp. 129-151.

Feldstein, M. and Horioka, C. (1980), 'Domestic Saving and International Capital Flows', *Economic Journal,* vol. 90, pp. 314-329.

Finn, M. G. (1990), 'On savings and Investment Dynamics in a Small Open Economy', *Journal of International Economics,* vol. 29, pp. 1-21.

Genberg, H. and Swoboda, A.K. (1992), 'Saving, Investment and the Current Account', *Scandinavian Journal of Economics,* vol. 94, pp. 347-366.

Ho, T.W. (1999), 'Export-orientation and Investment-Saving Correlation: A Case of Taiwan', *Applied Economics,* vol. 31, pp. 805-813.

Ho, T.W. (2002), 'The Feldstein-Horioka Puzzle Revisited', *Journal of International Money and Finance,* vol. 21, pp. 555-564.

Ho, T.W. (2002), 'A Panel Cointegration Approach to the Investment-Saving Correlation', *Empirical Economics,* vol. 27, pp. 91-100.

Hussein, K.A. (1998), 'International Capital Mobility in OECD countries: The Feldstein-Horioka Puzzle', *Economics Letters,* vol. 59, pp. 237-242.

Im, K.S., Pesaran, M.H. and Shin, Y. (1997), 'Testing for Unit Roots in Heterogeneous Panels', Discussion Paper, University of Cambridge.

Jansen, W.J. (2000), 'International Capital Mobility: Evidence from Panel Data', *Journal of International Money and Finance,* vol. 19, pp. 507-511.

Kao, C. (1999), 'Spurious Regression and Residual-based Tests for Cointegration in Panel data', *Journal of Econometrica,* vol. 90, pp. 1-44.

Kao, C. and Chiang, M.H. (1998), 'On the Estimation and Inference of a Cointegrated Regression in Panel Data', Working Paper, Center for Policy Research, Syracuse University.

Kao, C. and Chiang, M.H. (2001), 'On the Estimation and Inference of a Cointegrated Regression in Panel Data', in B. Baltagi (eds), *Advances in Econometrics*, Vol. 15, pp. 179-222.

Krol, R. (1996), 'International Capital Mobility: Evidence from Panel Data', *Journal of International Money and Credit,,* vol. 15, pp. 467-474.

Mackinnon, J.G. (1991), 'Critical Values for Cointegration Tests', in R.F. Engle and C.W.J. Granger (eds), *Long-Run Economic Relationship: Reading in Cointegration,* Oxford: Oxford University Press, pp. 267 – 276.

Miller, M.S. (1988), 'Are Saving and Investment Co-integrated?', *Economics Letters,* vol. 27, pp. 31-34.

Moosa, I.A. (1996), 'A Note on Capital Mobility', *Southern Economic Journal,* vol. 63, pp. 248-254.

Mundell, R. (1961), 'A Theory of Optimal Currency Areas', *American Economic Review,* vol. 51, pp. 657-665.

Murphy, R.G. (1984), Capital Mobility and the Relationship between Saving and Investment in OECD Countries', *Journal of International Money and Finance,* vol. 3, pp. 327-342.

Obstfeld, M. (1993), 'International Capital Mobility in the 1990s', NBER Working Paper No. 4534.

Oh, K., Kim, B., Kim, H. and Ahn, B. (1999), 'Savings-Investment Cointegration in Panel Data', *Applied Economics Letters,* vol. 6, pp. 477-480.

Pedroni, P (1995), 'Panel Cointegration Asymptotic and Finite Sample Properties of Pooled Time Series Tests with an Application to the PPP Hypothesis', Indiana University Working Paper in Economics No. 13.

Penati, A. and Dooley, M. (1984), 'Current Account Imbalances and Capital Formation in Industrial Countries 1949-81', *IMF Staff Papers,* vol. 31, pp.1-24.

Philips, P.C.B. and Perron, P. (1988), 'Testing for a Unit Root in Time Series Regressions', *Biometrika,* vol. 75, pp. 335-346.

Sachs, J. (1982), 'The Current Account in the Macroeconomic Adjustment Process', *Scandinavian Journal of Economics,* vol. 84, pp. 147-159.

Sarno, L. and Taylor, M.P. (1998), 'Savings-investment correlations: Transitory versus Permanent', *The Manchester School Supplement,* vol. 2025-2034 pp. 17-38.

Sinn, S. (1992), 'Saving-investment Correlations and Capital Mobility: On the Evidence from Annual Data', *The Economic Journal,* vol. 102, pp. 1102-1170.

Tesar, L.L. (1991), 'Savings, Investment and International Capital Flows', *Journal of International Economics,* vol. 31, pp. 55-78.

Tobin, J. (1983), 'Comment on 'Domestic Saving and International Capital Movements in the Long Run and the Short Run' by M. Feldstein', *European Economic Review,* vol. 21, pp. 153-156.

Vos, R. (1988), 'Savings, Investment and Foreign Capital Flows: Have Capital Markets Become More Integrated?', *Journal of Development Studies,* vol. 24, pp. 310-334.

Wong, D.Y. (1990), 'What do Saving-investment Relationships Tell Us About Capital Mobility?', *Journal of International Money and Finance,* vol. 9, pp. 60 74.

PART IV
CONTAGION AND THE CURRENCY CRISES

Chapter 11

Sources of the Asian Currency Crisis

Muhd Zulkhibri Abdul Majid and
Mohammed B. Yusoff

Introduction

Four waves of financial crises have hit international capital markets during the 1990s; the European Monetary System (EMS) crisis in 1992-1993, the collapse of the Mexican peso with 'tequilla effects' in 1994-1995, the Asian flu of 1997-1998 and the Russian virus in 1998. These financial crises stimulated the theoretical and empirical literature on the economics of the crises in several ways, among other things on the determinants of a crisis (Kaminsky and Reinhart, 1999), its impact on domestic output (Aghion, Bacchetta and Banerjee, 2001) and policy implications (Rogoff, 1999).

The East Asian financial crises have been one of the most serious and challenging economic events of the 1990s. The macroeconomic conditions of these countries namely Malaysia, Thailand, Indonesia and the Philippines are shown in Table 11.1. These newly emerging economies, which had succeeded in sustaining rapid growth through export promotion, had strong economic fundamentals before the onset of the financial crisis, but also shared some disturbing similarities.

First, all the four countries, except for the Philippines, experienced slowdowns in economic growth in 1996. Second, all four countries saw their current account deficits rose substantially due to sluggish growth in export earnings. As a percentage of Gross Domestic Product (GDP), Indonesia, Malaysia, the Philippines and Thailand saw their current account deficits deteriorate from 2.0 percent, 3.8 percent, 1.9 percent and 5.7 percent in 1992 respectively; to 3.4 percent, 4.9 percent, 4.7 percent and 4.7 percent in 1996 respectively. Third, the four countries accumulated large external debts. In 1996, Indonesia, the Philippines and Thailand had external debts amounting to US$102.2 billion, US$39.0 billion and US$78.5 billion respectively, which increased to US$137.1 billion, US$50.6 billion and US$93.0 billion respectively, in 1997. Fourth, the real exchange rates in all four countries appreciated markedly. Finally, the levels of international reserves as a percentage of yearly imports were falling in Malaysia, the Philippines, and Thailand from 1995 to 1996.

The economists were divided as to which models are relevant to the East Asian currency crises as they are uncertain whether the currency crisis was due to fundamental imbalances or contagious events. Systematic empirical research on these issues is only just emerging and the evidence is mixed. Eichengreen, Rose and Wyplosz (1995) and Kaminsky and Reinhart (1999) show that currency crises are frequently preceded by fundamental macroeconomic imbalances and early warning signs. On the other hand, Jeanne (1995) and Jeanne and Masson (1996) demonstrate empirically that the French crisis of 1992-93 had strong self-fulfilling characteristics.

This chapter examines the determinants of currency crises in for ASEAN countries: Malaysia, Thailand, Indonesia, and the Philippines (ASEAN-4). We develop a formal empirical model to analyse the determinants of currency crises. In addition, we would like to determine whether contagion effects exist in foreign exchange markets, in which a speculative attack in one country may spread to other countries. The currency crises of the 1997 have also raised questions about whether currency crises are predictable events with systematic early warning indicators or whether they are essentially unpredictable. This chapter will determine the ability of the model to predict the likelihood of currency crises in ASEAN-4 countries.

Literature Review

Currency crisis theories go back to the Salant and Henderson's (1978) model of speculative attack on the gold market, which Krugman (1979) applied to the foreign exchange market. In the model, the government runs a budget deficit, which is financed through additional money creation. The private sector will exchange this additional money creation for foreign currency and so they are steadily lost until reserves reach the threshold level. At that time, the demand for money falls, reserves fall to zero and a currency crisis occurs. This speculative attack is driven by the natural outcome of investors' maximisation and forward-looking behaviours.

The first generation models share the basic assumption of weak country fundamentals, which are known to be unsustainable in the context of a fixed exchange rate regime. This then establishes a unique relationship between the fundamentals and timing of the crisis. The strength of the models is that a sudden speculative attack and loss of reserves occur even though all the behavioural functions are continuous and the fundamentals develop predictably.

The limitations of first generation theories became evident after the EMS crisis in 1992-1993 since these models only allowed only for an exchange rate peg, which either is or is not sustainable under the given fundamentals. The second generation models take into account the possibility of self-fulfilling crises (Obstfeld, 1986, 1994, 1996 or Jeanne, 1997). An increase in devaluation expectations makes it more costly for the authorities to maintain an exchange rate peg. These costs rise as higher interest rates lead to unemployment. The government weighs the costs of defending the exchange rate against the benefits. Investors anticipate the government's calculation and this can raise the costs of defence even further and the crisis becomes self-fulfilling.

These second generation models introduce the possibility of multiple equilibria: one in which there are no attacks, no change in fundamentals and indefinite maintenance of the peg and another in which investors expect an attack. The new fundamentals in the second equilibrium are validated after the investors' expected change in the exchange rate actually occurs. The currency crisis is then modeled as a sudden jump from one equilibrium to another. And, the timing of crisis is no longer uniquely determined.

There are several factors that can create a situation of multiple equilibria and may cause a self-fulfilling currency crisis. In Obstfeld (1994) market participants expect the currency to be devalued at a given rate and set nominal interest rate to a higher level. Because of high unemployment or a large debt burden, the higher interest rates make the peg too costly for the government to keep. Another source of multiple equilibria is the government's expected desire to offset a negative output shock. Authorities' behaviour with regards to problems in the banking sector is another factor that can create a situation of multiple equilibria. As the central bank defends the peg, interest rate rise, which may cause losses to the banking sectors.

In emerging market countries willingness to decrease unemployment is not a key aspect of recent crises. Consequently, in a multiple equilibria model, Masson (1999) used a balance of payments approach to determine the country fundamentals. The cost benefits calculation is determined by the expected value of foreign reserves and the model does not include a direct escape clause for the government. The source of multiple equilibria is the higher debt service costs for the government due to depreciation expectations. The model is tested with recent crises in emerging markets and finds that the fundamentals of some crisis countries are inside the multiple equilibria region.

The recent crises in emerging markets have also inspired new theories, which includes the liberalisation of the financial system and the weaknesses in the banking sector are reasons for crises. Diaz-Alejandro (1985) cite the liberalization of financial markets and bad banking supervision as reasons for the banking and currency crises in Latin America. In addition, the public expects the government to intervene and save most depositors when financial intermediaries run into trouble, whether or not deposits are explicitly insured. The model by Calvo and Vegh (1993, 1999) points out that a non-credible stabilisation programme can be a reason why a consumption boom is followed by a drop in output and finally a currency crisis. Similarly, Kamin and Wood (1997) pointed out the boom and bust cycle of capital flows after liberalisation as a reason for currency crises.

Some progress in explaining recent crises and contagion effect have been made using models that contain financial diversification and the use of leverage by investors. These models are founded on the basic portfolio theory, where a representative investor weighs the effects of different portfolio management rules and margin calls. They find that diversification, together with leveraged investors, creates conditions for contagion effect. In the model by Calvo (1998) contagion effect is caused by margin calls by informed investors, who are then mimicked by uninformed investors. Calvo and Mendoza (2000) discussed optimal diversification as the number of possible investment countries grows. They show that costly information gathering might not be profitable when the number of countries grows. This might cause herding behaviour and contagion of currency crises.

Herding behaviour can be one reason for the large capital flows and contagion effect. Studies have found many theoretical reasons for this herding behaviour (Schafstein-Stein 1990, Banerjee 1992, and Devenow-Welch 1996). Krugman (1997) provided two reasons for the herding behaviour in the Asian crises. First, there is a bandwagon effect driven by investors' awareness of expectations that other investors have private information. Secondly, much of the money invested in emerging markets is managed by agents rather than directly by principals. These agents are compensated in accordance with comparisons with other money managers and so herding behaviour is quite rational.

Model Specification

In this chapter, a currency crisis is defined following the definition by Frankel and Rose (1996), which say that crisis is a nominal depreciation of at least 25 percent a year from the mean rate in the bilateral exchange rate *vis-à-vis* the U.S dollar. A currency crisis exists only when there is an abrupt change in the nominal exchange rate. The definition of crisis excludes the element of unsuccesful speculative attacks since it is very difficult and subjective to define when a speculative attack has occurred then ascertain whether the countries, Malaysia, Indonesia, Thailand, and the Philippines, are under the condition of currency crises before proceeding to analyse the model of currency crises and contagion effects.

Following Eichengreen, Rose and Wyplosz (1996), and Kruger, Osakwe and Page (1998), the model is written as

$$Crisis_{j,t} = \eta X(L)_{i,t-1} + \varphi R\,(Crisis_{j,t}) + \varepsilon_{i,t} \tag{1}$$

where φ is the coefficient on the regional contagion variable R, $(Crisis_{j,t})$; $X(L)_{i,t-1}$ is a vector of information set of lagged explanatory variables of economic fundamentals from country i in period $t-1$; η is the vector of coefficients on the lagged regressors and $\varepsilon_{i,t}$ is a normally distributed error term defined as,

$$\varepsilon_{i,t} = \alpha_i + v_{i,t} \tag{2}$$

where α_i is a random country specific effect and $v_{i,t}$ is a normally distributed error term with zero mean and unit variance. The i subscript indexes the individual countries of a cross-section and the t subscript indexes the time period in the available data. The variable *Crisis* takes a value of 1 if crisis exists and 0, otherwise. The regional contagion variables, $R\ (Crisis_{j,t})$, for country j, take a value of 1 if and only if, there is a crisis in at least one country other than j. If this condition is not satisfied, the contagion variable will take a value of 0 for the period.

The lagged values of the economic fundamentals are used to indicate that crises arise due to persistent deteriorations in economic fundamentals. This implies that it takes some time for deterioration in economic fundamentals to trigger a currency crisis. Besides, we do not expect a very brief and short-lived decline in fundamentals to result in a currency crisis. Using lagged economic fundamentals enable us to segregate the effects of economic fundamentals on currency crises, which also provide a simple test of the ability of the explanatory variables to predict future crises.

Sources of Data and Choice of Variables

The data used in this empirical analysis were obtained from the International Monetary Fund's (IMF) *International Financial Statistic*. The choice of variables used in the estimation is based on theoretical considerations and data availability, as suggested in previous studies, by Eichengreen, Rose and Wyplosz (1996), Sachs, Tornell and Velasco (1996) and Kaminsky and Reinhart (1999). Using quarterly data for Malaysia, Thailand, Indonesia, and the Philippines spanning the ten-year period from 1987 to 1997, this chapter hypothesises that the macroeconomic variables: the ratio of M2 to reserve; trade balance; the growth rate of domestic credit; the banks' claim on the private sector; domestic inflation; real exchange rate and regional contagion, cause the currency crises.

As in Sachs, Tornell and Velasco (1996), the ratio of M2 to international reserves is chosen as a measure of reserve adequacy. This variable has worked well in previous empirical studies and has been identified as a leading indicator of currency crises by Kaminsky and Reinhart (1999). The use of a broad measure of money, as opposed to monetary base, in the definition of the reserve adequacy variable can be rationalised on the grounds that it measures the potential amount of liquid monetary assets that agents can try to convert into foreign exchange. To reduce dispersion in this variable and to facilitate the interpretation of its associated coefficient, the log form is used and it is expected that this variable has a positive effect on the probability of crisis.

The trade balance and the real exchange rate are indicators of external competitiveness. Along with misalignment of the real exchange rate, trade imbalance could cause currency crisis. There is a fair amount of evidence showing that some currency crises are preceded by negative trade balance and volatile exchange rate. We expect a negative association of the trade balance and a positive association on the real exchange rate on the probability of crisis. The effects of monetary policies are captured by the growth rate of domestic credit and we expect it to have a positive effect on currency crises.

Banks' claims on the private sector are a measure of the health of the domestic banking system and are known as a lending boom variable. Sachs, Tornell and Velasco (1996), argued that lending booms increase the ratio of bad loans to total assets thereby weakening the banking system. A weak banking system increases the probability of speculative attack because investors know that the government will be reluctant to resist an attack by increasing interest rates since this would result in bankruptcies and a recession. In this case, the crisis is self-fulfilling. This variable is expected to have a positive effect on the probability of crisis.

Contagion effects are the most recent contribution of extended second-generation models or a third-generation model. There are several channels through which they may be transmitted across countries. Most explanations, however, imply that contagion effects tend to occur at the regional level. In order to capture the effects of contagion, we define a dichotomous variable that takes the value of 1 for countries where at least one other country has had one currency crisis in the quarter. We expect this variable to have a positive relationship on the probability of crisis.

Estimation Technique

Using pooled quarterly data for Malaysia, Thailand, Indonesia and the Philippines from 1987 to 1997, this chapter estimates explicitly the multiperiod probit model linking macroeconomic variables and a measure of contagion to the crisis index. Pooled quarterly data method is used to increase the number of observations and the number of crisis episodes. Three episodes were found each for Malaysia, Indonesia and Thailand, and four for the Philippines. Furthermore, probit with random effects is an appropriate method to estimate a model that has dependent binary, repeated variables and repeated observations of the same group countries over time.

Let P_i be the cumulative normal distribution, called Probit, for the *i*-th observations, then

$$P_i = F(x_i \beta) = \int_{-\infty}^{s} 1/(2\pi)^{1/2} \exp(-z^2/2) dz \tag{3}$$

where $s = x_i \beta$. The Probit Model is written as

$$\begin{aligned} y_t &= F^{-1}(P_i) + \varepsilon_i \\ &= x_i \beta + \varepsilon_i \end{aligned} \tag{4}$$

where $F^{-1}(P_i) = x_i \beta$ is the inverse of cumulative distribution $F(x_i \beta)$. The probit model is derived from a model involving the latent variable, say y_t^* such that

$$y_t^* = x_i \beta + \varepsilon_i \tag{5}$$

where $\varepsilon_i \sim$ normal (0, 1). The value of binary y_i depends on the value if y_i^* is greater than 25 percent devaluation (depreciation) and 0 otherwise.

Since the estimated coefficients in the probit model are difficult to interpret, the effects of one-unit changes in the regressors on the probability of crisis termed as marginal effects. The non-linear and the marginal contribution of each variable depends on the other explanatory variables in the models. In this chapter the marginal effect of x_i is calculated as

$$\delta E(y_i / x_i) / \delta x_i = [\delta F(x_i \beta) / \delta(x_i \beta)] \beta_i \tag{6}$$

where $\delta F(x_i \beta) / \delta(x_i \beta)$ is the density function associated with *F* (Greene, 1999). β_i is weighted by a factor, in this case a density function, which depends on all the values of *X*. As the density function is non-negative, therefore the direction of the effect of a change in β_i depends on the sign of β_i.

Results and Discussion

The regression results on the determinants of currency crises are reported in Table 11.2. Insignificant variables are subsequently excluded in each of the regression equations. The probit model with random effects is estimated utilising a maximum likelihood procedure. There are no specific overall goodness-of-fit measures for this methodology. Therefore, the pseudo R^2 and likelihood test ratio are used for the test of overall goodness-of-fit and the percentage of right prediction to predict the likelihood of currency crises.

Model 1 uses all explanatory variables as derived from the model formulation. The coefficients that are significant at 1 percent level are the ratio of M2 to reserve, real exchange rate, banks' claims on private sector, trade balance and regional contagion. These results support the findings by Kruger, Osakwe and Page (1998). But the growth rate of domestic credits and domestic inflation are insignificant at conventional levels. They all have the expected signs. The ratio of M2 to reserve has a positive coefficient and is significant at 1 percent level suggesting that countries with a low reserve relative to a broad measure of money are more likely to experience currency crises. The result is consistent with the view addressed in first-generation models of currency crises, that reserve inadequacy triggers a currency crisis. The result is also consistent with the findings of Caramazza, Rici and Salgado (2000), which state that reserve inadequacy triggers a currency crisis. The real exchange rate is significant at 1 percent level and has the expected sign indicating that misalignment of real exchange rate increases the probability of a currency crisis.

Domestic credit and domestic inflation are insignificant at conventional level. This is interesting given that these are important fundamental variables suggested in the theoretical literature. The result do not support the notion that inconsistency in macroeconomic policies leads to the countries experiencing in a speculative situation, suggesting that monetary expansion to finance the fiscal deficit does not increase the probability of currency crisis. On the other hand, trade balance variable is significant at 1 percent level and has a negative influence on the probability of a currency crisis, suggesting that a deteriorating trade balance is a risk factor.

The regional contagion variable has a positive sign and is significant at the 1 percent level, supporting the findings for industrial countries by Eichengreen, Rose and Wyplosz (1996). A currency crisis in neighbouring country increases the probability of a speculative attack on the domestic currency. Two channels of international transmission of speculative attacks have been identified in the literature. The first channel is trade links in which a currency crisis in an economy forces the government to devalue the domestic currency. The second channel is information effects, which hypotheses that a currency crisis in one country sends a signal to speculators that pegs in countries with similar macroeconomic policies are unsustainable.

Banks' claims on private sector is significant at 1 percent level confirming the belief that it is an important determinant of currency crises. This suggests that currency crises in Malaysia, Thailand, Indonesia and the Philippines are due to the weaknesses in the banking sector, supporting the hypothesis that lending booms in these countries weaken the structure of the banking sector and increase the probability of speculative attacks on the domestic currency.

In order to find a more parsimonious model, insignificant variables are excluded from our benchmark equation denoted as Models 2 and 3. Model 2 excludes the growth rate of domestic credit. The ration of M2 to reserve, banks' claims on private sector, trade balance, real exchange rate and regional contagion are all significant at the conventional levels. The likelihood ratio test with one degree of freedom for exclusion of money growth is insignificant at the 5 percent level. Model 3 excludes both the growth of domestic credit and domestic inflation from the equation and the results show that the rest of the variables are significant. The likelihood ratio test with two degree of freedom, for exclusion of the two variables, are not significant, suggesting that domestic credit and inflation can be excluded from the model.

Model 4 shows the results of logit model in which the estimates have been divided by 1.81 to make them comparable to probit results. The results generated by simple logit are similar to the probit with random effects, in terms of sign and significance of variables. All variables are significant at 1 percent and 5 percent levels except the growth of domestic credit and domestic inflation suggesting that the results are not driven by specific method of estimation.

Conclusion

This chapter examines the determinants of currency crises in Malaysia, Thailand, Indonesia and the Philippines in the period between 1987 to 1997, using quarterly panel data. The empirical findings indicate that reserve inadequacy, deteriorating trade balance, increases of banks' claims on private sector and misalignment of real exchange rate increase the probability of a speculative attack. The results also suggest that currency crises could be contagious.

The growth rate of domestic credit should capture the behaviour of monetary policies preceding the crises but the results do not support that lending booms in these countries weaken the structure of the banking sector and increase the probability of speculative attacks on the domestic currency. In addition, domestic inflation is not an important macroeconomic variable in determining the probability of currency crisis. The results do not supports the notion that inconsistency in macroeconomic policies leads to the countries being in a speculative situation suggesting that monetary expansion to finance the fiscal deficit does not increase the probability of currency crisis

It could be concluded that in the Asian currency crises, there is a linkage between the economic fundamentals and currency crises. The economic fundamentals are the ration of M2 to international reserve, trade balance, banks' claims on private sector and misalignment of real exchange rate as well as contagion effects. The contagion indicator suggests that the currency crises in Malaysia, Thailand, Indonesia and the Philippines were partly driven by the effect of economic disturbances in neighbouring countries. These results suggest that central banks in these countries should closely monitor the changes in these fundamental variables to prevent the occurrence of currency crises.

Table 11.1 Macroeconomic Indicators

	Year	Malaysia	Indonesia	Thailand	Philippines
Real GDP Growth Rate (percent)					
	1991	8.8	8.9	8.4	-0.2
	1992	7.8	7.2	7.8	0.3
	1993	8.4	7.2	8.3	2.1
	1994	9.4	7.5	8.8	4.4
	1995	9.4	8.1	8.6	4.8
	1996	8.6	8.0	6.4	5.5
	1997	8. 0	4.7	0.5	5.1
	1998	-7.4	-13.2	-10.2	-0.5
Current Account Deficits (percent of GDP)					
	1991	-8.9	-3.3	-7.7	-2.3
	1992	-3.8	-2.0	-5.7	-1.9
	1993	-4.5	-1.3	-5.1	-5.5
	1994	-5.9	-1.6	-4.6	-4.6
	1995	-9.9	-3.5	-2.7	-2.7
	1996	-4.9	-3.4	-4.7	-4.7
	1997	-4.8	-3.8	-4.0	-4.0
	1998	13.7	4.2	11.2	2.3
Real Effective Exchange Rate (1990=100)					
	1991	96.9	99.6	99.0	103.1
	1992	109.7	100.8	99.7	107.1
	1993	111.0	103.8	101.9	97.4
	1994	107.1	101.1	98.3	111.7
	1995	106.9	100.5	101.7	109.5
	1996	112.1	105.4	107.6	116.3
	1997	84.8	62.3	72.3	90.8
External Debts (US$ billion)					
	1991	16.0	76.1	37.6	30.4
	1992	16.4	84.4	43.4	30.6
	1993	19.2	90.3	50.6	32.6
	1994	22.9	89.1	62.1	34.3
	1995	27.4	97.6	67.1	37.9
	1996	28.5	120.2	78.5	39.0
	1997	44.9	137.1	93.0	50.6
	1998	42.5	187.1	86.1	53.2

Table 11.1 (continued)

Inflation Rates (percent)					
	1991	4.0	9.0	6.0	19.0
	1992	4.8	8.3	3.8	8.4
	1993	3.6	9.3	3.6	7.8
	1994	3.7	8.5	5.3	9.4
	1995	3.4	9.3	5.0	7.9
	1996	3.5	6.5	5.8	8.4
	1997	2.6	11.6	5.6	5.1
	1998	5.3	58.4	8.1	9.8
International Reserve (percent of import):					
	1991	34.4	42.5	51.4	29.4
	1992	34.3	44.2	52.0	28.3
	1993	33.3	44.2	50.6	30.2
	1994	35.3	43.4	50.5	30.5
	1995	34.4	45.4	49.4	29.8
	1996	33.5	47.0	44.0	29.3
	1997	33.9	47.6	42.7	28.7
	1998	54.3	39.5	42.0	33.9

Source: International Financial Statistics, IMF, various issues.

Table 11.2 Regression Results

Variables	Models (1)	(2)	(3)	(4)
Log M2/Reserve	0.7151*	0.7105*	0.6721*	0.6357*
	[2.0275]	[2.0372]	[1.9311]	[1.5943]
	(2.9524)	(2.9446)	(2.7663)	(2.6931)
Domestic Inflation	-0.00704	0.00672	-	0.00775
	[-2.0751]	[2.0024]		[2.0214]
	(-1.8075)	(1.7566)		(1.7138)
Trade Balance	-0.000376*	-0.000374*	0.000377*	0.000365*
	[-1.7757]	[-1.7858]	[-1.8060]	[1.5242]
	(-3.2529)	(-3.2765)	(4.6029)	(-3.2973)
Real Exchange Rate	-0.00692*	0.00702*	0.00617*	0.00678
	[-1.1228]	[1.1516]	[1.0143]	[0.9734]
	(-4.6887)	(4.47829)	(4.6029)	(4.3711)
Domestic Credit	2.3644	-	-	1.9621
	(0.2668)			[0.1877]
	(1.9241)			(0.8641)
Banks' Claims on Private Sector	0.000151*	0.000150*	0.000156*	0.000146*
	[1.7550]	[1.766]	[1.8358]	[1.5082]
	[3.5062]	(3.5428)	(3.7919)	(3.2973)
Regional Contagion	3.7022*	3.7028*	3.6369*	3.7243*
	[4.5257]	[4.5772]	[4.8768]	[4.0265]
	(3.9740)	(3.9583)	(4.3861)	(3.3233)
Pseudo R-Square	0.3548	0.2718	0.2623	0.3559
Likelihood Ratio Test	-	1.0658	4.2829	-

Notes: Asterisk (*) denotes statistically significant at 1 percent level. Figures in ( ) indicate the marginal effects while [ ] refers to the t-ratios to test the significance of initial coefficient. Likelihood ratio test for excluded variable(s) in the system. Model 4 is an alternative estimation by logit where the coefficients are divided by 1.8138.

References

Aghion, P., Bacchetta, P. and Banerjee, A. (2001), 'Currency crises and monetary policy in an economy with credit constraints', *European Economic Review*, vol. 45, pp. 1121-1150.

Banerjee, A. (1992), 'A simple model of herd behaviour', *Quarterly Journal of Economics*, vol. 107, pp. 797-817

Calvo, G. (1998), 'Capital flows and capital market crises: The simple economics of sudden stops', *Journal of Applied Economics*, vol. 1, pp. 35-54.

Calvo, G. and Mendoza, E.G. (2000), 'Rational contagion and the globalization of securities markets', *Journal of International Economics*, vol. 51, pp. 79-113.

Calvo, G. and Vegh, C. (1993), 'Exchange rate stabilization under imperfect credibility', in H. Frisch, and A. Worgotter (eds), *Open-economy macroeconomics*, MacMillan Press, London.

Calvo, G. and Vegh, C. (1999), 'Inflation stabilization and BOP crises in developing countries', NBER working paper No 6925.

Caramazza, F., Rici, L. and Salgado, R. (2000), 'Trade and Financial Contagion in Currency Crises', IMF working paper No. 55.

Corsetti, G.P., Pesenti, P. and Roubini, N. (1998), 'What Caused the Asian Currency and Financial Crises?', *Japan and the World Economy*, vol. 11, pp. 305-373.

Devenow, A. and Welch, I. (1996), 'Rational herding in financial economics', *European Economic Review*, vol. 40, pp. 603-615.

Diaz-Alejandro, C.F. (1985), 'Good-bye financial repression, hello financial crash', *Journal of Development Economics*, vol. 19, pp. 1-24.

Eichengreen, B., Rose, A.K. and Wyplosz, C. (1995), 'Speculative Attacks on Pegged Exchange Rates: An Empirical Exploration with Special Reference to the European Monetary System', Working Paper No. 4, Federal Reserve Bank of San Francisco.

Eichengreen, B., Rose, A.K. and Wyplosz, C. (1996), 'Contagious Currency Crises", *Scandinavian Economics Review*, vol. 98, pp. 463-484.

Frankel, J.A. and Rose, A.K. (1996), 'Currency Crashes in Emerging Markets: An Empirical Treatment', *Journal of International Economics*, vol. 41, pp. 351-366.

Greene, W.H. (1999), *Econometric Analysis*, New Jersey: Prentice Hall.

International Monetary Fund (1998), *World Economic Outlook*, IMF, Washington.

International Monetary Fund (1998), *International Financial Statistics*, IMF, Washington.

Jeanne, O. (1997), 'Are currency crises self-fulfilling? A test', *Journal of International Economics*, vol. 43, pp. 263-286.

Jeanne, O. and Masson, P. (1996), 'Currency crises, sunspots and Markov-switching regimes', CEPR Discussion Paper No. 2170.

Kamin, S.B. and Wood, P.R. (1998), 'Capital inflows. Financial intermediation and aggregate demand: Empirical evidence from Mexico and other Pacific Basin Countries', International Finance Discussion Papers 583, Board of Governors of the Federal Reserve System.

Kaminsky, G.L. and Reinhart, C.M. (1999), 'The twin crises: The causes of banking and balance-of- payments problems', *American Economic Review*, vol. 89, pp. 473-500.

Kruger, M, Osakwe, P.N. and Jennifer, P. (1998), 'Fundamentals, Contagion and Currency Crises: An Empirical Analysis', Bank of Canada working paper No.10, Ottawa.

Krugman, P. (1979), 'A Model of Balance of Payments Crises', *Journal of Money, Credit and Banking*, vol. 11, pp. 11-325.

Krugman, P. (1997), 'Currency crises', unpublished paper, MIT.

Masson, P. (1999), 'Contagion: Macroeconomic models with multiple equilibria', *Journal of International, Money and Finance*, vol. 18, pp. 587-602.

Obstfeld, M. (1986), 'Rational and self-fulfilling balance-of-payment crises', *American Economic Review*, vol. 76, pp. 72-91.

Obstfeld, M. (1994), 'The logic of Currency Crises', *Cashier Economiques Et Monetaires*, vol. 43, pp. 189-213.

Obstfeld, M. (1996), 'Models of Currency Crisis with Self-fulfilling Features', *European Economic Review*, vol. 40, pp. 1037-1047.

Rogoff, K. (1999), 'International institutions for reducing global financial instability', *Journal of Economic Perspectives*, vol. 13, pp. 21-24.

Sachs, J., Tornell, A. and Velasco, A. (1996), 'Financial Crises in Emerging Markets: The Lessons from 1995', *Brookings Papers on Economic Activity*, vol. 1, pp. 147-215.

Salant, S. and D. Henderson (1978), 'Market anticipation of government policies and the price of gold', *Journal of Political Economy*, vol. 86, pp. 627-648.

Scharfstein, D.S., Stein, J.C., (1990), 'Herd behaviour and investment', *American Economic Review*, vol. 80, pp. 465-479.

Chapter 12

The Economic and Financial Crisis in Malaysia

Hassanuddeen A. Aziz

Introduction

The last three decades of the 20th century witnessed tremendous economic growth achieved by nations of Asia. In 1995, the economic management practiced by Malaysia was referred as the best model of economic development among developing countries. This miracle was a perfect mirage until the financial crisis hit Asia in 1997. On 2 July 1997, the Thai Central Bank abandoned all efforts to defend the baht peg with the US dollar from speculative attack that started in May 1997. Consequently, it triggered global financial instability with stock market meltdown and market sentiments turned against the whole region.

Malaysia, which had strong fundamentals and enjoyed average annual growth of 8 percent since 1987 suffered severely as the stock market crashed and the ringgit had depreciated by some 80 percent. The government was totally unprepared to face the crisis. The massive outflows of short-term capital caused share prices to fall rapidly, aggravating the economic turmoil through rapid falls in market capitalization. The Composite Index plunged from 1000 points in early 1997 to 262 points in August 1998. Prior to the crisis, the ringgit was considered as a strong and stable currency and had been trading at around 2.50 against the US dollar for a long time. By April 1998, the economic crisis had worsened with the ringgit continuing to depreciate towards 4.80 against the US dollar. Stronger economies were also affected as the problems faced by individual neighboring economies quickly spread across the whole region. While Thailand, Indonesia, Malaysia and South Korea experienced the most severe impact, the crisis affected the performance of stronger economies such as Hong Kong, Singapore and Taiwan. While most of the countries turned to IMF for solutions, Malaysia refused to surrender its financial independence to the world's body and handle the crisis in its own way. The currency traders were blamed as the culprit of the crisis. However, it cannot be denied that these currency traders were able to manipulate the currency market since the opportunity arises from internal weaknesses of Malaysian economy. By not accepting aid from IMF, Malaysia developed its own way to curb the crisis and revive its economy. Indeed Malaysia has learned a lot from this precious experience in managing its economy in the era of globalisation.

This chapter describes the currency scenarios in Malaysia during the time of crisis. It examines the monetary policy that led to the ringgit crisis, the overheating hypothesis in terms of current account deficits and total factor productivity, the role of speculators, the contagion hypothesis in terms of herding mentality, the effects of rapid globalisation and financial system liberalisation, the problem of moral hazard in financial intermediaries and how it could lead to over-investment and over-pricing of assets which led to the predicament faced by the Malaysian financial sector during the crisis year.

Events Leading to the Ringgit Crisis

During the recession in mid 1980s, Southeast Asian countries underwent structural adjustment in order to remove market distortions and encourage capital flows. As a result of this adjustment, the region recovered well by the 1990s.

In 1990, the sum of all developing countries' capital account surpluses stood at US$ 48.7 billion, but by 1993 the figure trebled to US$ 62.9 billion. For Malaysia, the net capital inflows exploded from an annual average of RM 732 million between 1981 and 1990 to an annual average of RM 7,345 million from 1991 to 1993.

The Plaza Accord of 1985 forced the Japanese government to allow the value of yen to drastically appreciate against the dollar (Dester & Henning, 1989). The Plaza Agreement led to subsequent economic recession in Japan. This yen appreciation to the dollar triggered capital movement into Southeast Asia. Japanese multinationals were pressured to shift production lines to other countries such as Thailand and Malaysia. The huge inflow of capital in turn, exerted an upward pressure on the ringgit and an equal magnitude in the current account deficit. Exerting a downward pressure on the ringgit should have left the exchange rate as it was before.

From a balance of payments deficit of RM 1.1 billion in 1988, a surplus of RM 29.24 billion was posted in 1993 (refer to Table 12.1). Bank Negara refused to allow the ringgit to appreciate and continued to maintain the ringgit's target zone within the RM 2.49/55 range. The central bank had to supply more ringgit to the foreign-exchange markets. Since the increase in the supply of ringgit more or less matched that in demand, the exchange rate remained stable. Table 12.1 shows that reserves declined by RM 1.2 billion in 1988 but by 1993, it increased by RM 29.2 billion. The broad measure of money supply, while expanding by only 6.7 percent in 1988; was expanding at a rate of 26.6 percent in 1993. To keep the growth in money supply on track, the surplus had to be sterilized, as the focus of monetary management is to curb inflationary pressures and maintain price stability.

To neutralize the expansion, Bank Negara used sterilization by issuing debt securities to the banking sector in exchange for cash. The stock of sterilization debt was negligible in 1991, but by 1993, Bank Negara's borrowings amounted to RM 60.3 billion. This imposed a great burden, which was settled in 1994. Settling a sterilization debt creates high-powered money and artificially lowers interest rates. This can be observed by Bank Negara's discount rate which stood at 7.23 percent on average in 1990, and increased to 7.7 percent in 1991, and then fell to 4.51 percent by 1994. The artificially low interest rates fuel credit expansions.

In 1995, the previous yen-dollar relationship reversed. On 27th March 1995, the rate was 89.3 yen and by 25th March 1997 it had dropped to 124. This change threatened the growth of capital inflow from Japan and reversed the gain in competitiveness, which Southeast Asian countries had acquired during the yen's superiority.

The ringgit also appreciated against the currencies of other countries as a result of Bank Negara's convention of targeting the US dollar instead of a trade-weighted basket of currencies. Although the ringgit-dollar rate was stable, they were both appreciating against other major currencies. In 1996, these problems were compounded by an oversupply of electronics. The electronics market retarded while US dollar appreciated, which meant that the ringgit was over valued and downward pressure was exerted on the exchange rate.

If the ringgit was allowed to depreciate, Malaysia's export competitiveness would have been restored and import volumes would have mitigated. Aimed at the target zone, Bank Negara supported the ringgit by purchasing it in the foreign exchange markets and supplying foreign currency from its reserves. This should have led to a money-supply contraction and a rise in interest rates, which would have ceased credit creation, slowed down economic growth, reduced imports and moderated the current-account deficit in conformity with the adjustment process of a fixed exchange rate regime. However, this was not the case. Credit creation continued as a result of continued unwinding of the sterilized debt. Investments continued strongly but not in manufactured exports; much of the credit went into construction and equity-purchase.

In August 1994, Bank Negara lifted the restriction on foreign inflows of short-term funds with hope that it will increase foreign inflows and liquidity to boost the stock market since there was a slowdown in capital inflows from Japan (Gomez & Jomo, 1997). This could not continue for long because either the interest rates would have to rise or the exchange rate would have to be allowed to depreciate. Once the crisis started in Thailand, speculators turned their attention to Malaysia and other Southeast Asian countries. They knew that the Malaysian government had two choices: to maintain the currency at the cost of sharply lower growth or depreciate the currency. Knowing that the country would sacrifice the ringgit instead of economic growth, the speculators started offloading their holdings of the ringgit resulting in a self-fulfilling crisis.

Macroeconomic Indicators

The outbreak of crisis is unpredictable since there is no single indicator that can signal its occurrence. Economic theory suggests that a high current account deficit and low total factor productivity are signs of an overheating economy. The volatility of portfolio investments contributing to capital flights also indicates risks of a currency crisis. A large current-account deficit does not foreshadow a currency crisis; it depends on where the money is coming from. If flighty short-term capital rather than long-term foreign direct investment finances its current-account deficit, a country is vulnerable to sudden capital outflows.

When the exchange-rate crisis struck Thailand, the country had current-account deficits of 7 to 8 percent of GDP. Despite Thailand's 10 years of substantial growth, its economic fundamentals were weak. In the following sub-section we will analyze the balance of payment deficit, the total factor productivity, and capital flights aspects in the Malaysian financial sector.

Current Account Deficit

Malaysia's soaring Balance of Payments (BoP) deficits had caused much worry. BoP deficit grew from RM 11 billion in 1994 to RM 18 billion in 1995, an increase of 63.6 percent. The 1995 deficit was large relative to total trade volume and GDP, constituting 4.7 percent and 7.9 percent, respectively. The 1996 deficit was about 5.5 percent of GDP. The increase in Malaysia's BoP deficit sent signals that something was wrong. Since BoP records transactions between a country and the rest of the world, it reflects the health of its economy and should be interpreted carefully.

The Malaysian economy has been growing at a rate of 8 percent on average since 1987, with a GDP growth of 9.6 percent in 1995 and 8.6 percent in 1996. Its per capita income has rose from US$ 1,814 (RM 4,662) in 1987 to US$ 4,027 (RM 10,349) in 1995. The ratio of savings to GDP were high by international standards, which was around 34 percent showing high growth that was not devoid of strains such as infrastructure bottlenecks, environmental degradation and so on.

Prior to the crisis Malaysia had experienced BoP deficits before. Deficits in the service account were more than surpluses in the merchandise account. Current account deficits were acceptable in the late eighties or early nineties. Deficits then were little, partly because of increased imports of capital and intermediate goods, with the BoP adjusting itself with a time lag of 1 to 2 years. However, the BoP deficit during this period could not be attributed to the increased importation of capital and intermediate goods, which would have generated more exports. Imports of consumer goods were rising, which reflected the wealth of Malaysian consumers. Increased imports of capital goods associated with foreign investment activities are financed by foreign investors themselves. In this case, the deficit in the current account was offset by foreign capital flows in the capital account. Similarly, increased imports of intermediate inputs were not troublesome as long as they were converted into exports.

The increase in BoP deficit may be a sign of overheating. A weak correlation between GDP growth and BoP deficit increases this possibility. There are economies with low GDP growth and large BoP deficits (e.g. United States) and there are economies with high GDP growth and large BoP surpluses (e.g.

Taiwan). However, these observations do not disprove the overheating hypothesis. Overheating happens when high growth rate is not supported by economic fundamentals.

Mechanistic adjustment of exporting more and importing less is difficult. Cheap imports reduce domestic inflation and it is not easy to export more if the products are not internationally competitive. Exports cannot be priced competitively unless they are driven by productivity improvements. It is also not wise to reduce imports through restrictions, as it would cause misallocation of resources, shielding domestic industries from international competition as well as going against to multilateral forums commitments.

Malaysia's trade deficit with Japan has always been more than its current account deficit. However, this would not necessarily make Japan the source of its BoP problems. This is because most of the imports from Japan are re-exported to other countries after re-processing.

Construction contributed more to GDP growth than manufacturing did during the years prior to the crisis, which affected BoP. If its growth had slowed down, it would have reduced the import bill and released resources to increase exports.

The external deficit problem was serious even though it may not have been the main cause of the currency crisis. A deceleration of economic growth could have helped the economy to cool down and reduce the BoP deficit. Macroeconomic fine-tuning was necessary for the economy's stability. The authorities should have closely monitored macroeconomic variables to avoid market distortions that would negatively impact our BoP.

The Government should not have pursued high growth rates and ignored the signs of overheating. Decelerating during overheating and accelerating once the support mechanism had been restored was more appropriate. Import growth should be checked by making domestic substitution better for local consumers in terms of price and quality and not by introducing protectionism measures.

Capital Flights

Capital flight is "the result of individual agents reacting in the way that is posited as rational by economic theory and accepted as normal in industrial countries." (Lessard & Williamson, 1987). Approaches that are used to calculate capital flights are the total private capital outflows, the residual method, the hot method and the derived method.

In the present context capital flight is seen as "speculative capital." It is "hot money" that responds to various forms of domestic macroeconomic policy distortions. Capital flight is capital export by private non-bank sectors (and in some cases banks and official entities) plus the "errors and omissions" of the BoP entry (since capital flight is concealed). Using this approach, capital flight is usually measured as follows:

$$KF = STPCF + ECBP \qquad (1)$$

where:

KF : Capital flight
STPCF : short-term private capital flows (short-term capital of other sectors)
ECBP : errors and omissions in the balance of payments entry.

Table 12.2 (a) displays the total capital flight between 1990 and 1995. The inflows from 1991 to 1994 can be attributed to the factors laid out earlier. In 1995 there were already signs of capital outflows, two years before the outbreak of the crisis.

Malaysia has always relied on foreign investment, which comprises both direct and portfolio components to sustain its economic growth. Direct foreign investment inflows (DFI) are more important than portfolio foreign investment (PFI). However, the latter may exceeds the former sometimes. A case in point is in 1982-84 (see Table 12.2 (b)). DFI inflows grew rapidly, peaked in 1982 and declined thereafter until 1987, then peaked again in 1992 and have been declining since then. PFI inflows peaked in 1982 and in 1994. PFI typically shows a higher degree of volatility compared to direct investments. This is not surprising since portfolio investment can be withdrawn without much financial loss. However, direct investments entail physical sinking of capital in the form of plants, machinery and equipment. There were significant net outflows of portfolio investment in 1987 and 1988 and a small outflow in 1991 (Table 12.2 (b)).

Foreign portfolio investments are influenced by the market conditions facing local shares. The government's adoption of expansionary fiscal policies in the 1980s may have been associated with the substantial inflows of PFI. Bank Negara may have attributed the inflows in 1994 to the lifting of the restriction on foreign inflows of short-term funds. When the bubble burst in 1985 and the stock market remained sedated with low price, a withdrawal of foreign portfolio investment would have entailed huge capital losses for foreign investors. It made sense to wait until the stock market recovered to minimize losses, before funds were withdrawn in 1987 and 1988.

The movement of net factor payments abroad roughly corresponds to that of foreign direct and portfolio investment flows (see Table 12.2 (b)). Net factor payments (NFP), which are factor payments arising from previous investments that are unrelated to new capital inflows were more stable, as shown in Table 12.2 (b). NFP have almost always exceeded net capital inflows.

NFP abroad contributed to the country's current account deficits in the BoPs in several years. Such payments were larger than the current account deficit, which meant that there would be sizeable current account surpluses for these payments. However, in 1995, the deficits in the current account were financed by private capital inflows, both direct and portfolio not by the drawing down of reserves, as a comparison of columns 3 and 5 in Table 12.2 (b) would suggest.

Total Factor Productivity

Malaysia's 8 percent economic growth track and the belief that economic turmoil will never happen again was derailing during the period, as reflected in Malaysia's poor productivity. The labor market was exploited by employees asking for an increase in salary, while the level of productivity remained the same. Instead of adopting laborsaving methods like mechanization and automation to enhance the productivity of the workforce, employers opted for the easy way out - employ foreign workers, which would heavily strain the nation. This thinking was evident in the reluctance of many industries to invest in research and development despite the incentives given by the Government. The private sector was not as efficient as it ought to be. Malaysia at that time was competing with the developing countries only.

To compete in the world market, Malaysia should increase its total factor productivity (TFP). TFP can only be increased through the efficient usage of labor and capital. Productivity growth is associated with growth in capital intensity (CI) and growth in TFP. This indicates whether an enterprise adopts a CI, which provides capital, quality, volume and speed to improve productivity, or labor-intensive policy. Figure 12.1 shows the close relationship between changes in productivity, CI and TFP.

Productivity growth is the sum of the TFP growth and weighted CI growth. For a given productivity growth, the total percentage contribution from TFP growth and CI growth must add to 100. From Table 12.3, the average growth in TFP for 1987-96 was 1.7 percent and CI grew by 5.9 percent. Throughout this period, capital was the main source of growth with CI contributing 65 percent and TFP contributing 35 percent to the productivity growth of 4.7 percent. For the sub-periods 1987-90, average growth in TFP was 2.8 percent and CI grew by 2.9 percent, contributing 65 percent and 35 percent respectively to productivity growth of 4.3 percent. For the sub-period 1991-96, average growth in TFP was 0.9 percent and CI growth was 7.8 percent contributing 17 percent and 83 percent respectively to productivity growth of 5 percent. Importantly, the evidence suggests TFP had been decreasing for most part of the 1991-1996 period.

Spiraling wage cost that is unmatched by productivity growth is bound to lead to an increase in the price of goods and services. Therefore, the Government had refused to give higher wages and instead promised government servants only bonuses at the end of the year. Measures by the Government to raise the national savings rate, cut government expenditure and delay projects were designed to improve the country's BoP that would improve the performance of the local currency.

Malaysia's high GDP growth was mainly input-driven. In Table 5, the average growth in capital between 1986 and 1995 was 13.7 percent and that of labor was 10.6 percent, whereas the average annual growth for TFP was only 3.2 percent. This high output growth would have registered a slower growth, had it not been for the over presence of foreign workers, and there may have been some savings in the Services Account through less income remittances. The economy would have experienced discomforting structural adjustments but then it could have learned to produce more with less labor. The high growth also affected infrastructure and environmental resources. An economy needs to grow fast while keeping in mind the economic fundamentals.

High growth can be sustained if infrastructure, Research and Development (R&D) and Human Resource Development (HRD) also improve. TFP is determined by five major elements; demand intensity, education and training, economic restructuring, capital structure and technical progress. Technical progress relates to the effective and efficient utilization of technology, innovation, work attitudes and management and organizational effectiveness. The 35 percent TFP growth over the period of 1987-96 related to a negative 25.7 percent contribution from technical progress. This reflected low levels of R&D in the country during the studied period for long-term sustainability of the economy.

Foreign direct investment plays a critical role in the industrial development of Malaysia. Singapore and the United Kingdom are the most important sources of FDI due to historical reasons; the role of Japan has increased rapidly since 1985 arising from the Plaza Accord. This wave of Japanese FDI has been mainly concentrated in the electronics industry.

Speculative Attack

Information availability in the financial markets is vital for the investors. They will be able predict the stock, currency and market conditions, and act accordingly to make a profit with sufficient information. A speculator, acting as a rational human, however exploits the situation to his advantage.

Knowing that Thailand was already burdened by economic crisis and could not afford to devalue the baht, speculators moved into the money market agreeing to provide US dollars in return for a fixed amount of local currency to be given after a specified period of time. Thailand suffered and this was closely followed by the other Asian markets. The currencies of SEA countries compared to what they were worth a year before took a severe beating. The Thai baht was down by over 90 percent, the Indonesian rupiah by 200 percent, the ringgit by 80 percent and the Singapore dollar by 9 percent.

After Malaysia, Indonesia and the Philippines were hit by the crisis; many still refused to acknowledge that the problem is affecting the whole region. However, the blow on Hong Kong proved that regional markets are closely interconnected.

In 1997, Malaysia admittedly possessed economic weaknesses. However, the modus operandi of currency speculation and its devastating effects might have expedited the impact of the crisis swiftly. Millman (1995) stated that currency traders could move US$1 trillion around the world at the speed of light. Of this amount, only 1.5 percent goes into the payment of actual trade. The rest represent money being exchanged for money, short-term investments to earn higher interest and outright currency speculation. Speculators can leverage up to 20 times or more of the funds they deposit with their banks. The currencies trading as devised by the currency traders is such that they can borrow offshore money and sell in most cases to each other and every time they sell, the currency devalues by a number of points.

Malaysia could have learned from the events in Thailand. The second strategy for counter attack was to cut off the supply of money that speculators needed. This includes efforts by Bank Negara that would raise interest rates at a controlled and gradual level. Local banks would have to subscribe to these bonds, meaning that they would have less to loan out. Indirectly, this would lead to a more prudent lending policy, added to other recently introduced monetary policies during the time, which would help keep speculators at bay.

There are three ways to stabilize exchange rates: (a) credible fixed exchange rates - "irrevocably fixed" peg or currency board (gold standard); (b) capital controls and (c) formal institutions for intervention (Frankel, 1993).

An idea devised by James Tobin, a Nobel Laureate in economics, is to put a small tax on foreign-exchange transactions to make short-term speculation more costly while having little effect on long-term investment. The other measure is to limit short-term foreign borrowing, like what happened to Chile in 1982. All loans and bank deposits from abroad were taxed. Chile enjoyed steadier growth over the past decade. Whether that was a result of its capital controls is uncertain. Chile's experience suggests that capital controls may be difficult to enforce. But it does not mean that governments are at the mercy of sudden inflows and outflows of capital. It, however, means that the extent to which such capital movements are destabilizing depends on the strength of a country's financial system and the soundness of its economic policies.

Suppose that a country's fundamental tradeoff between the costs of maintaining the current parity and the costs of abandoning it is deteriorating, so that in the future the country would have to devalue even in the absence of a speculative attack; then speculators would try to get out of the currency before devaluation therefore worsening the government's tradeoff, leading to an earlier devaluation. Smart investors would try to get out earlier still - resulting in a crisis that ends the fixed exchange rate regime before the fundamentals make devaluation necessary. Given an inevitable eventual abandonment of a currency peg, and perfectly informed investors, a speculative attack on a currency will occur at the earliest date at which such an attack could succeed. The reason is essentially arbitrage: an attack at any later date would offer speculators a sure profit; this profit will be competed away by attempts to anticipate the crisis (Krugman, 1996).

In Krugman's scenario, the crisis is provoked by the inconsistency of government policies, which make the long-run survival of the fixed rate impossible. Defending the rate in a time of speculative attack is too expensive. The currency is then forced to float. The 1997 speculative attack on the currency of the region, driven by expectations of devaluation, was the main reason for devaluation.

Contagion Effect

According to the IMF, the Thai crisis was caused by high real exchange rates, large current account deficits, unhinged private sector foreign borrowings, weak banking systems and denial syndrome by authorities who delayed the needed policy changes. Malaysia on the other hand, was affected due to the contagion effect or the domino theory.

Why should a country's problem inflict casualty on neighboring countries? The Southeast Asian countries that were under speculative attack were selling similar products in world export markets. A Thai devaluation had depressed Malaysian exports. Similarly, the depreciation of the pound during the European crises of 1992-3 affected the trade and employment of France.

However, in the European and Asian, cases the trade links appeared fairly weak; and in the Latin American crisis of 1995, they were virtually nil. Mexico is neither an important market nor an important competitor to Argentina; why, then, should one peso crisis trigger another?

Countries are perceived as a group with some common observed characteristics. Once investors have seen one country from a group abandon its peg under pressure, they may revise their estimate downward of the willingness of the rest of the group. The political commitment to a fixed exchange rate is subjected to herding effects, where countries in the same region must be committed in pegging their currencies collectively. Contagion reflects irrational behaviour on the part of investors, either because individuals are irrational or because money managers face asymmetric incentives. South Korea had few strong trade links with the troubled economies of Southeast Asia. A fund manager, who did not reduce exposure in South Korea, would have been caught in a devaluation of the won. He might well be blamed for lack of diligence (Drazen, 1997).

There is also a positive side to herding. During the wave of optimism that followed Mexican and Argentine reforms in the early 1990s, countries that had done little actual reform, such as Brazil, were also lifted by the rising tide.

Herding Mentality

Like financial markets, foreign exchange markets also exhibit irregularities that compromise the efficiency hypothesis theory of markets. One such inefficiency would be herding behaviour. Shiller (1989) saw the stock market crash of 1987 as a clear example of market overreaction. He argued that neither changes in corporate performance, nor market discount rates, could account for the drastic fall in stock prices. Investors were responding to developments in the market itself. Since the market overreacted due to psychological or behavioural factors we can conclude that there was a possibility to consider policy responses to market inefficiency.

Investors move in herds, where any response taken by major investors will be quickly followed by others. Herding in markets with private information can create "hot money" that sometimes causing the foreign exchange markets to overreact to news about national economic prospects. This is consistent with individual rationality because the action by the individual is based upon their private information and self-interest.

In the Principal-agent theory, the agent's compensation may be tied to the performance of their funds relative to other fund managers. The internal struggle between agents with longer-term and shorter-term perspectives may also bring about the herding mentality in the foreign-exchange markets. Pension-fund managers investing in emerging market funds may not be willing to take the risk of staying in unpopular markets. They may act alike if the compensation of the fund-managers is based on comparison with other money managers even if they have information suggesting that the market's judgment is wrong.

Effects of Globalisation

Following the crisis, Malaysia did not adapt to global financial markets quickly. By increasing the speed and magnitude of market reaction, globalisation had magnified the costs of bad policies and weak institutions. If globalisation was handled well, the 1997 crisis could have been avoided.

World financial markets have been integrating since the 1990s, leading to surges in private capital flows into developing countries. Through this, Indonesia, Thailand and Malaysia each received about $65 billion of net private capital in the period 1990-96. Unlike the private capital inflows of the 1970s and early 1980s, funds during the 1997 period went to the private sector, instead of official agencies. Foreign direct investments and portfolio equity funds are non-debt creating, enabling countries to tap the growth of global capital to raise investment and give global investors the chance to reduce risk through portfolio diversification. Southeast Asian countries have also experienced indirect benefits such as the spillover effects in the form of new technology, managerial and organizational systems.

Improper management of integration and private capital negatively impacts a nation. To avoid this, flexible exchange rates are used to steer the economy through interest rates. However, Malaysia, Thailand, Indonesia and the Philippines kept their exchange rates pegged to the dollar resulting in borrowing from abroad without the fear of exchange-rate risks.

Increased foreign borrowing makes it easier for banks to increase the risk of their portfolio and incur sizable losses. This can be observed in Thailand when the bubble burst in the property sector. Malaysia lacked proper supervisory and monitoring tools with integration as the speed and magnitude of market reaction increased.

When the region's currencies came under speculative attack, the governments, unable to defend the peg had the currency float freely. Currency attacks spread to other parts of the region due to the contagion effect. Studies contended that the causes of such crises were fiscal deficit and other macroeconomics factors. In Malaysia, actions and incentives were impounded and the deficit was checked with more reduction expected by 1998. What triggered the lack of confidence of market players that led to that kind of savage attack on its currency? The answer may lie in the aftermath and the mandatory actions requested by IMF to the affected countries.

Moral Hazard and Overinvestment

As delegated monitors for individual savers who deposit their funds with them, financial intermediaries reduce the information costs of moral hazard and improve the channeling of funds from savers to borrowers. The cost of monitoring and enforcing debt contracts issued directly to investors is why raising funds through an intermediary can be superior. Debt contracts include contracts issued by financial intermediaries to borrowers (bank loans) and the contracts issued by financial intermediaries when they borrow from investors (bank deposits). Portfolio diversification within financial intermediaries facilitates a bank's transformation of loans that need monitoring and enforcement into bank deposits that do not. Investors who buy the secondary securities issued by intermediary may purchase the primary securities directly and save the intermediary's cost.

Banks and other financial intermediaries in Thailand, Indonesia and Malaysia, avoided their responsibilities as delegated monitors during the crisis. They channeled foreign capital into the domestic economy under distorted incentives. Most of the banks were under-capitalized, borrowing abroad and investing recklessly in the domestic market. If lending works, the bankers make money and if it fails the depositors and creditors lose money but the bank's owners bear little risk because they have little capital tied up in the bank.

Financial intermediaries, whose liabilities are guaranteed by the government, pose a problem of moral hazard. If the government bails the depositors and creditors, then they are secured from the risk. The Asian Miracle was propelled by an endless flow of outside capital that looked cheap. The problem was the availability of cheap funding; often the product is inconsistent with monetary policies. Southeast Asia kept open capital accounts to encourage capital to flow their way. That has made it easier for foreign banks to lend dollars and for foreign investors to invest in their equity markets. The money came in such abundance because the currencies of the region seemed to offer stability. While dollar/mark or dollar/yen rates gyrated unpredictably, moving against each other by as much as 50 percent in a matter of months, the Thai baht was locked in a narrow band against the American currency. The Indonesian rupiah gently depreciated by an orderly 5 percent or so every year to compensate for its higher rate of inflation. Borrowers could obtain dollars without worrying that they might need more of their local currency to repay them at the end of the day.

Asian economies pre-crisis had a class of financial intermediaries that were able to raise money at safe interest rates but lend that money at premium rates to finance speculative investments. They erased capital controls during the 1990s and consequently, inflows of foreign money amounted to 5-10 percent of GDP. The Jakarta stock market was 69 trillion rupiah in 1993 and increased to 260 trillion rupiah in 1996 with 80 percent to 90 percent of the volume accounted for by foreigners.

Moral hazard distorts investments in over-guaranteed and under-regulated intermediaries. It can lead to excessive investment by the economy (McKinnon and Pill, 1996). Asian banks and bank-like institutions lend money rather than buying capital assets. Amsden (1989) showed that lending to a very highly leveraged firm engaged in risky investment is de facto much like buying the capital directly. All capital ends up being purchased by guaranteed intermediaries. This is an extreme result, but it captures the tendency of Asian businesses to become extremely leveraged by Western standards. Investment is pushed to a maximum value resulting in the illusory of over-optimistic phenomenon.

The consequences of this distortion can be worsened by globalisation. Suppose a country does not have access to the world capital market and has to rely on a fixed supply of domestic savings. Unresponsive to the interest rate, the excessive investment demand generated by the intermediaries would not lead to excessive investment, but it would only drive up the interest rate.

Financial excess in Southeast Asian economies were translated into increases in actual volume of investment and in asset prices. This reflects that assets were imperfectly elastic in supply. Financial intermediaries have impacts on the quantities of investments and also prices. After the Southeast Asian crisis, there was a major change in the financial regime. Finance companies were closed. Banks were forced to curtail risky lending at best and closed their doors at worst. Even if the IMF did not insist on financial housecleaning as a condition for aid, implicit guarantees and easy lending for risky investment were over for some time.

The Southeast Asian crisis was a typical private sector external debt crisis. These countries allowed unrestricted access to external finance to the private sector. They did not take the difference between domestic and external debt seriously and excluded foreign exchange risks from their calculation. This resulted in an external debt by the private sector. Believing that there was no foreign exchange rate risk with the pegged and the overvalued nominal value of ringgit/dollar rate, even though the ringgit had been devalued, it was only rational for private sector to over-borrow. The rational thing then was to get more of it since the ringgit seemed to be cheaper in terms of dollar denomination. In case of a problem, the private external debts would eventually be nationalized and a de facto socialization of the banking system also provided incentive to over-borrow. Acquisition of property and securities by non-residents had sustained speculative bubbles in equity and property markets prior to the currency crisis. Traditional measures of vulnerability did not signal a crisis because the problem was off the government's balance sheet. The boom-bust cycle created by financial excess preceded the currency crises because the financial crisis was the driver of the process, with the currency fluctuations merely a symptom. The crisis's ability to spread without being noticed can be explained by the fact that the afflicted Asian economies were in a "meta-stable" state.

Mishkin (1992) argued that financial crises have severe effects on growth because they disrupt the productive activities of financial intermediaries. An important aspect of moral hazard is the bias in the type of investment undertaken. Some of the Asian crises were associated with unwise investments like office towers and auto plants rather than excessive investment per se. There were large changes in relative prices. Even if monetary factors were not crucial, the huge real depreciation associated with the crises in Southeast Asia played a role in explaining the financial crises' large declines in output. Seeing that capital was producing a poor return in Asia, investors would put their money elsewhere. Investors were erratic, swayed by waves of excessive optimism followed by waves of excessive pessimism. And it was impossible to totally eliminate moral hazard, which caused people to take excessive risks in the expectation that the central bank or the IMF would bail them out when things went wrong. These factors can mean that market forces do not allocate capital perfectly around the world. The Asian crises have portrayed that intermediaries will "almost always" require a bailout, since competition pushes them to the point where they do not earn economic profits in any state of the world, and cover their costs only in the most favorable possible state. Overinvestment and overvaluation of assets in Southeast Asia on domestic financial intermediaries were an important cause for the 1997 crisis.

Conclusion

How bad was the 1997 crisis in Malaysia? For it to be bad, the benchmark would have to be the mid-80s recession. Fortunately for Malaysia, Thailand was hit first in the crisis, so Malaysia was able to anticipate the necessary measures to be taken. Malaysia was able to analyze the steps Thailand took and found out beforehand which worked and which didn't, unlike what happened in the mid-80s when it took years before Malaysia could correct the situation. Bank Negara had opted for measures, which would not jeopardize growth that the economy needed to maintain albeit at a slower pace. To get as bad as predicted in the future, Malaysia would have to go to a very low percentage of growth for 1998, which the numbers and statistics simply do not support.

During the period, Malaysia was stronger than Thailand and Indonesia economically and worked through the crisis remarkably. Malaysia's economy was solid and prudently managed. Malaysia also did not seek any financial aid from the IMF following its currency problem. The fundamentals of the economy can cope with its problems especially after measures taken to strengthen the financial sector and limit credit expansion. Malaysia's long tradition of sound microeconomics policies and prudent management of the economy was in solid condition, but still suffered from the contagion effects of its neighbors.

Unlike the 1985/86 recessions, Malaysia was more resilient facing the 1997 crisis. Firstly, it had a strong manufacturing sector contributing a sizable sum to the national coffers as evidenced in the increase in long-term direct foreign investment. Furthermore, Malaysia had diversified its exports, which enabled it to cushion the volatility in certain markets. Malaysia's financial turmoil did not derail it from achieving the long-term development goals.

Malaysia needed prudence with spending. The construction of shopping malls, hotels and commercial centers stopped since there was already an oversupply of them. Malaysia gave priority in investing in things that would generate future income.

As human resource is a vital if not the most important asset in any economy, the Government has always invested more in education and training of workers. Investment in infrastructure was also given due attention to sustain growth. Malaysia also reduced unskilled foreign labor as they increased wages. The dependency on foreign labor had lulled us into complacency instead of making giant strides in capital-intensive ventures. This had to be stopped and greater emphasis must be placed on automation and other technology-driven economic activities. To achieve this, indigenous science and technology must be allowed to flourish. More incentives must be given to encourage more research and development (R&D).

To win confidence back, Malaysia had reprioritized its development projects. The projects were not based on the strength of who-you-know but what-you-know. The respective players in the finance sector concurred that there was greater need for transparency and accountability - both in the private and public sectors - to win over outsiders, including foreign fund managers. Professional bodies must be equally ethical when reporting about their clients' companies performances. To make the economy vibrant, Malaysia would need more than strong savings. Non-performing companies and non-productive activities must be stopped altogether to prevent further bleeding of the economy.

The increase in the supply of Malaysian Government Securities would have effectively mopped up liquidity. The lack of liquidity will led to higher interest rates. A high interest rate and lower ringgit would attract investment, but on the other hand the cost of borrowing would also be high. High interest rates would also deter currency speculators who borrow on a short-term basis. As for local banks, a report by rating agency Standard and Poor said that Malaysian banks were not likely to face the same level of problems as those in Indonesia, where 16 sick banks were forced to close following market volatility. The agency said Indonesia's and Thailand's financial sectors were most affected by the 1997 market volatility due to excesses in non-performing loans funded by foreign currency and real estate speculation prior to the devaluation of the baht. Asia's impressive growth in recent years before the crisis came partly from its ability to borrow cheaply from abroad. Companies in Thailand, for example, were able to borrow overseas at about half the rate they would need to pay at home; in Indonesia, the cost of borrowing from foreign sources was one-third the local rate.

The lesson learnt from this crisis is the need for transparency on the part of government and speculators. Regulations and discipline are diligently required for the currency markets to prevent anarchy in the economies of countries particularly the developing ones, without hampering the dynamics of currency trading. The most important thing is to adopt proper policy and take care of the financial sector.

Table 12.1 Balance of Payments (RM million)

	1988	1993
Current account	4344	-6439
Trade balance	14524	8193
Services balance	-10180	14951
Transfers	395	409
Long-term capital account	-3218	4415
Basic balance	1521	8066
Overall balance	-1104	29239
Net change in reserves	-1177.3	29182.1

Source: Department of Statistics and Central Bank of Malaysia

Table 12.2 (a) Capital Flight - The Hot Money Method

Year	Amount(Us$ Million)
1990	-22
1991	136
1992	1295
1993	6473
1994	4038
1995	-893

Source: IMF IFS Yearbook 1997

Table 12.2(b) Capital Inflows and Current Account Balance

Year	DFI (1)	Portfolio (2)	Total (US$ million) (1)+(2)=(3)	Net Factor Payment Abroad (US$ million) (4)	Current Account (US$ million) (5)
1980	934	-11	923	584	-285
1981	1265	1131	2396	5574	-2486
1982	1397	1804	3201	8343	-3601
1983	1261	1410	2671	8109	-3497
1984	797	1003	1800	5368	-1671
1985	695	335	1030	5508	-613
1986	489	599	1088	4780	52
1987	397	-948	-551	5270	2572
1988	611	-966	-355	5423	1184
1989	1668	107	1775	4866	315
1990	2332	255	4362	5064	-870
1991	3998	-170	3828	6800	-4183
1992	5183	1122	6305	8006	-2167
1993	5006	709	5715	8256	-2991
1994	4342	1649	5991	9087	-4520
1995	4132	440	4572	9526	-7362

Source: International Financial Statistics, various issues

Table 12.3 Average Growth of Productivity, CI and TFP

	Productivity (percent)	TFP (percent)	CI (percent)
1987-96	4.74	1.66	5.86
1987-90	4.31	2.85	2.91
1991-96	5.02	0.86	7.82

Source: National Productivity Corporation, Malaysia

Table 12.4 Growth Rate in Real Added Value, Capital, Labor and TFP

Year	Real Added Value	Real Capital	Labor	TFP
1986	8.9	2.8	0.1	7.4
1987	6.8	2.5	7.5	1.9
1988	16.7	7.5	16.9	5.0
1989	25.3	10.8	17.2	11.9
1990	18.2	19.2	20.8	-1.7
1991	22.3	23.9	16.2	1.7
1992	14.0	21.0	4.7	0.1
1993	17.1	17.9	10.6	2.4
1994	14.6	14.6	5.3	3.9
1995	12.0	16.3	6.9	-0.5
Avg. 86-95	15.6	13.7	10.6	3.2

Source: National Productivity Corporation, Malaysia

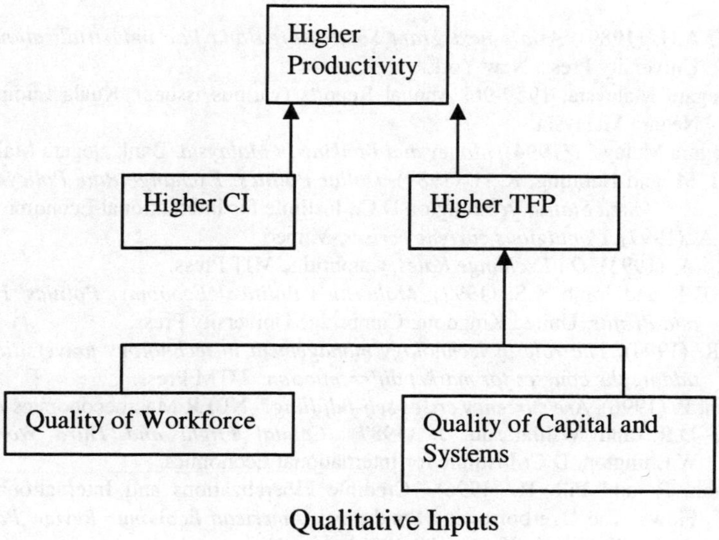

Figure 12.1 Relationship between Productivity, CI and TFP

References

Amsden, A.H. (1989), *Asia's next grant South Korea and late industrialization*, Oxford University Press, New York.

Bank Negara Malaysia, 1959-96, Annual Reports (various issues), Kuala Lumpur, Bank Negara Malaysia.

Bank Negara Malaysia (1994), *Money and Banking in Malaysia,* Bank Negara Malaysia.

Dester, I. M. and Henning, R. H. (1989), *Dollar Politics: Exchange Rate Policymaking in the United States*, Washington D.C., Institute for International Economics.

Drazen, A. (1997), *Contagious currency crises,* Mimeo.

Frankel, J.A (1993), *On Exchange Rates*, Cambridge MIT Press.

Gomez, E.T. and Jomo K.S. (1997), *Malaysia's Political Economy: Politics, Patronage and Profits,* United Kingdom: Cambridge University Press.

Ismail, R. (1994), *The role of technology management in technology universities: value-adding the courses for market differentiation.* UTM Press.

Krugman, P. (1996), *Are currency crises self-fulfilling?* NBER Macroeconomics Annual.

Lessard, D.R. and Williamson, J. (1987), *Capital Flight and Third World Debt*, Washington, D.C: Institute for International Economics.

McKinnon, R. and Pill, H. (1996), 'Credible Liberalizations and International Capital Flows: The Overborrowing Syndrome', *American Economic Review Papers and Proceedings*, vol. 87, pp. 189-193.

Millman, J.G. (1995), *The Vandals' Crown: How Rebel Currency Traders Overthrew the World's Central Banks,* New York: Simon & Schuster Inc.

Mishkin, F. (1992), 'Anatomy of a Financial Crisis', *Journal of Evolutionary Economics*, vol. 2, pp. 115-130.

Shiller, R. (1989), *Market Volatility,* Cambridge: MIT Press.

Tobin, J, (1996), *Essays in economics: National and International.* MIT Press, Cambridge, Massachusetts.

Subject Index